CONTENTS

D0545198

List of Figures

List of Profiles

List of Tables

PREFACE

Access to History Context

Structure

In some ways *Access to History: Context* volumes are similar to most textbooks. They are divided into chapters, each of which is focused on a specific topic. In turn, chapters are divided into sections which have self-explanatory headings. As is the case with most textbooks, *Context* authors have organised the chapters in a logical sequence so that, if you start at the beginning of the book and work your way through to the end, everything will make sense. However, because many readers 'dip' into textbooks rather than reading them from beginning to end, care has been taken to make sure that whichever chapter you start with you should not find yourself feeling lost.

Special Features in the Main Text

Points to Consider – at the start of each chapter this shaded box provides you with vital information about how the chapter is organised and how the various issues covered relate to each other.

Issues boxes are a standard feature of each chapter and, like Points to Consider boxes, are designed to help you extract the maximum benefit from the work you do. They appear in the margin immediately following most numbered section headings. The question(s) contained in each issues box will tell you which historical issues(s) the section is primarily going to cover. If the section you intend to start with has no issues box, turn back page by page until you find one. This will contain the questions the author is considering from that point onwards, including the section you are about to read.

Boxed sections appear in both the margin and the main column of text. In each of the boxes you will find a self-explanatory heading which will make it clear what the contents of the box are about. Very often, the contents of boxes are explanations of words or phrases, or descriptions of events or situations. When you are reading a chapter for the first time you might make a conscious decision to pay little attention to boxed entries so that you can concentrate your attention on the author's main message.

Q-boxes appear in the margin and contain one or more questions about the item they appear alongside. These questions are intended to stimulate you to think about some aspect of the material the box is linked to. The most useful answers to these questions will often emerge during discussions with other students.

Activities boxes – as a general rule, the contents of activities boxes are more complex than the questions in Q-boxes, and often require you to undertake a significant amount of work, either on your own or with others. One reason for completing the task(s) is to consolidate what you have already learned or to extend the range or depth of your understanding.

Profiles – most of these are about named individuals who are central to an understanding of the topic under consideration: some are about events of particular importance. Each Profile contains a similar range of material. The two aspects you are likely to find most useful are:

▼ the dated timeline down the side of the page; and

▼ the source extracts, which provide you with ideas on what made the subject of the Profile especially notable or highly controversial

Profiles also provide useful points of focus during the revision process.

End-of-chapter Sections

The final pages of each chapter contain different sections. It is always worthwhile looking at the **Summary Chart** or **Summary Diagram** first. As their names suggest, these are designed to provide you with a brief and carefully structured overview of the topic covered by the chapter. The important thing for you to do is to check that you understand the way it is structured and how the topics covered inter-relate with one another.

The **Working on...** section should be studied in detail once you have finished your first reading of the main text of the chapter. Assuming that you read the Points to Consider section when you began work on the chapter, and that you followed any advice given in it when you read the chapter for the first time, the Working on... section is designed to suggest what form any further work you do on the chapter should take.

The **Answering extended writing and essay questions on...** sections, taken as a whole throughout the book, form a coherent body of guidance on how to tackle these types of examination questions successfully.

The same is true of the **Answering source-based questions on...** sections which have been carefully planned bearing in mind the ways you need to build on the skills you have already developed in this area. You may find these sections particularly helpful during the time you are preparing for an exam.

The last part of each chapter contains a **Further Reading** section. These are of vital importance to you in chapters covering topics you are expected to know about in some detail. To do well in any History course it is essential to read more than one book. However, it is possible to find individual books which can act as your guide and companion throughout your studies, and this is one of them. One of the major ways in which it fulfils this function is by providing you with detailed guidance on the way you can make the most effective use of your limited time in reading more widely.

This book is an integral part of the *Access to History* series. One of its functions is to act as a link between the various topic books in the series on the period it covers, by drawing explicit attention in the Further Reading sections to where, within the series, other material exists which can be used to broaden and deepen your knowledge and understanding. Attention is also drawn to the non-*Access to History* publications which you are likely to find most useful. By using material which has been written based on the same aims and objectives, you are likely to find yourself consistently building up the key skills and abilities needed for success on your course.

Revision

Context books have been planned to be directly helpful to you during the revision period. One of the first things many students do when starting to revise a topic for an examination is to make a list of the 'facts' they need to know about. A safer way of doing this (because it covers the possibility that you missed something important when you originally worked on the topic) is to compile your lists from a book you can rely on. *Context* volumes aim to be reliable in this sense. If you work through the chapter which covers the topic you are about to revise and list the events contained in marginal 'events lists' and in boxed lists of events, you can be confident that you have identified every fact of real significance that you need to know about on the topic. However, you also need to make a list of the historical issues you might be asked to write about. You can do this most conveniently by working through the relevant chapter and noting down the contents of the 'issues boxes'.

For almost everybody, important parts of the revision process are the planning of answers to all the main types of structured and essay questions, and the answering of typical questions (both those requiring extended writing and those based on source material) under exam conditions. The best way to make full use of what this book has to offer in these respects is to work through the two relevant sets of end-of-chapter sections (Answering extended writing and essay questions on... and Answering source-based questions on...) in a methodical manner.

Keith Randell

THE BRITISH ECONOMY IN THE NINETEENTH CENTURY

CHAPTER 1

POINTS TO CONSIDER

Among the factors that shape a nation's history and character three are outstanding – its **economy**, its political system and its relations with other countries. In this opening chapter you will be introduced to the first of those factors – the economy. The period covered by this book was an extraordinary time for Britain's economy. To help you understand why this was, five of the major developments that took place during the nineteenth century have been selected for study:

1. Britain's population grew dramatically – more than doubling in size from about twenty million to about forty-six million
2. Britain changed from an agricultural and rural society into an industrial and urban one
3. Britain became the world's major trading nation
4. British merchant ships carried the majority of the world's traded goods
5. Britain became the world's largest investor in overseas markets and the world's financial centre.

Introduction

In order to study economic history, we need to refer to facts and figures and so we will be meeting lots of these as we go along. These should be regarded as the necessary tools of the trade. Another important point to remember is that economic growth is seldom uniform. Growth can occur in one part of the country while decline takes place in another. Wages may rise in one industry while they fall in another. One social class may benefit from a particular economic change while another may suffer. The biggest oddity, and one which often baffled or angered nineteenth-century observers, is that great wealth and extreme poverty frequently exist side by side. How contemporaries responded to that situation is the theme of Chapters 4 and 7 in this book.

THE ECONOMY

An effective way of defining what is meant by the British economy is to ask a set of questions. What resources, human and material, did Britain have? How did it use these? How did its people earn their living? What conditions did they live and work in? What goods and materials did Britain produce, and in what quantities? How much did it consume? How did it perform as a trading nation? How wealthy was Britain, and how was its wealth distributed among the people? How involved was government and parliament in directing or controlling economic affairs? It is questions such as these that economic historians attempt to answer.

ISSUE
Why did the population increase to such a remarkable extent in the nineteenth century?

1 Population

From 1801, the year of the first national census (held every tenth year from then on), we have reliable statistics regarding the growth of the population in Britain. The figures show that between 1811 and 1911 the population increased by nearly two and a half times.

Table 1 The population of the UK, 1811–1911.

Year	England and Wales	Scotland	Ireland	Total
1811	10,164,256	1,805,864	5,937,856	17,907,976
1821	12,000,236	2,091,521	6,801,827	20,893,584
1831	13,896,797	2,364,386	7,767,401	24,028,584
1841	15,914,148	2,620,184	8,196,597	26,730,929
1851	17,927,609	2,888,742	6,574,278	27,390,629
1861	20,066,224	3,062,294	5,798,967	28,927,485
1871	22,712,266	3,360,018	5,412,377	31,484,661
1881	25,974,439	3,735,573	5,174,836	34,884,848
1891	29,002,525	4,025,647	4,704,750	37,732,922
1901	32,527,843	4,472,103	4,458,775	41,458,721
1911	36,070,492	4,760,904	4,390,219	45,221,615

Q Why did the death (mortality) rate fall?

The explanation is not that the *birth rate* increased – in fact, after a spurt in the middle years of the century, it fell sharply after 1871 – but that the *death rate* consistently declined across the greater part of the century.

Figure 1 Graph showing birth and death rates, 1780–1960.

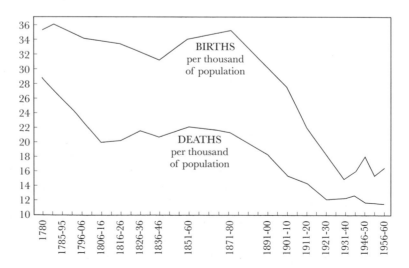

The essential cause of the declining death rate was the drop in infant mortality. Children survived to be become adults who in previous generations would have died during their first twelve months. This raises the question of why fewer infants died. The main reason was that there was a general improvement in the standard of people's health. Mothers were healthier and gave birth to healthier babies, more of whom consequently survived. This process had begun around the middle of the eighteenth century as Figure 2 shows:

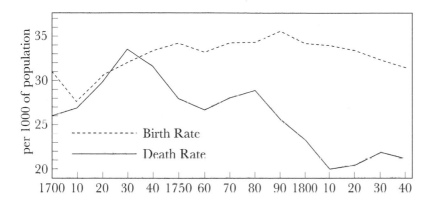

Figure 2 Graph showing birth and death rates, 1700–1840.

The reasons for this remarkable improvement in health can be listed under four headings:

a) *diseases became less virulent*
b) *medical knowledge and treatment improved*
c) *public health regulations created a less infectious and contagious environment*
d) *nutrition improved.*

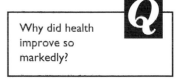

Why did health improve so markedly?

a) Medical historians now suggest that by the end of the nineteenth century, the major diseases such as cholera and typhoid, which had frequently reached epidemic proportions in earlier generations, had become less deadly. This had been brought about by the weakening in the strains of the diseases and by the greater resistance to infection that people had developed.

b) Historians also suggest that the deepening of medical knowledge played a part. Vaccination against smallpox became possible early in the nineteenth century and, while the breakthrough in antibiotics, which was to provide cures for all the major epidemic diseases, did not come until well into the twentieth century, doctors in the nineteenth century had already become conscious of the need for preventative medicine. If people adopted healthier living habits they would be less likely to contract diseases in the first place.

MALTHUSIANISM

The initial reaction to the evidence of mounting numbers of people was one of anxiety. In the early nineteenth century there were widespread fears that food supplies would soon be outstripped by the demand for more mouths to be fed. The most influential figure to advance this theory was the Reverend Thomas Malthus. In his published writings he argued that no matter how well Britain might increase its food production it could never keep pace with the rate of human reproduction. Britain was therefore doomed to poverty and mass starvation unless it could limit its birth rate. His solution was not contraception but 'moral restraint', by which he meant that couples should marry later and have sex less frequently. His pessimistic view of population growth became known as Malthusianism. Although subsequent developments were to show that he had exaggerated the crisis, the controversy he started is by no means dead. There are neo-malthusians today who warn that the world's population explosion threatens to destroy human civilisation.

c) This was particular evident in regard to public health. Government measures throughout the Victorian period showed an increasing recognition of the need to combat ill-health by organised programmes to promote hygiene. (This theme is explored in greater detail on pages 90–96.) The greatest need was for a clean and regular water supply. Without this there was no prospect of combating the diseases that ravaged the population. In Victorian Britain ordinary people were often referred to as 'the great unwashed'. This may have been a cruel description but it was an accurate one. Disease thrives in dirt. Once the authorities in Victorian Britain had grasped this fact, they began to make efforts to provide clean water and effective sewerage. Judged by its beneficial effects, the wc (water closet) lavatory, with its ability to flush away human waste, ranks as one of the modern world's greatest inventions. Its widespread adoption in Britain marked a major step forward in the fight against poor health.

d) Historians now suggest that of all the factors that produced better health in the nation, improved nutrition may have been the most significant. Until recently this was a controversial claim as some writers considered that there was insufficient reliable evidence to support it. But in the 1980s and 90s findings revealed that the average height and weight of the population showed a marked increase in the second half of the nineteenth century. Since the correlation between better eating habits and height and weight increase is now an accepted medical fact, there is a strong case for arguing that improved nourishment was producing a people better able to resist disease.

However, it has to be stressed that the advances we have described were by no means available to all. Whether individuals or families had access to fresh water and sanitation depended on where they lived and what their level of income was. Local authorities differed widely in the speed and willingness with which they undertook the task of improving public health. The public health acts which were passed were not always mandatory; that is to say, they did not require the local authorities to respond, but merely encouraged them and gave them permission to introduce health measures if they so wished. In 1914 most working-class houses still lacked an inside lavatory and a third of them did not have piped water supplies. Slums, squalor and poverty were still grim features of Britain's industrial cities and urban areas. Life remained hard and insecure for the majority of the population in 1914. But everything is relative. Compared with the situation a century earlier conditions were vastly better. During the century from 1815 to 1914, the population had doubled but the amount of goods and services it consumed had multiplied by seven.

To put this another way, the population as a whole was three and a half times better off in 1914 than it had been a century earlier.

Does this mean that each individual man, woman and child was three and a half times better off? The short answer is no, for the simple reason that wealth and resources were not evenly distributed across the population. In terms of need, some people received too much and others too little. In a pioneering study of social conditions in Britain in 1900, Seebohm Rowntree concluded: 'In this land of abounding prosperity, probably more than one fourth of the population are living in poverty'. Whether the state had the right or the duty to correct this imbalance became one of the great political issues in the late Victorian and Edwardian periods. (See the analysis of this theme on pages 196–99.)

ACTIVITY

1. Look back at the population tables and graphs in this section and then tackle the following questions:
   ▼ How would you explain the widening gap between the birth and death rates in the period 1760 to 1840?
   ▼ What do you notice about the population trend for Ireland as compared with that for England and Wales and Scotland?
   ▼ What do you understand by Thomas Malthus's theory of population? How convincing do you find his arguments?
2. Having studied Figure 3, describe what you think the cartoonist's intentions were. You may care to suggest what each of the figures represents, what experiences and knowledge of city life the artist was drawing on and what audience he was expecting to reach.

FATHER THAMES INTRODUCING HIS OFFSPRING TO THE FAIR CITY OF LONDON.
(A Design for a Fresco in the New Houses of Parliament.)

Figure 3 'Father Thames introducing his offspring to the fair city of London', a *Punch* cartoon, 1852.

ISSUE
How far was the
change in the
distribution of the
population the result
of industrialisation?

2 Industrialisation

The population not only increased in size; it also underwent an important shift in its location and concentration. This was largely a result of the change in work patterns. What the nineteenth century witnessed was a considerable extension of the factory system. Rather than working at home as they traditionally had, large numbers of people, both men and women, became employed in factories. It was a change not so much in what people worked at as where they worked. This is clear from the pie charts in Figure 4 which show that already by the 1830s a large proportion of the population was engaged in the manufacture of goods and that this proportion had only slightly increased by 1914.

Figures 4a and 4b Pie charts showing the occupations of British workers in 1841 and in 1914.

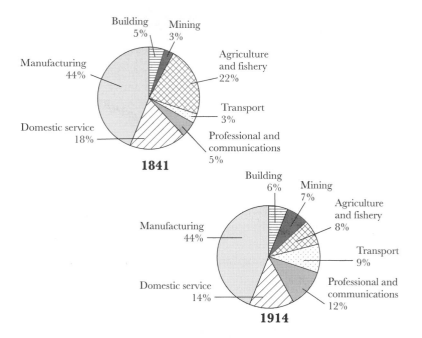

Figure 5 Graph showing the decline in the number of agricultural workers, 1841–1911.

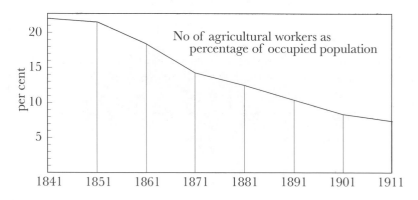

The charts also reveal that by 1914 the number of agricultural workers had dropped to nearly a third of its 1841 figure. This represents the movement of people away from the land to the urban industrial areas, a movement which is further shown in Table 2.

Table 2 Population growth in British cities, 1811–61.

	1811	1821	1831	1841	1851	1861
Birmingham	83,00	102,00	144,00	183,00	233,00	296,000
Glasgow	101,00	147,00	202,00	275,00	345,00	420,000
Leeds	63,00	84,00	123,00	152,00	172,00	207,000
Liverpool	104,00	138,00	202,00	286,00	376,00	444,000
Manchester	89,00	126,00	182,00	235,00	303,00	339,000
Sheffield	53,00	65,00	92,00	111,00	135,00	185,000

(figures drawn from the census returns for these years)

This expansion of the industrial cities became particularly marked after 1871 with the development of what became known as the conurbations – the densely-populated regions that grew up around the centres of manufacturing, mining and ship building.

Table 3 The growth of the conurbations in late-Victorian and Edwardian Britain, 1871–1911.

Year	Greater London	S.E. Lancs	W. Midlands	W. Yorks	Merseyside
1871	3,890,000	1,386,000	969,000	1,064,000	690,000
1901	6,856,000	2,117,000	1,483,000	1,524,000	1,030,000
1911	7,256,000	2,328,000	1,634,000	1,590,000	1,157,000

ACTIVITY

1. Account for the remarkable growth in the urban areas as shown and described in this section.
2. What social problems do you think would be likely to follow such a rapid and sustained rise in the size and density of the population?

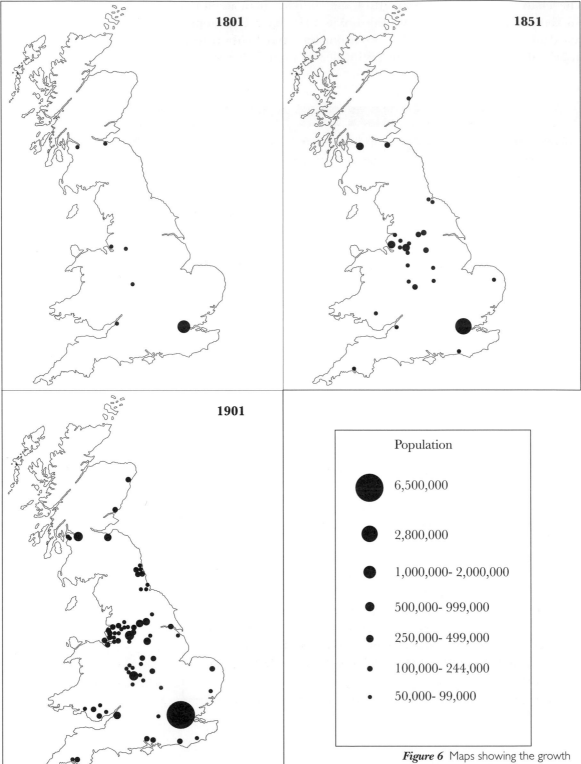

Figure 6 Maps showing the growth of British cities, 1801, 1851, 1901.

The factor that explains the changing location of the population was the impact of the machine. The celebrated Scottish writer, Thomas Carlyle, captured the way that mechanisation altered the lives of people in the nineteenth century.

It is the Age of Machinery, in every outward and inward sense of that word; the age which, with its whole undivided might, forwards, teaches and practices the great art of adapting means to ends. Nothing is now done directly, or by hand; all is by rule and calculated contrivance. Our old modes of exertion are all discredited, and thrown aside. On every hand, the living artisan is driven from his workshop, to make room for a speedier, inanimate [lifeless] one. The shuttle drops from the fingers of the weaver, and falls into iron fingers that ply it faster.

These things indicate a mighty change in our whole manner of existence. For the same habit regulates not our modes of action alone, but our modes of thought and feeling. Men are grown mechanical in head and in heart, as well as in hand. They have lost faith in individual endeavour, and in natural force, of any kind. Their whole efforts, attachments, opinions, turn on mechanism, and are of a mechanical character.

Source A Adapted from *Signs of the Times* by Thomas Carlyle, 1829.

Modern researches have confirmed the accuracy of Carlyle's observations. The following passage summarises how historians now view the picture:

A large proportion of rural workers had long been used to manufacturing through their own part-time employment within the domestic system. Two things were different in factory labour. First, there was the relentless discipline of mechanisation. Here was the origin of the conveyor-belt mentality where man, the creator of the machine, was made its servant. The discipline of the machine was reinforced by the authority of master or overlooker and the sombre instructions of the factory bell, summoning hands, not people. Second, the decision of whether and when to work was taken out of the hands of the individual and placed at the whim of impersonal market forces. An independent handworker worked when he pleased; a factory operative could only work when required to do so by the demands of the market.

Source B From *The Evolution of the British Welfare State* by Derek Fraser, Macmillan 1973.

ISSUES

How was Britain able to establish itself as the workshop of the world in the nineteenth century? Why was it unable to maintain that position into the twentieth century?

KEY STAGES IN BRITAIN'S POSITION AS WORKSHOP OF THE WORLD

1850 –63 coal production rose from 45 to 100 million tons per annum;

1850 –73 textiles overtaken by machinery and heavy industrial goods as Britain's main and most profitable exports;

1851 the Great Exhibition in London displayed Britain's technical and industrial achievements;

1852 by this date 7,000 miles of railway track had been laid;

1851 –75 steel output rose from 40,000 to 1,250,000 tons per annum;

1873 by this date 14,000 miles of railway track had been laid.

3 Trade and Commerce

In the eighteenth century Britain had been the first nation to begin to undergo an 'industrial revolution'. Some historians are unhappy with this term, which they suggest over-dramatises the process it describes. However, others still regard it as a convenient way of referring to the wide range of advances in technology and applied science, which, by the middle years of the nineteenth century, had made Britain the world's leading industrial power. This process began around the middle of the eighteenth century with the textile industry. But a century later it was heavy industry, driven by the steam engine, powered by coal and served by a rapidly expanding communications network, that enabled Britain to rejoice in the description 'the workshop of the world'.

This description referred to the lead in industrial production and international trade which Britain had established by the middle years of the nineteenth century. The expansion of its road and waterway network and the development of its railways, ports and shipping allowed Britain to export its manufactured goods in such volume that for much of the century it was a long way ahead of its nearest commercial rivals.

Britain's industrial and commercial leadership did not last. Between 1870 and 1914 there occurred what has been called the 'the late-Victorian recession'. Britain was overtaken in the volume of its iron and steel output by Germany and the USA. In the same period Britain's rate of industrial growth was only half that of the USA. Furthermore, by 1910, British industrial exports made up only 10 per cent of world trade compared with figures of 20 per cent for German and 40 per cent for American. Despite these facts, many modern economic historians have challenged whether there really was a recession. They point out that British industry was still growing in this period and was more efficient (i.e., it produced its goods more cheaply while maintaining higher quality) than American and German industry. They suggest that, although the British economy

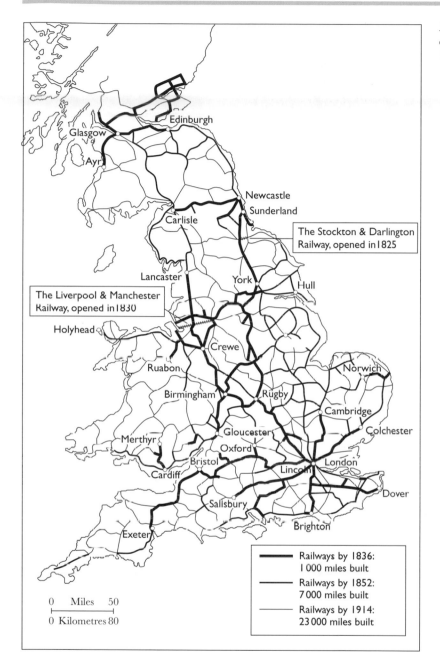

Figure 7 Map of railway development between 1825 and 1914.

The Stockton & Darlington Railway, opened in 1825

The Liverpool & Manchester Railway, opened in 1830

Railways by 1836: 1 000 miles built

Railways by 1852: 7 000 miles built

Railways by 1914: 23 000 miles built

0　Miles　50

0 Kilometres 80

was in relative decline compared with that of Germany and America, this was only to be expected given the larger populations and greater natural resources of Germany and America.

However, at the time, British industrialists genuinely believed that the trade figures indicated that they could not compete with their American and German rivals in the open market. They urged the government to bring in measures to protect their manufactures

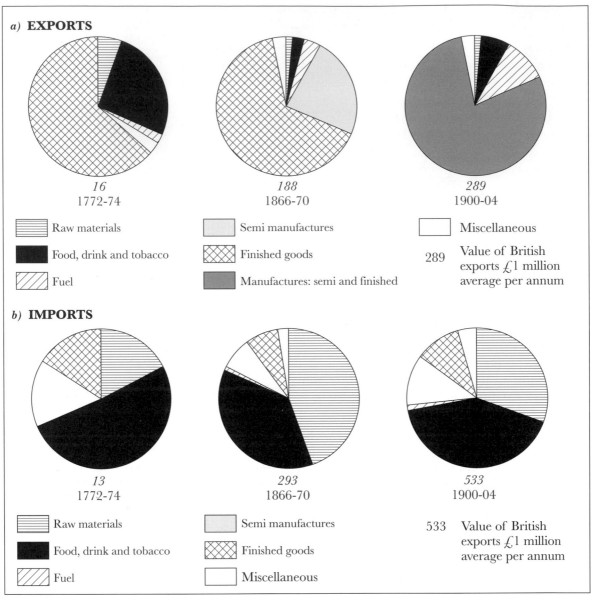

a) **EXPORTS**

16
1772-74

188
1866-70

289
1900-04

	Raw materials		Semi manufactures		Miscellaneous
	Food, drink and tobacco		Finished goods	289	Value of British exports £1 million average per annum
	Fuel		Manufactures: semi and finished		

b) **IMPORTS**

13
1772-74

293
1866-70

533
1900-04

	Raw materials		Semi manufactures	533	Value of British exports £1 million average per annum
	Food, drink and tobacco		Finished goods		
	Fuel		Miscellaneous		

Figures 8a and 8b Pie charts showing Britain's major imports and exports by type of commodity.

against foreign competition. This brought the debate about what economic policy Britain should follow to a full circle. Throughout the nineteenth century there had been a constant argument between the landed classes, who wanted **protection**, and the manufacturing classes, who wanted **free trade**.

By the 1840s the principle of protection had been undermined by a series of financial reforms which had abolished a whole range of tariffs and import duties. The Corn Laws began to look increasingly out-of-date as an economic policy and in 1846 they were repealed.

Q

Why was there a clash between Free-Trade and Protection?

ACTIVITY

1. What connections can be drawn between the statistics on city and conurbation growth, given in Tables 2 and 3 and Figure 6, and the map in Figure 7 showing railway development?
2. Having studied the charts in Figure 8, attempt the following exercise:

    Write two or three sentences on each of the terms 'raw materials', 'manufactures', and 'semi-manufactures' to show that you understand the differences between them.

For the next two generations Britain allowed a policy of free trade to operate. This period between the 1840s and 1880s broadly coincided with the period of Britain's pre-eminence as an industrial trading nation, but the consensus among economic historians is that the repeal of the Corn Laws played little part in bringing this about (see page 47).

FREE TRADE

A notion closely associated with the Scottish economist Adam Smith, one of the great influences on economic thinking in the nineteenth century. He had argued in his book, *The Wealth of Nations*, (1776) that trade flourished best and brought the largest returns when it was left entirely free of government interference. He explained that tariffs and duties on imported goods, which were imposed to protect home products, impeded the flow of trade and so reduced the scope for British manufacturers to export their goods. Smith's argument that free trade encouraged business and therefore higher profits was championed by most manufacturers and industrialists.

THE MANCHESTER SCHOOL

The name given to the believers in free trade in the middle of the nineteenth century. The leading members of the school were the Manchester-based politicians John Bright (1811–98) and Richard Cobden (1804–65), who gained a formidable reputation as the chief spokesmen for the Anti-Corn Law league, the mass movement which campaigned for the repeal of the Corn Laws in the late 1830s and early 1840s.

PROTECTION

In 1815 Parliament, which was dominated by the landed and farming interests, passed the Corn Laws. These were an attempt to protect the British farmers from being undersold by cheaper grain from the continent. The Corn Laws placed a high tariff on foreign corn thus making it unprofitable to import. However, in practice the Corn Laws did not lead to prosperity for the farmers. Chronic low wages meant that the workers simply did not have enough money to buy bread at the inflated prices that would have brought profits to the corn growers. The grim result was bread shortage and hunger for the working classes without any real financial gains for the farmers. Nonetheless, the landed classes clung on to protection in the mistaken belief that it would preserve the profits that were made from the sale of the agricultural produce grown on their estates.

Why was there a late-Victorian recession?

The economic argument took another turn during the period of 'the late-Victorian recession'. By the 1890s the Conservatives and a considerable number of Liberals had begun to follow the lead set by the radical politician, Joseph Chamberlain, in demanding that Britain's perceived industrial and agricultural decline could be halted only by

KEY STAGES IN BRITISH ECONOMIC POLICY

1815 the Corn Laws re-imposed a protectionist policy on Britain;

1823 –27 reforms introduced by William Huskisson at the Board of Trade reduced duties on a whole range of imported goods, thus undermining protection as a principle;

1842 –46 Robert Peel's free-trade budgets extended Huskisson's reforms;

1846 the Corn Laws were repealed;

1846 –73 British commerce and farming flourished, the free-trade ideas of the Manchester school predominated;

1851 the Great Exhibition celebrated Britain's position as 'workshop of the world'

1853 –60 the free-trade budgets of W.E. Gladstone completed the work of Huskisson and Peel;

1860 the Cobden-Chevalier reciprocity treaty led to Britain and France abolishing duties on each other's goods;

1870 -1914 the 'late-Victorian recession' – falling prices, low productivity, and rising unemployment – undermined the belief in free trade;

1896 -1914 the tariff reform (protection) versus free trade dispute became a dominant issue in British politics.

a return to a policy of protection. Tariffs on imported foreign goods would have to be reimposed. Such a view was strongly opposed by many traditional Liberals. 'Tariff Reform versus Free Trade' became one of the most controversial political issues in the generation before 1914.

Key factors in the late-Victorian recession, 1870–1900

▽ the opening up of the prairies in the USA and Canada flooded the world's agricultural markets with cheap grain – free trade Britain, in particular, found it increasingly difficult to compete;

▽ an agricultural depression in Britain, caused by bad harvests, foreign competition and falling land prices;

▽ American and German iron and steel output overtook British;

▽ the machines and industrial processes which had earlier given Britain its lead became outdated, particularly in the coal and textile industries;

▽ too little capital was put into developing new machinery and methods;

▽ many British manufactured goods became more expensive than foreign ones, which led to lower exports and higher imports;

▽ the falling prices at home of both food and goods benefited the consumers initially but led to lower profits, lower investment and the laying off of workers;

▽ unemployment remained high (average of 12%) in this period.

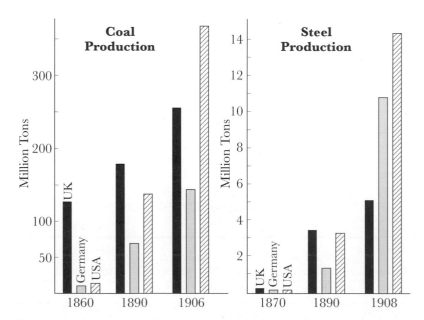

Figure 9 Graphs showing British, American and German coal and steel production 1860–1908.

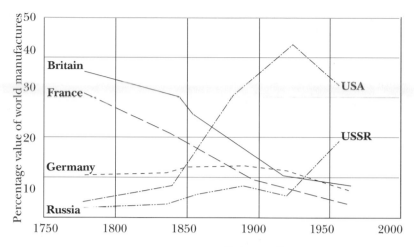

Figure 10 Graph showing Britain's share of world trade.

Bernard Partridge

Figure 11 'The Uncommercial Traveller', *Punch* cartoon, 1901.
Mr Punch: 'Now, Mr Bull, Wake up! You'll have to keep your eye on that chap. He's always at it, speaks their languages and knows their money.'
John Bull: 'Pooh! My goods are better than his!'
Mr Punch: 'I daresay – but you've got to make them understand it!'

Year	domestic production	imports
1837–41	3,070,000	390,000
1842–45	3,140,000	280,000
1846–48	2,920,000	480,000
1849–54	3,620,000	860,000
1862–68	2,960,000	1,430,000
1869–75	2,550,000	2,570,000

Table 4 Wheat supplies in Britain (annual average in tons), 1837–75.

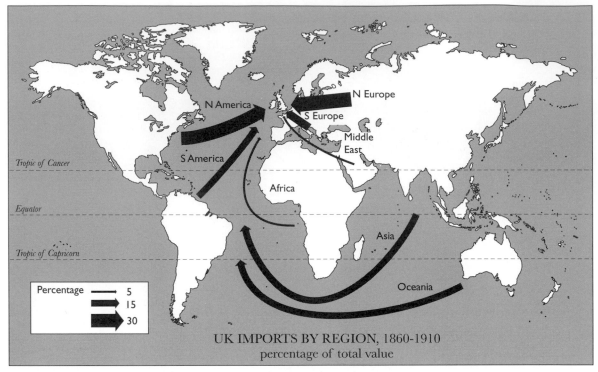

Figure 12 Map showing where Britain's imports came from.

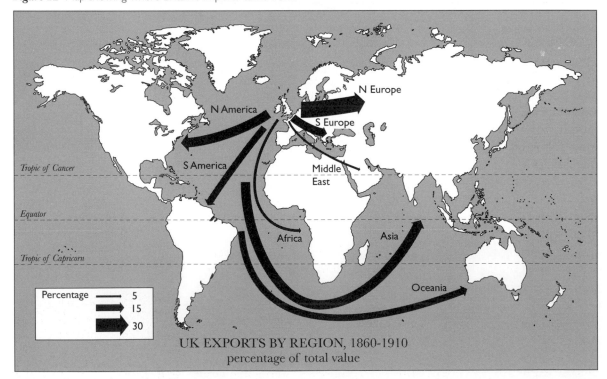

Figure 13 Map showing where Britain's exports went to.

1840	328p	1860	219p	1880	221p
1845	228p	1865	194p	1885	173p
1850	220p	1870	213p	1890	151p
1855	361p	1875	215p	1895	104p
1859	208p	1879	215p	1899	133p

Table 5 Wheat prices per quarter bushel (converted into decimal currency), 1840–99.

ACTIVITY

1. In the light of the statistical information in Figures 9 and 10, how valid do you judge Mr. Punch's concerns about the threat to British trade to have been. Use the other information in this section in compiling your answer. Reference to the views of modern analysts, as described on page 12, would be particularly appropriate.
2. Study Tables 4 and 5 and then answer the following questions:
   a. Explain the changing balance between the domestic wheat production and wheat imports in the period 1837–75.
   b. How far do these figures support the notion that i) the abolition of the Corn Laws in 1846 ushered in a long period of cheap wheat and ii) there was a late-Victorian recession?

4 Shipping

The remarkable increase in Britain's overseas trade has two main explanations. By the middle of the nineteenth century industrial output had outstripped demand at home and had encouraged the view that exports were the chief means by which profits could be increased. British manufacturers felt they were ideally placed to satisfy the growing international demand for industrial goods. But, just as the initial burst of internal trade in the eighteenth century had required an effective communications network to distribute goods around Britain, so the industrial boom that began about 1850 needed reliable means of carrying the goods to overseas buyers. It was here that the position of Britain as an island nation with a strong naval and ship-building tradition proved invaluable. The most significant technical advance which made possible the huge increase of tonnage conveyed on the world's oceans was the development of the steel-built steamship. When the nineteenth century opened, British ships had been short and bulky, built of wood and powered by sail. In 1900 98 per cent of British carrying vessels were long, large vessels, built of iron and steel and driven by steam.

KEY STAGES IN BRITISH SHIPPING

1800 Lloyds of London became the world's leading ship insurers;
1800 largest ships – 700 tons;
1800–25 large extension of London's docks;
1802 first steam ship built;
1825 first iron ship floated;
1838 Brunel's *Great Western* iron paddle steamer;
1840s British iron-hulled sailing clippers were able to carry commodities from China to England in only 90 days;
1849 the Navigation Laws repealed;
1850s screw propellers replaced paddles as chief means of propulsion;
1854 piston-cylinder engine increased the speed of steam ships;
1860s steel began to replace iron as the chief material for ship building;
1869 the opening of the Suez Canal shortened the journey to India and the Far East;
1876 The Merchant Shipping Act created basic safety standards by imposing the Plimsoll line limit on loading;
1897 first marine turbine engine greatly improved the speed and efficiency of ships;
1900 largest ships – 70,000 tons.

ISSUE
How was Britain able to establish itself as the world's leading commercial nation?

5 Finance

Between 1830 and 1850 Britain considerably increased its national income by achieving a positive balance of payments. What that means is that the value of the goods it exported exceeded the cost of the goods it imported. This provided British banks and finance houses with a capital surplus which they re-invested in overseas markets and ventures. Among the enterprises in which British firms put their capital abroad were mines, chemical works, railways, rubber plantations, engineering works, and timber production. During the second half of the nineteenth century British financial and commercial concerns invested five billion pounds overseas in this way. This was not done for selfless reasons – profit was always the aim – but it did result in a number of other countries being able to mount their own industrial revolutions.

What helped to give strength and security to British investment abroad was the nation's position for much of the century as the world's leading shipping nation. Until late in the century ship-building and goods-carrying remained highly profitable activities. It was still the case in 1900 that half of all the world's merchant ships had been built in British shipyards. Even when that favourable position began to be threatened in the late Victorian years by foreign competition, British companies continued to draw considerable profit from their foreign investments. The reason relates to what are referred to as **'invisible' exports**.

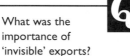

What was the importance of 'invisible' exports?

INVISIBLE EXPORTS

The term for the capital income that came from the repayment of the interest on the loans that had been advanced. The more British financiers loaned the more they received in repayments. Nor did the advantage stop there. 67 per cent of the capital that Britain's financiers advanced was spent by the borrowing countries on buying British industrial products.

2. Show that you understand the term, 'invisible exports', by defining it in your own words.

3. In what ways might invisible exports compensate for a decline in the overseas sales of agricultural and industrial products?

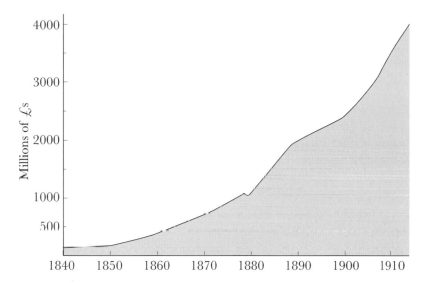

Figure 14 Graph showing British investment overseas, 1840–1914.

THE BANK OF ENGLAND

At the beginning of the nineteenth century this had simply been a commercial bank but by 1900 it had become the institution on which governments relied to control and safeguard the nation's finances. It issued the only legal currency in England and Wales, supervised the exchange rates, protected Britain's bullion reserves, maintained the **gold standard**, and gave assistance to other banks in time of difficulty. By 1900 it had established itself as the most dependable of the world's financial institutions.

A major role in sustaining the value of Britain's invisible exports was played by **the City** and the **Bank of England**. The reliability of the Bank of England encouraged a large number of countries to invest in British enterprises, since they judged that their money would be secure. The common expression 'as safe as the Bank of England' conveyed the confidence people around the world had in Britain as a financial centre. Britain's merchant banks and insurance houses flourished as foreign businesses and companies chose to protect themselves by taking out British insurance policies. Lloyds of London, the marine insurers, was an outstanding example. The reputation which these developments gave to Britain encouraged many foreign banks to set up their own branches in the City. There was very little international financial business that did not go through the City at some stage. The result of all this was a very substantial swelling of Britain's invisible exports.

Britain's being on the gold standard was usually thought of as an advantage since it gave strength to the British currency. However, a major drawback was that high prices had to be charged by British exporters. This was because the real gold value of Britain's pound sterling was so much higher than other currencies that foreign traders had to match it by paying larger amounts of their own

THE CITY

The term used to describe the large number of banks and finance houses concentrated in the small area of the historic City of London. The main bank was the Bank of England.

THE GOLD STANDARD

The term refers to the position in which a nation's currency – in Britain's case the pound sterling or sovereign coin – has a fixed gold content. In 1821 the sovereign was 92 per cent pure gold. Between that date and 1914 all British coinage had an exact gold value. The gold standard gave Britain's currency such a strength and reliability that foreign investors rushed to buy it and to use it as the common form of exchange. By 1914 nearly all trading nations had followed Britain in adopting their own gold standard, which gave great stability to international commerce. It was the economic disruption caused by the First World War that made it impossible for countries to maintain their gold standards.

currency when purchasing British goods. This was an obvious disincentive to their buying British. In the last quarter of the nineteenth century Britain's exporters found that the gold standard was pricing their goods out of the market.

Figure 15 Pie charts showing regional spread of Britain's capital exports.

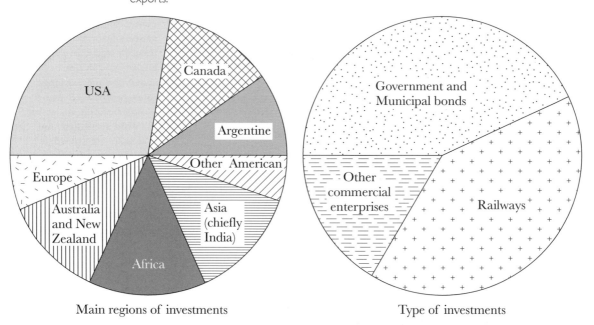

Main regions of investments   Type of investments

ACTIVITY

Having read section 5, answer the following questions:

1. What contribution did the City make to Britain's development as a trading nation in the nineteenth century?
2. Draw up two lists, showing a) the advantage and b) the disadvantage for Britain of being on the gold standard.

Summary of The British Economy in the Nineteenth Century

Year	Population Growth	Industrialisation and Urbanisation	Trade	Shipping	Investment and Finance
1800				largest ships – 700 tons	Lloyds of London the world's largest marine insurers
1811	17,907,976				
1815			Corn Laws introduced		
1821	20,893,584				
1823–27			free-trade reforms of the Liberal Tories	Navigation Laws relaxed	
1825			railways began to provide the chief means of moving goods to the ports for export	major extension of London docks completed	
1831	24,028,584				
1836			by this date 1,000 miles of railtrack built		
1838				Brunel's 'Great Western' launched	
1840s				British sailing clippers dominate world's carrying trade	
1841	26,730,929	agricultural workers made up 22% of work force; manufacturing workers 44%; domestic servants 18%			total British investment abroad – £100 million
1846			the repeal of the Corn Laws mark climax of Peel's free trade policies		
1849				Navigation Laws repealed	
1851	27,390,629	agricultural workers made up 21% of work force	the Great Exhibition; by this date 7,000 miles of railtrack built		total British investment abroad – £150 million
1853–60			Gladstone's free-trade budgets complete Peel's work		

Year	Population Growth	Industrialisation and Urbanisation	Trade	Shipping	Investment and Finance
1861	28,927,485	agricultural workers make up 17% of work force			total British investment abroad – £450 million
1866–70			value of average annual exports – £188 million, imports – £293 million		
1869				Suez Canal opened	
1870–1900			the 'late-Victorian recession' – Britain's share of world trade drops from 25% to 15% in this period		
1871	31,484,661	growth of conurbations began about this date, e.g. Greater London 3,890,000			total British investment abroad – £800 million
1876				Merchant Shipping Act	
1881	34,884,661	agricultural workers made up 12% of work force			
1891	37,732,922	agricultural workers made up 10% of work force			total British investment abroad – £1,000 million
1896–1914			the free-trade versus protection dispute		
1900–04			value of average annual exports – £289 million, imports – £533 million		total British investment abroad – £2,500 million
1901	41,458,721	Greater London 6,856,00			by now the Bank of England established as the world's most dependable bank
1911	45,221,615	Greater London 7,256,000; agricultural workers made up 8% of work force; manufacturing workers 44%; domestic servants 14%	by this date 22,000 miles of railtrack built	largest ships – 70,000 tons	total British investment abroad – £3,900 million

▼ Working on The British Economy in the Nineteenth Century

The purpose of this opening chapter was to introduce some of the key economic developments which occurred in this period and which underlay the politics and the social movements of the time. It was meant to provide a set of references and pointers for you to look back on when dealing with other themes in this book. Politics will tend to dominate our study of the nineteenth century so it is vital to remember that so much of politics is a reaction to the prevailing economic situation.

As a review exercise to make sure that you have grasped the essential material in this chapter, check back over the five key economic themes with which the chapter deals – population, urbanisation, industrialisation, trade, and finance. Make sure you understand what the main developments were. Then begin the process of assessing their significance in the light of the themes you know will be covered in later chapters. Of course, at this stage, this can be only a partial exercise since obviously you have not yet studied the material in the rest of the book. However, you could usefully start formulating your ideas about such questions as:

▼ In what ways were party politics in the nineteenth century affected by the economic changes occurring at the time?

▼ Why was the question of poverty such a big political issue in the nineteenth century?

▼ Why did the pressure for reform of parliament become so strong in the Victorian period?

▼ Trace and explain the swings in British economic policy between protection and free trade.

▼ What grounds are there for regarding British imperialism between 1870 and 1914 as a policy of economic exploitation?

Answering extended writing and essay questions on The British Economy in the Nineteenth Century

The following list shows the different style of questions you are likely to encounter on the topic of the British economy in the nineteenth century. Seven types of issue have been selected. You will find that these form the basic pattern of approach in all the end of chapter review sections.

Type of Issue	Examples of typical questions
1 causes/reasons/motives	Explain why the population of Britain increased in size by nearly two and a half times between 1811 and 1911
2 course of events	Trace the key developments in British economic policy in the nineteenth century.
3 consequences/results/effects	What were the major social and economic consequences of the growth of the conurbations in Britain in the nineteenth century?
4 success/failure	How successfully did the British manufacturing industry meet the challenge of foreign competition between 1870 and 1914?
5 significance/importance	How significant were the population theories of Thomas Malthus?
6 comparison	Why was Britain subsequently unable to sustain its position as 'the workshop of the world' that it had gained in the middle years of the nineteenth century?
7 right/wrong (moral/ethical judgments, assessing validity)	How accurate is it to suggest that there was a 'late-Victorian recession'?

You will immediately notice that these questions vary in difficulty. For our first exercise in essay preparation, let us take number 2, which is one of the more straightforward questions. Here you are being asked to describe the responses to the major economic developments of the period. Notice how broad the question is. It covers a whole century. This means that you have to be very selective in choosing the points you want to include. You do not have the time or space to digress or to give extended treatment to any particular point. In a question this wide there are no factors that are so essential that if you were to omit them you would necessarily write a poor answer. Nevertheless, there are certain points that suggest themselves. The list on page 14 will obviously be helpful here. Your answer could be well structured around the following: protection, the Corn Laws and their repeal, mid-Victorian prosperity, the late-Victorian recession, and free trade versus tariff reform. If these are linked together in an informed chronology they will go a long way towards meeting the requirements of the question.

Answering source-based questions on The British Economy in the Nineteenth Century

You will have learned from the Preface that source-based questions are graded in degrees of difficulty. The following questions, which are meant to test your basic understanding, relate to Thomas Carlyle's description of the social impact of the machine (page 9). Before attempting them, re-read the passage and the accompanying material on pages 6–9.

▼ QUESTIONS ON THE SOURCES

Explain in your own words what you understand Carlyle to mean by the following:
1. 'all is by rule and calculated contrivance' (line 4) **[2 marks]**
2. 'the same habit regulates not our modes of action alone, but our modes of thought and feeling' (line 11) **[3 marks]**
3. 'Men are grown mechanical in head and in heart, as well as in hand.' (line 12) **[3 marks]**

Points to note about the questions

In this instance the questions are entirely concerned with comprehension. Understanding is, of course, basic to source analysis. It is the essential first step. In subsequent chapters questions will become more difficult, but no matter how they are phrased or what particular skills on your part they call for, they will not be manageable unless you have fully understood the meaning of the material you are studying. That is why it is a very effective basic rule to turn any difficult passage into your own words. That way you will avoid assuming that you have understood when in fact you have not. So do not take these first questions lightly. Another key point is that you should judge how much you should write by the mark allocation in the square brackets. For 2 or 3 marks only, no more than a sentence or two is necessary. An example of how you might turn Carlyle's words into your own modern version is: **3.** People have become regimented in the way they think and feel as well as in the way they work.

Coursework

As you know, the choice of what you do for coursework is very much in your hands. The hope is that you will choose a theme that genuinely interests you and then research into it. Start from the known. Do not select a topic merely because you like the sound of it. You need to find out whether you have sufficient material of the appropriate kind. The suggested reading at the end of each chapter is meant to point you in the right direction by suggesting books and articles which will stimulate your interest. In all the recommended books you will find helpful and often quite extensive bibliographies.

Further Reading

Books in the 'Access to History' series

The Industrialisation of Britain, 1780–1914 by Phil Chapple covers all the five themes in this chapter. Chapters 1 and 2 of *Poverty and Welfare, 1830–1914* by Peter Murray deals with the effects of industrialisation as does Chapter 1 of *Labour and Reform: Working Class Movements, 1815–1914* by Clive Behagg. A helpful analysis of trade and commerce is included in Chapters 5 and 6 of *Whigs, Radicals and Liberals, 1815–1914* by Duncan Watts.

General

Informative analyses of population, shipping and trade are to be found in *The Age of Reform 1820–50* and *The Edwardian Age*, both books by Vyvyen Brendon (Hodder & Stoughton, 1994 and 1995). Very useful on population is *The Rise of Industrial Society in England 1815–1885* by S.G. Checkland (Longmans, 1964). Particularly helpful maps and charts on population and trade are to be found in *Atlas of British Social and Economic History since c.1700* by Rex Pope (Routledge, 1989). *The Years of Expansion Britain 1815–1914* edited by Michael Scott-Baumann (Hodder & Stoughton, 1995) has informative sections on the economy in this period. The growth of transport in this period is well covered in *British Transport and the Economy* by H.J. Dyos and D.H. Aldcroft (Leicester University Press, 1971). There is an excellent treatment of the effects of industrialisation and of Malthus's ideas in *Early Victorian Britain, 1832–51* by J.F.C. Harrison (Fontana, 1988). *Victorian Cities* by Asa Briggs (Penguin, 1978) is a modern classic on nineteenth-century urbanisation while *The People and the British Economy 1830–1914* by Roderick Floud (OPUS, 1998) is highly recommended as an up-to-date and readable study of all five themes of this chapter. A work which will prove very helpful as a source of reference throughout this book is *The Complete A–Z: 19th & 20th Century British History Handbook* by Eric Evans (Hodder & Stoughton, 1998).

POLITICS AND PARTIES I, 1815–46

CHAPTER 2

POINTS TO CONSIDER

In this chapter you will be introduced to the two parties which dominated politics in the first half of the nineteenth century – the Whigs and the Tories. After a brief introduction, three key areas will be presented for study:

1. The rule of the Tories between 1815 and 1830, which is divided into a) the 'reactionary' Tories, b) the historical debate on the 'reactionary' Tories, and c) the 'liberal' Tories
2. The Whig reforming governments of 1830–41, including a sub-section a) on the influences behind reform
3. Robert Peel's Conservative government of 1841–6, including a sub-section a) on the repeal of the Corn Laws.

You will immediately notice that a new party, the Conservative Party, has appeared on the scene. In the 1830s the Tory party changed its name to Conservative and began to alter its character in a number of ways. The Whig party also went through a transition and by the second half of the century had been transformed into the Liberal party. This illustrates an important characteristic of British politics that you will observe throughout this book. Parties never stand still; they are always adapting themselves to changing circumstances. The chapter describes how the political parties, whether in power or in opposition, responded to the pressing economic and social problems that are analysed in Chapters 1 and 4.

Introduction

Historians usually put their material into compartments with such labels as politics, economics, social issues, and foreign affairs. They do this in order to make analysis easier. But they also frequently warn that it would be wrong for us to think of these compartments as watertight. There is a great deal of spillage. Major issues are a combination of factors. This chapter is a good example of this. The economic, social and international situations affected the way political parties thought and behaved. In turn, the attitude of politicians affected the way they interpreted the economic, social and international questions they confronted.

Politics is essentially about power and the way it is distributed. At the beginning of the nineteenth century those who held political power were invariably those who had wealth. The formal expression of their power was Parliament. This was composed of two chambers, the House of Commons and the House of Lords. The Commons was an elected body of MPs while the Lords was made up of hereditary peers. The great majority of MPs were landed gentlemen who looked upon their membership of Parliament as one of the accompaniments of wealth and social position. It is true that the MPs in the Commons had to be elected, but so few people could vote that most elections were a foregone conclusion. Voting was done by a show of hands; the secret ballot did not come in until the 1870s. This meant that bribery and intimidation of voters was a regular occurrence. Such was the degree of control exercised over voters in some constituencies that they were known as 'pocket' or 'rotten' boroughs.

The two largest political parties in Parliament at the beginning of the nineteenth century were the Tories and the Whigs. These were groups that had originally developed out of the struggle between King and Parliament in the seventeenth century. In general terms, the Tories were those who believed in the combined authority of monarch, Anglican Church and Parliament to rule the nation. The Whigs were those who believed that Parliament was the major authority and were suspicious of the monarch and the Church having too much power. But these are broad distinctions. It would be wrong to think of the Whigs and Tories being divided over these questions on deep ideological grounds. The feature that strikes us now is how similar the members of both parties were in their wealth and social backgrounds. Even those who made their money from industry tended to use their profits to buy land so that they became almost indistinguishable in their life-style from the established landed class. An interesting example is Robert Peel, a successful cotton manufacturer whose son, also called Robert, was to become leader of the Conservative Party and the outstanding British statesman of the first half of the nineteenth century. Peel senior made sure that his son received the public school and university education that the landed classes traditionally regarded as the necessary stepping stones to high office and position in later life.

A distinction that can be made between the parties is that the Tories tended to be more resistant to change and slower to accept new ideas than were the Whigs. The Tories had been firmly opposed to the French Revolution which began in 1789. The ideals proclaimed by the revolutionaries of liberty and equality and the attack upon the French aristocracy had frightened the Tory government

What were the major parties?

into abandoning any thought of reform in England. William Pitt, the Tory Prime Minister during much of the struggle with France, had expressed this well when he explained that it was unwise to repair one's roof in the middle of a storm.

1 The Tories, 1815–30

ISSUE
How reactionary were the Tories before 1822?

a) The 'Reactionary' Tories, 1815–22

After a long period of Whig dominance in the eighteenth century, the Tories had come into power in 1783 and continued in office until 1830. They were therefore well established when our period opens. Since 1812 they had been led as Prime Minister by Lord Liverpool. The Tories under him faced serious social and economic problems after 1815. The end of the Napoleonic War in that year brought in an economic recession.

Reasons for the Post-1815 Depression

The war had created a demand for industrial goods; this sharply declined with the coming of peace. Workers were either laid off or had their wages reduced. Their plight was worsened by job competition from the demobilised troops who returned looking for work. Low wages and unemployment were also experienced by agricultural workers. The wartime blockades which had prevented imports coming easily into the country had created a boom time for British food producers. But British farmers after 1815 had again to compete with foreign produce which was often cheaper than its British counterpart. This resulted in an agricultural depression.

An important reaction to the depression on the part of the land owners who dominated Parliament was to introduce the Corn Laws in 1815. The main purpose of these was to impose tariffs on foreign grain to keep its price artificially high and therefore not worth importing. One result of this was to raise the price of bread, the staple diet of the working classes, at a time when wages were falling. In addition, the government resorted to increased taxation to pay the massive **National Debt** caused by its heavy borrowings during the French wars. However, since Parliament refused to renew income tax, the only alternative was a substantial increase in indirect taxation, levied on such basic items as tea, sugar, tobacco, beer and candles. The tax burden, therefore, fell disproportionately on the

Q How did the Tory Government respond to the depression?

THE NATIONAL DEBT
The total outstanding of all the money borrowed by the central government which it has to pay back with accumulated interest.

How was the
Government's
response received?

poorer classes. It was hard not to conclude that the poor were being taxed for the benefit of the rich.

Many became convinced that government and Parliament did not care about the difficulties being experienced by the workers. A radical figure who gave voice to such bitterness was the writer, William Cobbett. A fierce opponent of corruption in high places, Cobbett thundered against the iniquities of a system that allowed the deprived many to starve while the privileged few grew fat. The passion and power of Cobbett's arguments is evident in the following extract in which the particular object of his hatred is taxation:

> As it is the labour of those who toil which makes a country abound in resources, so it is the same class of men, who must, by their arms, secure its safety and uphold its fame. With this correct idea of your own worth in your minds, with what indignation, must you hear yourselves called the Populace, the Rabble, the Mob, the Swinish Multitude; and, with what greater indignation, if possible, must you hear the projects of those cool and cruel insolent men, who, now that you have been, without any fault of your own, brought into a state of misery, propose to narrow the limits of parish relief, to prevent you from marrying in the days of your youth, or to thrust you out to seek your bread in foreign lands, never more to behold your parents or friends? But suppress your indignation, until we return to this, after we have considered the cause of your present misery and the measures which have produced that cause.
>
> It is the *enormous amount of taxes*, which the government compels us to pay for the support of its army, its placemen [appointees], its pensioners etc. and for the payment of the interest of its debt. That this is the *real* cause has been a thousand times proved; and it is now so acknowledged by the creatures of the government themselves. The tax gatherers do not, indeed, come to you and demand money of you: but, there are few articles which you use, in the purchase of which you do not pay *a tax*.

Source A From William Cobbett's newspaper, the *Political Register*, 2 November 1816.

ACTIVITY

Study the passage above and then state briefly in your own words the main points made by Cobbett. What type of tax is he condemning?

Cobbett's harsh view of the government helped create a particular and lasting image of Lord Liverpool's administration. Until recently historians tended to repeat the charge that it was reactionary and harsh. The grounds for this accusation were the various repressive measures introduced to control the disturbances that occurred. More recently historians have begun to show a greater understanding of the difficulties facing the Tories and more sympathy towards the policies they followed. Before looking at this interpretation it would be worthwhile considering the disturbances of the time and the measures which Liverpool's government took to put them down.

LUDDISM

A movement that was said to be led by the mythical 'King Ludd' of Sherwood Forest. The Luddites were largely drawn from the Nottinghamshire handloom weavers, highly-skilled craftsmen whose previously highly-profitable work had been made obsolete by the introduction of mechanical looms. Between 1811 and 1817, groups of Luddites attacked cotton factories in Nottinghamshire, smashing the knitting frames and destroying the stocks of cloth. Their example was copied by groups in Lancashire and Cheshire. Luddism, meaning determined resistance to technological progress, added a new word to the language.

Peterloo, 1819

A mass meeting to demand reform was held at St Peter's Fields in Manchester. It was addressed by Henry 'Orator' Hunt, a leading radical and an associate of William Cobbett. It was intended to be a peaceful demonstration, but the size of the crowd frightened the authorities into sending in cavalry with drawn swords to disperse it. In the disorder and panic that followed, eleven people, including two women and a child, were killed and four hundred were injured. The government's immediate reaction was to introduce the Six Acts. Opponents of the government christened the event 'Peterloo', a mocking comparison with the British victory at Waterloo in 1815.

MAJOR DISTURBANCES

1811–17 Nottinghamshire Luddites were responsible for organising attacks on factories and machine wrecking;

1815 violent protests occurred in London against the Corn Laws;

1816 a meeting of Spencean radicals in London's Spa Fields got out of hand and led to riots and looting;

1817 troops used force to disperse the 'Blanketeers' march; unemployed textile workers in Derbyshire, led by Jeremiah Brandreth, attempted unsuccessfully to capture Nottingham Castle;

1819 the 'Peterloo' massacre in Manchester;

1820 conspirators met in Cato Street (London) to devise a plan to assassinate all the members of Liverpool's cabinet;

1821 riots accompanied the attempt of the divorced Queen Caroline to disrupt George IV's coronation service.

THE BLANKETEERS

The Blanketeers were unemployed workers who planned to march from Manchester to London to present a petition to the Prince Regent asking him to consider their grievances. The use of troops against them meant that few got further than Manchester itself. One man did reach London where he handed in his petition but it is unlikely that the Prince Regent ever saw it.

Figure 16 A cartoon of the time, showing the Peterloo massacre, 1815. The captain is shouting 'Down with 'em! chop 'em down my brave boys. Give them no quarter'.

SPENCEAN RADICALS

Spencean Radicals (or philanthropists) were the followers of Thomas Spence who believed that the land should be nationalised and that all taxes, except those on the income of the rich, should be abolished.

ISSUE

Does the Tory government of 1815–22 deserve the harsh criticism it has customarily received?

ACTIVITY

The contemporary depiction of Peterloo in Figure 16 has been described as 'ironic'. Check the meaning of that word in the dictionary (a handy book to have around whenever and whatever you are studying), and then say how the cartoonist displays his irony.

b) The Historical Debate on the 'Reactionary Tories'

The modern historian, George Kitson Clark, once shrewdly observed that before condemning an apparently oppressive regime we should always ask what its measures were aiming to protect. That is very much the line now taken by modern writers who urge that in judging the policies of Liverpool's government we should always bear in mind the severity of the problems that confronted it. They emphasise that the primary duty of any government is to keep the peace and maintain law and order. The resources for doing this were very limited in the period 1815–22. Most notably, there were no police forces. These would not be established until the late 1820s and it would take another twenty years before they became nationwide and effective. In the absence of civilian police, the only force to which the authorities could turn was the army. But at this time Britain did not have a large regular army in permanent readiness. Troops could be called out to deal with serious disorder at home. But this invariably took time and was used only as a last resort. This meant that when faced by the threat of disorder, the local magistrates, who were responsible for keeping the peace, were very restricted in what they could do. It is noticeable that the troops used at Peterloo were

Figure 17 A cartoon, drawn in 1819, by the satirist, Cruikshank. It shows the Tory government thrown into panic by the threat of radicalism.

largely drawn from the Manchester Yeomanry, which was a volunteer cavalry force. Few other parts of Britain had even an irregular force of this kind on which they could call.

ACTIVITY

Having studied Figure 17, answer these questions:

1. Why do you think radicalism is depicted as a guillotine?
2. What recent events might the satirist have had in mind?

If disorder was difficult to control once it had broken out, the obvious policy was for the government to prevent its occurring in the first place. This was the thinking that lay behind the Tories' supposedly tough measures, such as the suspension of Habeas Corpus, the use of *agents provocateurs* and the introduction of the Six Acts. Here, too, it should be stressed that these were temporary adjustments introduced to meet a particular crisis, not permanent changes in the law. Moreover, if one looks at the Six Acts they do not now appear especially oppressive. For example, the bans on keeping arms and maintaining private armies are the type of restriction that, arguably, any government in an ordered society has the right, perhaps even the duty, to impose. We should also bear in mind that, in an age before regular policing, the propertied classes had a deep-rooted fear of social disorder. When Cobbett spoke of 'the Rabble, the Swinish Multitude' he was deliberately using the language and imagery with which the authorities traditionally expressed their fear of mob rule. In view of such attitudes, the treatment of those arrested during the disturbances was not particularly vindictive. Norman Gash, one of the major modern authorities on this period, suggests that, judged by the standards of its day, Tory policy was remarkably lenient. He says in a deliberate understatement that 'it was not exactly a reign of terror'.

Yet there is still the charge that Liverpool's government thought only in terms of repression and did not attempt to tackle the root problems that had caused the unrest. The accusation obviously has weight. The Corn Laws and the increase in indirect taxation seemed calculated to deepen, not lessen, the hardships experienced by the poorer classes. But historians now urge us not to be retrospective in our judgments, not to apply twentieth-century welfare notions to a period in which they were unknown. To deal effectively on a national scale with problems such as poverty, unemployment, homelessness and ill health requires a vast bureaucracy of specialist departments and agencies. In 1815 this infrastructure, as it would now be called,

GOVERNMENT MEASURES AGAINST THE DISTURBANCES

1816 Lord Sidmouth, the Home Secretary, introduced a system of 'agents provocateurs' (informers who deliberately caused unrest in order to expose trouble makers);

1817 suspension of habeas corpus (the law which required that a person could not be arrested unless he was formally charged with an offence); a Seditious Meetings Act prohibited gatherings of more than 50 people;

1819 the Six Acts:
– restrictions on public meetings called to draft petitions
– magistrates empowered to confiscate arms
– magistrates empowered to confiscate seditious literature
– increased stamp tax on newspapers and pamphlets (a move intended to make such publications so expensive that only the relatively well-off could buy them)
– increased powers for the prosecution in treason cases
– training of private armies prohibited.

simply did not exist. Also missing was the attitude of mind that thinks in terms of state-provided welfare. It is true that radicals argued that there was more than enough wealth in the nation to meet all its needs. But it was not yet a commonly-held view that it was the task of government to concern itself with such issues. The conviction that government was ultimately responsible for the economic and social welfare of its citizens had yet to take hold. Indeed, that is the story of the nineteenth century – the gradual realisation that the seriousness of the social problems that plagued industrial Britain could only be properly dealt with by the government because the government was the only agency large and powerful enough to be able to do so.

ACTIVITY

In the light of the arguments just outlined, say how convincing you find the modern defence of Tory policies? Write down a list of arguments under two headings: strength of the defence – weakness of the defence. Your own views are particularly useful here since you are being asked not only to recount facts but also to make value judgments.

ISSUE
How liberal were the Liberal Tories?

c) The 'Liberal' Tories, 1822–30

The Government are as strong as any Government can wish to be, as far as regards those who sit facing them; but in truth the real opposition of the present day sit behind the Treasury Bench [the government front bench in the House of Commons]; and it is by the stupid old Tory party, who bawl out the memory and praises of Pitt while they are opposing all the measures and principles which he held most important; it is by these that the progress of the Government in every improvement which they are attempting is thwarted and impeded. On the Catholic question; on the principles of commerce; on the corn laws; on the settlement of the currency; on the laws regulating trade; on colonial slavery; on all these questions, and everything like them, the Government find support from the Whigs and resistance from their self-denominated friends.

Source B From a letter by Viscount Palmerston to William Temple, 17 July 1826.

The writer of this letter was later to switch parties and become a Whig leader and Prime Minister, but at this time Palmerston was a Tory MP and Secretary for War. His description therefore provides a valuable insider's view of the reforms introduced by the liberal Tories. In 1822 Lord Liverpool had re-shaped his Government, bringing in some younger, more progressive, ministers. It was they who were largely responsible for introducing the reforms passed in the next eight years.

LEADING LIBERAL TORIES

William Huskisson – Secretary of the Board of Trade
Robert Peel – Home Secretary
Frederick Robinson (Viscount Goderich after 1827) – Chancellor of the Exchequer
George Canning – Foreign Secretary

The Major Reforms of the Liberal Tories

Financial and economic reforms

1822   many tariffs and restrictions on imports were removed;

1823   the Corn Laws were modified by substituting a sliding-scale for the previous fixed rate. As British wheat rose in price, the duty on foreign wheat was reduced;

1823   the Reciprocity of Duties Act relaxed the Navigation Laws and allowed foreign ships to carry goods into British ports.

Reforms of the law

1823   the English penal code, with its antiquated laws and punishments, began to be overhauled and simplified under the direction of Robert Peel; the death penalty was removed from over 100 offences;

1824   measures were taken to improve conditions in prisons;

1829   the Metroplitan Police Force was established in London.

Religious reforms

1828   the Test and Corporation Acts, which had required all those holding public office to be practising members of the Anglican Church, were repealed;

1829   the Catholic Relief Act granted emancipation, i.e., the right of Catholics to sit in Parliament and hold public office (see page 120).

It should be stressed that what had prompted the Liberal Tories to consider reform was an improvement in the economy. The severity of the postwar depression began to ease considerably in the 1820s. This lessened social unrest and enabled the political repression to be lifted. It was this that encouraged the new ministers to embark on measures that were notably different from those before 1822. However, as Palmerston pointed out, not all Tories approved of these reforms. What he referred to as 'the stupid old Tory party' were unhappy with the measures. Palmerston's words highlight the difficulty facing the Tory party. By tradition it was committed to preserving the existing political and social system. When its more progressive members wanted to introduce essential reforms they found

Why did the government adopt reform in the 1820s?

it hard to do so without appearing to betray party principles. It was, as Palmerston indicated, religious issues that caused the most serious division among the Tories. To understand why religion had such political significance at this time, it is worth studying the following letter from George Canning, who succeeded Liverpool as Prime Minister in 1827:

1. The Catholic question is to remain an open question, upon which each member of the Cabinet is at perfect liberty to exercise his own judgement.
2. The inconvenience of having one open question in the Cabinet, makes it the more necessary to agree that there should be no other. All the existing members of the Cabinet are united in opposing the question of Parliamentary Reform, and could not acquiesce in its being brought forward or supported by any member of the Cabinet.
3. The present members of the Cabinet are also united in opposition to the repeal of the Test Act.

Source C Adapted from a letter by George Canning to the Marquess of Lansdowne, 23 April 1827.

Canning's letter described the three critical issues dividing the Tories – Catholic Emancipation (see page 120), Parliamentary reform, and the Test Act. The traditional Tories opposed religious and parliamentary reform on the grounds that it would alter the character of the nation for the worse. They looked on the monarchy, the Anglican Church and Parliament as the essential parts of the constitution and feared that the social and political privileges that they enjoyed under the existing system might well be threatened if it was altered in any important respects. That is why they were concerned to preserve the exclusive rights of the Anglican Church as the official state religion. For centuries it had been necessary for people to be professed Anglicans if they wished to have influence or position in public life. If equal rights were now to be granted to non-Anglican Christians, such as Catholics or Dissenters, all that would be undermined. As we shall see later in this chapter (page 40), it was the same fear of losing their privileges that lay behind the Tories' opposition to the reform of the electoral system.

By the time of Canning's death in September 1827, after only six months as Prime Minister, the issues which he had highlighted had already begun to destroy Tory unity. When the Duke of Wellington became Prime Minister early in 1828 he had to turn to the Whigs to fill four of his Cabinet posts. Wellington, the military hero who had defeated Napoleon, was not a natural leader in peacetime. He was aloof and dictatorial. It was said that he had 'a social contempt for his intellectual equals, and an intellectual contempt for his social

DISSENTERS
Members of Protestant denominations, such as Methodists, Congregationalists and Baptists, who did not accept the authority of the established Anglican Church.

THE TEST AND CORPORATION ACTS, 1661 AND 1673
These Acts prevented non-members of the Anglican Church from holding public office in local or central government.

equals'. But he did possess one important political gift: he had a sense of realism that allowed him to judge when a position was capable of being defended and when it was not. This proved vital in his approach to the demanding religious questions which he inherited from Canning. In 1828 his government decided not to oppose the Bill, introduced by the Whigs in the Commons, for the repeal of the Test and Corporation Acts.

On the surface this measure amounted to little more than the removal of laws which had not been invoked for generations. But the repeal had wider repercussions than expected. If the civil rights of Dissenters were now legally recognised, it was illogical not to extend these liberties to Catholics. The repeal of the Test Act thus gave increased strength to the argument for Catholic Emancipation. However, in the end it was not argument but force that carried the day. Since 1800, when Pitt's government had failed to honour its promise to grant Emancipation in return for Union, agitation had been mounting in Ireland (see page 120). By the late 1820s the Catholic demand was unstoppable.

The Catholic Association scored a remarkable victory with the election of their leader, Daniel O'Connell, as MP for County Clare. As the law stood, O'Connell as a Catholic could not take his seat at Westminster. But such was the atmosphere in Ireland following his triumph that civil war threatened if he were to be denied. Wellington tried to convince his government colleagues that Emancipation could not now be withheld. He argued that it was not a question of justice but of the appalling consequences if the Government refused. Robert Peel, who had originally strongly opposed Emancipation, became convinced that safety and public order demanded it. Bitterly contested though it was, this argument was eventually accepted. In March 1829, Peel himself introduced the Emancipation Bill. Despite meeting fierce opposition in both Houses, it eventually became law in June 1829. The frustrated high Tories gained their revenge a year later by joining with the Whigs in defeating the government in the Commons. Wellington resigned, thus opening the way for the Whigs to take office after nearly fifty years in opposition.

Besides causing the downfall of the Tories in 1830, the battle over Emancipation had a wider significance. It revealed that many previously firm opponents of reform were, in the end, willing to give way if the alternative entailed a greater social danger. Rather than face serious disorder they were prepared to make concessions on principles they had once regarded as sacrosanct. This grudging willingness to concede reform became a characteristic of politics in the nineteenth century.

Q

Why was the repeal of the Test and Corporation Acts so important?

Q

Why did Emancipation have such political significance?

ACTIVITY

Now that you have read section 1, trace the steps by which the Tories came to lose power in 1830. You need not make your analysis a long one – four or five brief paragraphs should be sufficient – but do remember to include personalities as well as issues.

2 The Whig Reforming Governments, 1830–41

Apart from a brief time in 1834–5, the Whigs were in power for eleven years after 1830. It proved to be a remarkable period of reform.

a) Parliamentary Reform

The question of reforming the electoral system in Britain had been raised on a number of occasions before the 1830s, but no government had persevered with any serious proposal for change. However, in 1830, the action of the diehard Tories rebounded on them. Their defeat of Wellington brought in a Whig government under Earl Grey pledged to introduce parliamentary reform.

The electoral system that operated down to 1832 was based on the assumption that there were two types of locality needing representation – counties and boroughs (towns and cities which had been granted royal charters allowing them to run their own affairs). Voting rights, especially in boroughs, had developed in an unplanned way over the centuries and had resulted in a shapeless and illogical pattern. The franchise (entitlement to vote) was not a basic legal right. It was usually limited to a minority of inhabitants and often depended on local custom and tradition, which varied from constituency to constituency. One of the biggest anomalies was that the membership of the House of Commons did not reflect the distribution of the population. The growth and shift of the population which accompanied the development of industry had glaringly exposed the unrepresentative character of Parliament. There were large areas of high-density urban population, such as Manchester, Birmingham, and certain districts of London, which had no MPs, while some of the existing rotten and pocket constituencies, which often had only a handful of voters, still returned MPs.

Q What was wrong with the unreformed Parliament?

In the unreformed Parliament, an informal alliance had developed between the aristocracy of the counties and the commercial interests in the boroughs. The two groups had enough in common to make their relations broadly harmonious; they had no reason to consider parliamentary reform. However, by the end of the eighteenth century, new social forces had begun to challenge this monopoly. The industrial cities and towns had created a new middle class which demanded to be represented in Parliament. In addition, the new class of skilled industrial workers had begun to form what contemporaries called a 'labour aristocracy'. Clearly such groups would not long remain content with the corrupt electoral system. If

Q Why had the demand for reform developed?

they were denied representation, their thoughts would turn to disruption if not revolution. That was the fear that convinced the majority of the Whigs that reform of Parliament was a practical necessity. It was not a theoretical question about political rights. Reform was necessary in order to avoid social upheaval.

The Whig reformers had to engage in a fierce struggle before they were finally able to achieve the reform of Parliament. The battle raged over fifteen months between March 1831 and May 1832. It required the drafting of three separate reform Bills and the formation of three separate governments, involved a bitter contest between the Commons and the Lords, and witnessed fierce confrontations between the supporters and opponents of reform.

Even after a third Bill was eventually passed by the Commons, it was still within the Lords' power to reject it since the Upper House had an absolute veto over measures passed to it by the Commons. But Earl Grey, the Whig Prime Minister, obtained William IV's royal promise that he would create enough pro-reform peers to swamp the House of Lords and drive the Bill through. Faced with this, Wellington and the other peers who opposed reform, stayed away from Parliament, thus allowing the Bill to become law.

Why was reform eventually accepted?

TROUBLES OVER REFORM

After the defeat of the first Reform Bill in October 1831, the disturbances in Bristol were so violent that it needed a cavalry charge to restore order. In London, the Duke of Wellington, a firm opponent of the Bill, became so unpopular that iron shutters had to be fitted over the windows of his house in Piccadilly to protect him from the mob.

The Main Terms of the First Reform Act, 1832

the right to vote was granted in the counties to adult males who:
– owned land of an annual value of £2 or more; or
– held a lease on property of an annual value of £10 or more; or
– were tenants on land of an annual value of £50 or more
in the boroughs to adult males who
– owned or occupied a house of an annual value of £10.

redistribution of seats
56 rotten and pocket boroughs were totally disfranchised;
30 boroughs lost one member (each borough normally returned two MPs);
22 new boroughs were created, with 2 members each;
20 new boroughs were created, with 1 member each;
25 counties were sub-divided, with each division having 2 members;
7 counties were given a third member.

In its introduction, the Reform Act declared its intention to be:

> To deprive many inconsiderable Places of the Right of returning
> Members, to grant such Privilege to large, populous, and wealthy
> Towns, to extend the Elective Franchise to many of His Majesty's
> Subjects who have not heretofore enjoyed the same, and to diminish
> the Expense of Elections.

At first glance these seem remarkable changes. Parliament appears
to have reformed itself extensively. But most modern writers emphasise that in practice the changes brought about by the 1832 Act were
far more limited. The following facts have to be noted:

Limitations of the 1832 Act

▼ The pre-reform electorate numbered 435,000; after 1832 it was
652,000, an increase of only just over a third.
▼ Five out of six adult males were still without the vote.
▼ The middle classes had gained influence in the boroughs, but the
landed classes were even more dominant in the counties.
▼ The working classes had been largely ignored.
▼ As there was still no secret ballot, electoral corruption remained
as entrenched after 1832 as before.

Why, then, was the
First Reform Act
such a significant measure?

This list of limitations seemingly undermines the notion of 1832 as a
revolution. But it is arguable that this is a case where the detail is less
important than the principle. The crucial point was that Parliament
had accepted the need to reform itself. The redistribution of seats
and the attempt to rationalise voting qualifications were admissions
that a corrupt House of Commons was no longer politically defens-
ible. In acknowledging this, Parliament established an important
principle – when circumstances warranted it, change would be introduced. This was the justification for all the reforms that government
and Parliament introduced from then on. The 1830s and 40s are
often appropriately referred to as 'the age of reform'. But none of
the many important social, economic and administrative changes
that were introduced would have been possible had not the First
Reform Act opened the door in 1832.

It is important not to misunderstand the character of reform in
this period. The Tory and Whig reformers seldom embraced reform
as a matter of principle or social justice. We can use a seeming
contradiction to make our point here. If 1832 was a revolution, it was
a revolution to avoid a revolution. The point of the paradox is that

the reformers of the 1830s and 40s were prepared to introduce change in order to prevent the build up of radical and revolutionary pressures. Reform was essentially a preventative move. It was thought better to introduce reform from above than be swept away by revolution from below. This point comes across clearly in the following extract from the celebrated writer, Thomas Macaulay, who, in 1831 as a young Whig MP, represented those who believed that reform was unavoidable:

> The middle class of England, with the flower of the aristocracy at its head, and the flower of the working classes bringing up its rear has taken its immovable stand between the enemies of all order and the enemies of all liberty. It will have Reform: it will not have revolution. All the observations that I have been able to make on the present state of the country have convinced me that the time has arrived when a great concession must be made to the democracy of England; that the question, whether the change be in itself good or bad, has become a question of secondary importance; that good or bad, the thing must be done; that a law as strong as the laws of attraction and motion has decreed it.

Source D Adapted from a speech of Thomas Macaulay in the House of Commons, 16 December 1831.

ACTIVITY

Study this passage in the light of the information in this section and then explain in three or four paragraphs what you understand Macaulay to mean when he says that 'the time has arrived when a great concession must be made to the democracy of England'.

When considering parliamentary reform we should keep sight of those who opposed it. Although they lost the debate, it helps maintain historical balance if we take note of their arguments. One of the most notable speeches in defence of the unreformed electoral system was given by the Tory MP, Sir Robert Inglis:

> Our Constitution is not the work of a code-maker; it is the growth of time and events beyond the design or the calculation of man: it is not a building, but a tree. It has adapted itself, almost like another work of nature, to our growth. The House of Commons is now the most complete representation of the interests of the people, which was ever assembled in any age or country. It comprehends [includes] within itself, those who can urge the wants and defend the claims of the landed, the commercial, the professional classes of the country, the privileges of the nobility, the interests of the lower classes, the rights and liberties of the whole people. It is the very absence of symmetry in our elective franchises which admits of the introduction to this House of classes so various.

Why was the Reform Bill resisted so strongly?

Source E From a speech of the Tory MP, Sir Robert Inglis, in the House of Commons, 1 March 1831.

Views such as those of Inglis have long ceased to be fashionable, but it is important for historical perspective to appreciate the conviction with which such beliefs were held at the time. The resistance to the Reform Bill was not simply blind reaction and self-interest, though of course these were present. As this extract shows, there was a logic to it. History's losing causes demand as much attention as those that triumphed. An especially notable opponent of reform was the young William Gladstone, later to be the Liberal leader and arguably the greatest British statesman of the century. As a Tory MP in the 1830s, he was appalled by the Reform Act and the other Whig measures, particularly the Church reforms, which he denounced as 'godless' since they involved the state's encroaching on the rights of the Church. He declared that the world around him was 'dying in sin'.

ACTIVITY

Reform is an appropriate topic for a group debate. A proposition such as, 'The grounds for opposing the reform of Parliament in 1832 were just as strong and just as valid as the argument for supporting it' should be provocative enough to arouse genuine discussion. Your own views are obviously important, but do try to understand how contemporaries approached the question so that you can introduce their ideas into the debate.

---

b) Reform of Local Government

The reform of Parliament in 1832 was followed three years later by the reform of local government under the Municipal Corporations Act of 1835. Until the 1830s local government was an extraordinary picture of confusion. This was because the rapid and uncontrolled growth of the industrial towns had made nonsense of the old boundaries that dated back to medieval times. At the beginning of the century there were 246 towns and cities possessing their own charters. They were known legally as incorporated boroughs and each had its own council elected by a small group of residents whose right to vote was based on a variety of antiquated qualifications. Some of these towns were very small and yet they retained their rights as corporations even though there were large teeming industrial centres, such as Manchester and Birmingham, which had no representative local government. The Municipal Corporations Act began the task of remedying the situation.

The Municipal Corporations Act, 1835

– 178 old borough corporations were abolished,

– these were replaced by borough councils elected by all the male ratepayers in the area;

– the elected concillors would then elect their own aldermen (higher officials to hold office for six years) and mayor;

– the councils were empowered to take over the work of the local Improvement Commissioners who had been responsible for such matters as roads and water supplies;

– the councils were to form watch committees to organise local police forces;

– the councils were entitled to raise loans and receive grants from the central government;

– towns which lacked a council were entitled to petition to become boroughs (Birmingham and Manchester did so by 1839).

At first the Act disappointed those who had hoped that its passing would lead rapidly to widescale improvements in the physical conditions of the towns. In the late 1840s, well over a decade after the Act had been in force, a third of Britain's towns still lacked adequate water supplies and sewerage. But the importance of the Act was long term not short term. It established the means of eventual improvement. The Act was a key first step in encouraging a sense of local responsibility and involvement which enabled genuine reform of urban conditions to be undertaken.

Interestingly, at the time the Act was passed its attraction to the Whig government was not that it was an important extension of democracy but that the reformed voting system now provided an opportunity to undermine the traditional dominance of the Tory Party in the localities. There was also a feeling among people of property that a reformed and efficient local government system would make it far easier to police the localities and combat crime.

c) Other Major Reforms under the Whigs

The passing of the Reform Bill in 1832 was followed by a range of important economic, administrative, social and religious changes. Many of these are analysed in other chapters of this book but it is helpful to have a list of them to hand (see page 44).

d) The Influences behind the Whig reforms

Historians now broadly agree that there were two main influences that shaped the reforms of this period, utilitarianism and humanitarianism. Some modern commentators also argue that to these should be added a third equally important influence – the cross-party fear of

ISSUE
What inspired the reforms of the period?

MAJOR WHIG REFORMS

1832 First Reform Act;

1833 Abolition of slavery in the British Empire. £20 million was paid in compensation to the dispossessed slave owners. This marked the success of the humanitarian campaign led by William Wilberforce;
Factory Act (see page 99);
Education grant (see page 103);

1834 Poor Law Amendment Act (see page 88);

1835 Municipal Corporations Act;

1836 Registration of Births, Deaths and Marriages Act – compulsory registration provided the statistical evidence for social reform;

1836 The Ecclesiastical Commission, first set up under Peel's Government in 1834, began to overhaul the Church of England's out-dated system of sees and parishes. Among its most important measures was the Tithe Commutation Act which attempted to rationalise the Church's finances.

1840 Penny Post introduced – postal services made more efficient and cheaper by use of pre-paid stamps affixed to the mail.

ISSUE
How far was this ministry a fulfilment of the commitment made by Peel in the Tamworth Manifesto of 1834?

what would happen if reform were not introduced. They suggest that the age of reform began not with the First Reform Act of 1832, but with the Tory surrender over Catholic Emancipation three years previously. According to this view, the age of reform should not be interpreted as a period of enthusiastic pursuit of change. Outside the ranks of the radicals, contemporary observers looked upon most of the reforms as grudging concessions not eager crusades. The purpose of most politicians in the first half of the nineteenth century was to preserve as much of the structure of Church and State as they could in a time of growing public disturbance. Although later generations have seen it as an unwarranted and exaggerated anxiety, there was in the 1830s and 40s a real fear that the growth of radicalism and unrest, associated with such movements as Chartism and the Anti-Corn Law League, was a portent of revolution. It is in this context that the readiness of the Whig and Conservative parties to undertake reform has to be understood.

It should also be stressed that although the Whig central government tends to be given the credit for the reforms of the period, it was often the vigorous championing of reform by individual radical MPs, sometimes in the face of government indifference, that enabled the measures to pass successfully through parliament.

ACTIVITY

On pages 87 and 97 you are given definitions of utilitarianism and humanitarianism. Using that information, compile a list of the Whig reforms and attach to each one a brief statement indicating whether you think it was inspired by utilitarian or humanitarian thinking. You might, of course, consider both influences to have been at work in some of the reforms.

3 Robert Peel's Conservative Government, 1841–6

By 1841, after eleven years of government the Whigs had little enthusiasm for continuing. However, their defeat in the election of 1841 and their replacement by the Conservatives under Peel did not mean an end to the age of reform. In fact Peel's government of 1841–6 proved to be one of the major reforming administrations of the century. The clue to why this was so lies seven years earlier. In 1834, while in opposition, Peel had issued his Tamworth Manifesto, from which the following is a key extract:

I consider the Reform Bill a final and irrevocable settlement of a great Constitutional question – a settlement which no friend to the peace and welfare of this country would attempt to disturb.

Then, as to the spirit of the Reform Bill, and the willingness to adopt and enforce it as a rule of government: if, by adopting the spirit of the Reform Bill, it be meant that we are to live in a perpetual agitation; that public men can only support themselves in public estimation by promising the instant redress of anything which anybody may call an abuse, – by abandoning the respect for ancient rights, and the deference to prescriptive authority; if this be the spirit of the Reform Bill, I will not undertake to adopt it. But if the spirit of the Reform Bill implies merely a careful review of institutions, civil and ecclesiastical, undertaken in a friendly temper, combining, with the firm maintenance of established rights, the correction of proved abuses and the redress of real grievances, – in that case, I can for myself and colleagues undertake to act in such a spirit and with such intentions.

Source F Adapted from Sir Robert Peel's election address to the constituents of Tamworth in Staffordshire, 1834.

ACTIVITY

Peel's statement is quite a difficult piece of prose to understand, but since it is a landmark document it repays study. Read it through as often as you need to make sure you have grasped its meaning. Then jot down a few sentences of your own to explain what Peel meant when he spoke of accepting 'the spirit of the Reform Bill'. The following analysis should help you to do this.

The most striking feature of Peel's election address, which became known as the Tamworth Manifesto, was its acceptance of the Reform Act. Having fought against the Bill and lost, the Tory party was faced with the dilemma of what its attitude should be in the reformed Parliament. Peel's response was clear. He and his colleagues, in what from now on we call the Conservative Party, would not attempt to reverse the changes made. Peel accepted that the 1832 Reform Act had introduced a new principle, that of Parliament's duty to redress genuine grievances. In stating this, Peel committed his Party to the cautious acceptance of essential reform. The Tamworth Manifesto had thus created a formula by which the Conservative Party could make the transition from the old Toryism which had resisted change to the new Conservatism which was willing to initiate necessary reform.

It was such reasoning that led Peel to turn immediately to reform in 1841. His main aim was to tackle the poverty and hardship of the

MAJOR REFORMS UNDER PEEL

1841 indirect taxation on essential foodstuffs reduced;

1842 the first of a series of budgets that continued the process begun by Huskisson in the 1820s of stimulating trade by substantial reductions in the import duties on a wide range of goods; to make up for the loss of revenue income tax was re-introduced at 7d (approx 3p) in the £; Mines Act (see page 98);

1844 the Bank Charter Act limited the issuing of bank notes to the Bank of England – this brought stability and security to the banking system; Factory Act (see page 98);

1846 repeal of the Corn Laws.

time, known later as 'the hungry forties', by reducing taxation and stimulating trade. This was a move away from protection towards free trade (see page 13). The logic of this was that at some point Peel would have to face the question of whether to keep the Corn Laws. It was not simply an economic question. The Corn Laws had come to represent the basic interest of the landed class, the backbone of the Conservative Party. If Peel were to repeal these Laws, he would in the eyes of traditional conservatives be betraying the Party he led.

a) The Repeal of the Corn Laws, 1846

ISSUES
What led Peel to repeal the Corn Laws? How far was repeal due to the agitation of the Anti-Corn Law League?

In 1820 a parliamentary committee had been asked to consider how well the Corn Laws, introduced five years earlier, were operating. The committee's answer was that they were not working. The monopoly given to the growers had not guaranteed their profits. The price of corn fluctuated so much that farmers were often unsure whether they would be able to sell at a profit, which discouraged them from producing on a large scale. This had meant that the corn merchants did not receive sufficient supplies; in order to maintain their trade the merchants often turned, therefore, to foreign suppliers of wheat. What made things worse was that the attempt to impose protection by means of the Corn Laws led to retaliation by other countries; they imposed tariffs on imports from Britain. The reaction was not confined to wheat; foreign countries began to discriminate against a variety of British goods and manufactures.

The committee's findings were exactly the arguments that were taken up by what proved to be one of the first great lobby or pressure groups in modern British history – the Anti-Corn Law League. The League was founded in 1839 and was led by two prominent MPs, Richard Cobden and John Bright. They were highly successful factory owners and businessmen who represented the interests of the manufacturing and commercial classes. From their base in Manchester they used the funds donated to them by the business world to conduct a national campaign against protection, with the Corn Laws as their chief target.

TECHNIQUES OF THE ANTI-CORN LAW LEAGUE
Two particular developments around this time helped the League to distribute its literature nationwide – the reduction of duty on newspapers and the introduction of a cheap postal system (pre-paid adhesive stamps greatly reduced the cost of postage in Britain). The League also made effective use of the growing railway system to send speakers around the country to spread the free trade message.

The League's constantly repeated argument was that the Corn Laws did not protect the profits of the growers, caused continuing distress to the poor by keeping the price of bread artificially high, and prevented Britain from developing into the great commercial nation that it could be. Cobden and Bright stressed that these were not only economic failings but were also moral ones. To deny the people of Britain their daily bread was an indefensible outrage, while to use protection against other nations was to increase the risk of international conflict.

Because of the considerable impact the Anti-Corn Law League

made both in Parliament and in the country at large there has been a tendency to regard it as having been the main influence persuading Peel and his government to repeal the Corn Laws in 1846. This is an understandable but not entirely accurate viewpoint. Historians now stress that the League was only one of the pressures on Peel, and that, in any case, his introduction of a progressive series of free-trade budgets during his 1841–6 government had taken him ever closer to the logical final step of abandoning the Corn Laws as the remnants of an outdated protectionism. Moreover, in the thirty years since their introduction in 1815 the Corn Laws had been modified so often that they had a very limited effect in practice.

Peel's problem was not whether to repeal them but when. He was aware that despite their restricted economic significance the Corn Laws remained for the traditionalists in the Conservative Party a powerful symbol of their interests as a landed class. Peel's intention in 1845 was to delay repeal until after the next general election, scheduled for 1847, by which time the Conservatives would have gained a mandate for Repeal from the electorate. His plan was not simply to remove the Corn Laws, but to make their abolition part of a much larger integrated economic scheme which would offer something to all classes. The scheme was described in a memo written by Prince Albert, Queen Victoria's husband:

> Sir Robert has *an immense scheme in view*; he thinks he shall be able to remove the contest entirely from the dangerous ground upon which it has got – that of a war between the manufacturers, the hungry and the poor against the landed proprietors, the aristocracy, which can only end in the ruin of the latter; he will not bring forward a measure upon the Corn Laws, but a much more comprehensive one. He will deal with the whole commercial system of the country. He will adopt the principle of the League, *that of removing all protection and abolishing all monopoly*, but not in favour of one class and as a triumph over another, but to the benefit of the nation, farmers as well as manufacturers.

Source G Memorandum of Prince Albert, 25 December 1845.

Whether Peel's scheme would have worked cannot be known for in 1846 his hand was forced not by the Anti-Corn Law League but by the onset of the famine in Ireland. The desperate situation there obliged Peel to rush through repeal in a belated attempt to get corn and other food supplies into Ireland (see pages 122–26). The Whigs supported him, but repeal involved a fierce fight both within the Cabinet and within the Conservative Party in Parliament. As he had feared, Peel was able to carry repeal through only at the cost of splitting his Party. In the Commons two-thirds of the Conservative MPs

Q

How successful was the Anti-Corn Law League?

ACTIVITY

Study the memorandum and then suggest what insights it offers into Peel's approach to protection and free trade.

turned against him. He was subjected to withering attacks from those who believed he was abandoning Conservative principles. Foremost among these was a group known as Young England, whose outstanding spokesman was the flamboyant MP, Benjamin Disraeli, destined twenty years later to become the leader of what remained of the Conservative Party.

Wellington's comment on the repeal crisis was:

> Rotten potatoes have done it all! They have put Peel in his damned fright.

Source H the Duke of Wellington, speaking in 1846.

Figure 18 'Papa Cobden taking Master Robert for a Free Trade Walk', a *Punch* cartoon, 1845
Papa Cobden: 'Come along Master Robert, do step out.'
Master Robert: 'That's all very well, but you know I cannot go as fast as you do.'

ACTIVITY

Study the Punch cartoon and then consider the following question: What point is the cartoonist making about the relationship between Peel and Cobden? In the light of the other information in this section, comment on the accuracy of the cartoonist's depiction.

Summary of Politics and Parties 1, 1815–46

Year	Reactionary Tories	Liberal Tories	Whigs	Peel
1811 & 1817	Luddite disturbances			
1815	Corn Laws passed			
1816	Spa Fields riot; Sidmouth introduces system of *agents provocateurs*			
1817	Blanketeers march; the Derbyshire rising; habeas corpus suspended; Seditious Meetings Act			

Year	Reactionary Tories	Liberal Tories	Whigs	Peel
1819	Peterloo 'massacre'; the Six Acts			
1820	Cato Street Conspiracy			
1821	Queen Caroline affair			
1822		leading reformers join the Cabinet – Peel, Huskisson, Robinson, Canning; Corn Laws modified		Peel became Home Secretary
1823		reform of the Penal Code begun; Reciprocity Act		
1828		Test and Corporation Acts repealed		
1829		Metropolitan Police formed; Catholic Relief Act		Catholic Emancipation Bill introduced by Peel
1830			Whigs take office	
1831			Reform Bill introduced	
1832			Reform Bill passed	
1833			Slavery abolished in British Empire; Factory Act; Education grant	
1834			Poor Law Amendment Act	Tamworth Manifesto; Peel's Government, 1834–35
1835			Municipal Corporations Act	
1836			Registration of Births, Deaths and Marriages Act	
1840			Penny Post introduced	
1841				Peel took office; began series of free-trade reforms
1842				first of Peel's free-trade budgets; Mines Act
1844				Bank Charter Act; Factory Act
1846				repeal of the Corn Laws

▼ Working on Politics and Parties 1

To help draw your thoughts together, trace the development of the parties in relation to their attitude towards reform. The pattern of the summary could be very useful here. Using that as a guide, try constructing a set of brief notes covering the period, 1815 to 1846. The following is meant to give you a push by offering an example of how you might group your material.

▼ Why was reform not contemplated by the Tories, 1815–22?
  Re-read pages 29–31.
  List the problems facing Liverpool's government.
▼ Why did the liberal Tories introduce reform after 1822?
  Re-read pages 33–37.
  List the main reforms and the reformers.
▼ Why did the Whigs under Grey introduce the Great Reform Bill?
  Why did the Tories oppose it?
  Re-read pages 38–42.
  List the main reasons.
▼ Why were so many reforms passed while the Whigs were in office between 1830 and 1841?
  Re-read pages 43–44.
  List the main reasons.

Example of notes in response to the last question:
– the Great Reform Act had cleared the way and pointed the path to further reform
– utilitarianism and humanitarianism helped create a mood for reform
– the blue books (check page 84) had begun to show the need for social reform
– reform seen as necessary in order to prevent serious social unrest
– the Conservatives under Peel accepted the principle of reform (e.g. Tamworth Manifesto) and so rarely opposed the Whig measures
– reforms owed much to the work of dedicated individual radical MPs.

Answering extended writing and essay questions on Politics and Parties 1

You will be familiar now with the way we break down essay questions into their types. The following list shows the style of questions you are likely to encounter on the topic of party development between 1815 and 1846.

Type of Issue	Examples of typical questions
1 causes/reasons/motives	What were the main influences behind the Whig reforms of the 1830s?
2 course of events	Trace the changing character of the Tory Party between 1815 and 1830.
3 consequences/results/ effects	In what sense did the Tamworth Manifesto of 1834 mark a turning point in the development of the Tory Party?
4 success/failure	How far did Robert Peel achieve his objectives during his 1841–6 ministry?
5 significance/importance	'Despite its high profile, the Anti-Corn Law League played only a very minor part in bringing about the repeal of the Corn Laws in 1846.' Discuss.
6 comparison	'The age of reform began not with the Whig Reform Act of 1832, but with the Tory surrender over Catholic Emancipation three years previously.' Discuss.
7 right/wrong (moral/ ethical judgments)	'What the Whigs did was necessary; what the Tories said was right.' Consider this view of the conflict over the First Reform Act.

Let us examine possible ways of approaching question 4, the type that calls for an assessment of success or failure. A very good rule of thumb here is that success should always be judged against the aims and objectives of the person or people concerned. To measure the success of anything, whether it be an idea, a programme, a period of government, a foreign policy, a military campaign, a treaty, or any of the other events or topics you are likely to be questioned on in your study of history, ask how far results matched intentions. In this particular question you need to explain what you think Peel's major aims were. It would be a good idea to separate these into economic and political objectives. Having jotted down a list of Peel's aims you can tick or put a cross against each one denoting success or failure.

Your task is then to explain your verdicts. Again, before beginning the essay proper, it would be worthwhile and would save time overall if you were to put a brief comment against each of your ticks or crosses. These would then become your notes around which the essay could be coherently structured.

You may find that the economic aims are the easier to pass judgment on. A strong case could be made for saying that Peel's intention was to move away from protection towards free trade and that this he largely achieved by a series of measures which reduced tariffs and taxation rates. The repeal of the Corn Laws, though forced upon Peel in ways that he would not have wished, may be seen as the climax of this. However, there is a qualification. You have to decide how much weight to give to the grand scheme that Prince Albert's memorandum cited. If it was indeed Peel's aim to introduce an integrated economic scheme in 1847, then the eruption of the Irish crisis forced him to introduce repeal prematurely. Does this limit his success? Here you might address the key political point. There is no doubt that repeal split the Conservative Party. Can this be counted a failure of political objective? Peel clearly knew that the Conservatives would fracture over repeal yet he still went ahead with it. Does this mean that for him party political considerations were secondary to the needs of his economic programme? If so, then was repeal really a political failure? These are the issues you should address. Your verdict is your own, of course, but it needs to be based on sound reasoning.

Answering source-based questions on Politics and Parties 1

The following exercise is based on the speeches on reform of Thomas Macaulay and Robert Inglis, both delivered in 1831. Re-read these (on page 41), and then answer the question below.

How far do these extracts indicate that, despite being on opposite sides of the debate, both Macaulay and Inglis were concerned with preservation rather than change? **[12 marks]**

Points to note about the question

In the source-based analysis in Chapter 1 your task was to show that you had understood the contents of the individual sources. Here we move on to the more difficult problem of comparing sources. Comprehension, as always, is essential but now you are required to build on you knowledge. Notice that 12-mark tariff requires a substantial answer from you.

Suggested response

In Inglis's view, the growth of the English Constitution has been organic and unregulated, at no time conforming to the concept of direct representation. This has been its strength. Its historical adaptability has enabled it to adjust to changing circumstance and has allowed Parliament to remain truly representative of the widest social strata. Such flexibility has given the upper, middle, and lower orders a genuine voice in the House. The Commons was never intended to be a uniform body structured in accordance with notions of balance; indeed, it has been this very lack of 'symmetry' that has preserved it as the guardian of English liberties. For Inglis, therefore, there is no need to change from outside a system that regulates itself by organic change from within.

Macaulay's essential argument was that in the prevailing atmosphere, what he called a 'concession to democracy' was no longer a matter of choice but of necessity. Parliamentary reform, and reform as a principle in itself, must be accepted; whether the changes involved were good or bad was not the issue; to resist reform would be to invite the most dangerous social disorder. Macaulay provides a revealing insight into the sense of anxiety that led a number of parliamentarians and public men to contemplate reform not as an ideal but as the lesser of two evils. Although it is a paradox, Macaulay wants change in order to preserve.

The difference between Inglis and Macaulay is a subtle one. They both agree that the basic constitution must be saved. But whereas Inglis believes that this is best achieved by allowing the system to adjust itself as it always has, Macaulay considers that the constitution can only be preserved if its defenders make the necessary alterations to it before it is overwhelmed by the forces of disruption from outside.

Further Reading

Books in the 'Access to History' series

The Great Reform Bill is examined in Chapter 3 of *The Growth of Democracy in Britain* by Annette Mayer and in Chapter 2 of *Labour and Reform Working-Class Movements 1815–1914* by Clive Behagg. The reform of central and local government in the 1830s and 40s is the subject of Chapters 3 to 5 of *Government and Reform 1815–1918* by Robert Pearce and Roger Stearn. The development of the Tory Party between 1815 and 1846 is covered in Chapters 2 and 3 of *Tories, Conservatives and Unionists* by Duncan Watts, while the same author's *Whigs, Radicals and Liberals 1815–1914*, Chapter 3, deals with the Whig Reforms. The social reforms of the period are covered in Chapters 2 and 3 of *Poverty and Welfare 1830–1914* by Peter Murray.

General

An excellent short study with which to start is *Regency England: the Age of Lord Liverpool* by John Plowright (Lancaster Pamphlets, 1996). *Party Politics 1830–52* by Robert Stewart (Macmillan, 1989) is strongly recommended as are the classic works by Norman Gash, *Lord Liverpool* (Weidenfeld, 1984), *Peel* (Longman, 1973) and *Reaction and Reconstruction in English Politics, 1832–1865* (OUP, 1965). Also highly valuable is *Peel and the Conservative Party* by Paul Adelman (Longman, 1987). The *Age of Reform* by Vyvyen Brendon (Hodder & Stoughton, 1994) deals with reforms in the 1830s and 40s. *The Years of Expansion Britain 1815–1914* edited by Michael Scott-Baumann (Hodder & Stoughton, 1995) describes the development of the parties between 1815 and 1846. The growth of the Conservative Party is analysed in *The Conservative Party from Peel to Major* by Robert Blake (Fontana, 1996). The 1832 Reform Act and party developments up to that time are examined by Eric Evans in his *The Great Reform Act* (Lancaster Pamphlets, 1994), and *Britain before the Reform Act: Politics and Society 1815–1832* (Longman, 1989). A particularly helpful text is *How Tory Governments Fall, The Tory Party in Power since 1783* edited by Anthony Seldon (Fontana 1996). There are excellent chapters on party politics before 1850 in *Britain's Century: A Political and Social History 1815–1905* by W.D.Rubinstein (Arnold, 1998). Articles that will prove particularly helpful to students are ' "Liberal" and "High" Tories in the Age of Lord Liverpool' by G. Goodlad, in *History Review*, November 1995, 'The Premiership of Lord Liverpool' by Eric Evans in *History Review*, April 1990, and 'Lord Liverpool' by John Plowright in *History Review*, September 1997.

POLITICS AND PARTIES 2 – DISRAELI AND GLADSTONE

CHAPTER 3

POINTS TO CONSIDER

This chapter continues the examination, begun in Chapter 2, of the main developments in British politics in the nineteenth century. The connecting theme is again the manner in which the parties responded to the pressing economic and social needs of a nation that was becoming increasingly industrialised and urbanised. This means that the material in Chapters 1, 4 and 7 will be particularly important and relevant. You will, therefore, find it helpful to make cross references to those parts of the book. The key areas selected for study are Disraelian Conservatism and Gladstonian Liberalism. There were, of course, other important individuals and movements in this period but Disraeli, the Conservative leader, and Gladstone, the leader of the Liberals, dominated the politics of their time. In studying them we go to the heart of the major issues of the second half of the nineteenth century. The chapter has an introduction which surveys the political scene between 1846 and 1867, the period in which Disraeli and Gladstone rose to prominence, and seven other main sections: 1 the Era of Gladstone and Disraeli; 2 Disraeli and the Second Reform Act, 1867; 3 Gladstone's first ministry, 1868–74; 4 Disraeli's reshaping of the Conservative Party; 5 the Conservatives in Office, 1874–80; 6 Gladstone's Midlothian campaign, 1879; 7 Gladstone's later ministries.

Introduction

a) Divisions within the parties, 1846–67

The repeal of the Corn Laws proved to be a critical event in party political history. Peel's 'betrayal' in introducing Repeal split the Conservatives into two main groups, the free trade supporters of Peel, known as the Peelites, who included Gladstone, and the protectionists, among whom Disraeli was a prominent figure. There were also serious divisions in the Whig Party, which included conservatives such as Palmerston who was opposed to reform in domestic affairs, and liberals, such as Cobden and Bright, who pressed for reform. Party labels were, therefore, no longer a very accurate way of defin-

> **ISSUES**
> Why were changes of government so frequent in the period 1846 to 1868?
> Why were there fewer social and economic reforms in this period?

ing the political beliefs and attitudes of those to whom they were applied. The result of this party splintering was that during the period 1846–68 there were no less than nine separate governments, many of them being coalitions drawn from the various groups.

b) Palmerston's Influence on Reform

Although there were some important reforms in the period, which are analysed in Chapters 1, 4 and 7, the years 1846–67 saw a marked slowing down in the pace of reform when compared with the preceding period, 1830–46. A major explanation for this relates to the dominant politician of the age – Lord Palmerston, who was Prime Minister for nearly half the period. Despite his reputation as a progressive in foreign policy, Palmerston was a typically old-fashioned Whig in domestic affairs; he was suspicious of reform and regarded the radical movements of the day as highly threatening. His strong belief in *laissez-faire* proved a check on state action in the field of social reform and he was firmly opposed to further parliamentary reform.

1 The Era of Disraeli and Gladstone, 1868–86

What characterised the period 1846–67 was a falling off of reform legislation and a softening of the hard lines distinguishing the parties. What characterised the succeeding period, 1868–86, was quite the opposite – a marked quickening in the pace of reform and the hardening of party divisions. From the uncertainties of party alignment following the break-up of the Conservatives over the Corn Law issue in 1846, there emerged twenty years later two clearly distinguished parties, the Conservatives and the Liberals. The chief reason for this is to be found in the personalities of the respective leaders of these parties, Benjamin Disraeli and William Ewart Gladstone. Disraeli led the Conservatives from 1868 to 1880, while Gladstone was the Liberal leader for most of the period 1865–94. Their personal rivalry gave definition to the age. Differences of principle are to be found between the parties, but a point that is now strongly emphasised by historians is the critical importance of personalities in determining the electoral support the parties gained. Whether electors voted Conservative or Liberal was much more likely to be decided by whether they liked Mr Disraeli or Mr Gladstone than by whether they supported a particular set of party policies. Disraeli and Gladstone personalised politics in such a way that the principles and programmes they advocated became identified with them as individuals.

BENJAMIN DISRAELI (1804–1881)

-*Profile*-

Disraeli was born into a middle-class Jewish family which converted to Anglicanism (when Benjamin was aged thirteen) in order to avoid the social and legal barriers which faced practising Jews in the early nineteenth century. Until he became Chancellor of the Exchequer in 1852 at the age of 48, Disraeli had not had a proper job. He had survived by borrowing heavily and by writing. By the 1840s he had established a reputation as a political novelist. After four unsuccessful attempts, he had eventually won a seat as a Conservative MP in 1837.

As a young politician, Disraeli deliberately adopted an outrageous style of dress in order to make himself known. He was particularly fond of green velvet jackets and yellow waistcoats. Such self-publicity sometimes brought him derision, but few doubted that he was a person of outstanding ability. A local paper described him on the hustings in Dorset in 1835:

> He commenced in a lisping, lackadaisical tone of voice. He minced his phrases in apparently the most affected manner. He would lean affectedly on the table, supporting himself with his right hand; anon he would push aside the curls from his forehead. But as he proceeded all traces of the dandyism and affectation were lost. His voice gradually became full, musical and sonorous. The dandy was transformed into a practised orator and finished elocutionist.

Source A From the *Dorset County Chronicle*, 30 April 1835.

In the 1830s and 40s, Disraeli expressed a deep distrust of utilitarianism which he considered was changing British society for the worse. In response he became a leading member of Young England. This was a group of Tories who reacted against the 1832 Reform Act and the utilitarianism of the age by looking back to a mythical golden English past which they believed could be restored by an enlightened aristocracy leading the working classes in re-establishing the nation's traditional values.

Robert Blake, his authoritative modern biographer, remarks that Disraeli's only certain feature in his early years was an 'unrelenting determination to get to the top'. Young England provided him with a base from which to attack Robert Peel, the Conservative leader, for betraying his party over the repeal of the Corn Laws. Yet once Disraeli had risen to the top of the Conservative Party by the late 1860s, he adopted policies that were essentially a continuation of what Peel had begun. As Peel had done, he came to recognise that the economic and social

1804 born in London into a genteel Jewish family;

1817 his family converted to Christianity;

1832 stood for Parliament as a radical but was unsuccessful;

1837 entered Parliament at the fifth attempt as Conservative MP for Maidstone;

1841 –46 became a leading figure in the Young England movement;

1844 –47 his three major novels, *Coningsby, Sybil* and *Tancred*, published;

1845 –46 led a campaign against Peel over repeal of the Corn Laws;

1852 Chancellor of the Exchequer in Derby's government;

1858 –59 Chancellor of Exchequer in Derby's second government;

1866 –67 pushed through the Second Reform Bill;

1868 became Prime Minister for the first time, but was defeated in the subsequent general election;

changes that industrialisation had brought to Britain made it vital that the Conservative Party adjust its policies. This was the essence of what Disraeli termed 'Tory democracy'. He believed that the Conservatives should not resist the widening of the franchise or the introduction of further social reform, but should aim to win the support of the newly enfranchised voters, especially after the passing of the Second Reform Act in 1867, by appealing to their traditional respect for Britain's institutions.

Disraeli scholars differ in their judgement of his policies but they agree in accepting that it was his personality that made him so distinctive. This view is well expressed in Paul Smith's biography:

> Disraeli's art and legacy lay not in the manufacture of measures but in the management of impressions ... Disraeli lives on as a source of political inspiration less because of his contributions to Conservative strategy ... than because of the brilliance and excitement that he found in, and imparted, to life.

Source B From *Disraeli: A Brief Life* by Paul Smith, 1996.

1868 –74 rejuvenated the Conservative Party in Opposition;

1872 made a series of key speeches redefining the role of the Conservative Party;

1874 became Prime Minister for the second time;

1874 –80 led one of the major reforming ministries of the century;

1876 raised to the peerage as Lord Beaconsfield;

1878 brought back 'peace with honour' from the Congress of Berlin;

1880 Conservatives defeated in the general election;

1881 died.

Figure 19 A drawing of Disraeli from the early 1840s, which seeks to capture the flamboyance and confidence with which the aspiring politician faced the world.

BENJAMIN DISRAELI AS A YOUNG MAN.

ACTIVITY

Having read the extract from the Dorset Chronicle in the profile and examined Figure 19, say in what way the two sources give a complementary picture of the young Disraeli.

The national institutions that Disraeli revered were:
▼ The Crown, the symbol of the nation's identity;
▼ The Established Church, which provided a moral framework for society;
▼ The House of Lords, which symbolised the virtues of the aristocratic hereditary principle;
▼ The Justices of the Peace in the counties, who guaranteed the rule of law.

What were Disraeli's political principles?

Yet while these were the great traditions that he admired, Disraeli showed himself very willing to adapt to change. He was an opportunist. He devoted considerable time, particularly in the early 1870s, to redefining the objectives of Conservatism; but his greatest achievement was not as a political thinker but as a practical politician who was always ready to adjust to changed circumstances. He had a sense of right timing and of knowing how to respond to the public mood. Disraeli's relatively humble class origins and the fact that he was a Jew made it difficult for him to gain full acceptance within the Conservative Party. Lord Salisbury, who was to be the Conservative leader later in the century (see page 201), remarked of him:

Why was Disraeli not fully trusted by the Conservatives?

> If I had a firm confidence in his principles or his honesty, or even if he were identified by birth or property with the Conservative classes in the country – I might in the absence of any definite professions work to maintain him in power. But he is an adventurer: & as I have too good cause to know, he is without principles and honesty.

Source C From a letter by the Marquess of Salisbury to Mr. Gaussen of the Hertfordshire Conservative Association, April 1868.

It was also the case that Disraeli's manner and style made him unpopular with some Conservatives. They would love to have been rid of him, but his talents meant that they could not do without him. This is what Robert Blake had in mind when he described Disraeli as having been 'an indispensable liability to the Conservative Party'.

A story goes that Disraeli once enquired why Gladstone regularly tramped the streets of London. 'He is saving bad women', he was told. 'Really', said Disraeli, 'then pray ask him to save me one'. But Disraeli had no need of such favours. A particularly fascinating aspect of his character was the way he excelled in the company of women. He had a great capacity for winning their affection. In a touching love letter to Mary Wyndham Lewis, his future wife, Disraeli wrote:

> I cannot reconcile love and separation. My ideas of Love are the perpetual enjoyment of the society of the sweet being to whom I am devoted, the sharing of every thought and even every fancy, of every charm and every care. Perhaps I sigh for a state which can never be mine, which never existed. But there is nothing in my own heart that convinces me it is impossible, and if it be an illusion it is an illusion worthy of the gods. I wish to be with you, to live with you, never to be away from you – I care not where, in heaven or on earth or in the waters under the earth.

Source D From a letter by Disraeli to Mary Wyndham Lewis, October 1838.

Marie Louise, one of Queen Victoria's granddaughters, related: 'after sitting next to Mr. Gladstone I thought he was the cleverest man in England. But after sitting next to Mr. Disraeli I felt I was the cleverest woman in England.' His subtlety worked particularly well on the Queen. He knew how to charm her and to say what she wanted to hear. She loved his flirtatious flattery as much as she loathed Gladstone's solemn sermonising. Disraeli was always careful to slip into their conversations frequent references to her beloved Albert, the Prince Consort, from whose death in 1861 she never fully recovered emotionally. As Disraeli himself lay dying in 1881 he was asked whether he would welcome a visit from the Queen. 'No', he replied, 'she would only ask me to take a message to Albert'. Roy Jenkins, the noted politician and biographer of Gladstone, considers that the Queen's affection for Disraeli and distaste for Gladstone made her sympathetic to Conservatism and distrustful of Liberalism.

Q Why was Disraeli's relationship with women important?

ACTIVITY

Having read section 2, explain in three or four paragraphs why Disraeli's public style and personal characteristics were so important politically.

WILLIAM EWART GLADSTONE (1809–1898)

-Profile-

Gladstone was born in 1809 into a prosperous merchant family of Scottish origin, whose wealth had been originally derived from the slave trade. He was deeply religious and regarded every moment of life as a gift from God. That was why throughout his life he kept a diary, which he called his 'account book with God'. The entries reveal his abiding sense of his own sinfulness. On the night of his honeymoon Gladstone recorded in his diary:

> the beloved [his bride, Catherine] sleeps for a while on the sofa – we have read the two second lessons [of the Prayer Book] together.
> She has less cause to rejoice as well as more to weep: but with me the joy is not tempered enough, I fear & hardly belongs to a follower of the Crucified, much less to one so false in his profession.
> She sleeps gently as a babe. O may I never disturb her precious peace but cherish her more dearly than myself.

Source E From Gladstone's diary entry for 25 July 1838.

The diary entries provide a fascinating picture of a man who had originally intended to enter holy orders but then decided that he could carry out God's will best by serving Him in the field of politics. That was why he lived his life with such extraordinary moral intensity. He had phenomenal energy. For recreation, he thought nothing of walking ten miles in a day. As for work, contemporaries spoke in awe of Gladstone's ability to do in one hour what it took everyone else two hours to accomplish and to sustain that output for 18 hours a day. One example of this is that during his lifetime he read some 20,000 books, an average of five a week. All this could be extremely irritating to observers who were unable to match his output. His ever-patient wife once remarked: 'Oh William dear, if you weren't such a great man, what a terrible bore you would be'. Disraeli observed more bitingly that Gladstone did not possess 'a single redeeming defect'. In a more recent judgment, Roy Jenkins in his 1995 biography described Gladstone as 'the most remarkable specimen of humanity of all the fifty who have so far held the office of British Prime Minister'.

1809 born into a merchant family
1832 entered Parliament as a Tory MP;
1843 President of the Board of
–46 Trade under Peel;
1852 Chancellor of the
–55 Exchequer
1859 Chancellor of the
–65 Exchequer;
1868 became leader of the Liberal Party;
1868 his first ministry;
–74
1875 retired from politics;
1876 wrote *The Bulgarian Horrors and the Question of the East*;
1879 undertook the Midlothian campaign;
1880 his second ministry;
–85
1884 Third Parliamentary Reform Act;
1886 became Prime Minister for the third time; his first Irish Home Rule Bill defeated in the Commons;
1892 his fourth ministry;
–94
1893 Second Home Rule Bill defeated in the Lords;
1894 resigned as Prime Minister and finally retired from politics;
1898 died.

Figure 20 Gladstone introducing his first Home Rule Bill in the Commons in 1886. It was his power as an orator that enabled him to dominate the House of Commons for so much of his career. His outstanding ability as a public speaker greatly helped him to become 'the people's William' (see page 73).

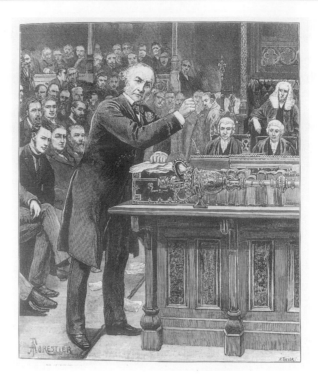

What were Gladstone's early political attitudes?

As a young reactionary Tory, Gladstone was outraged by the Reform Act of 1832 and by the Whig reforms of the 1830s, particularly those concerning the Church. It was his profound admiration for Robert Peel, whom he served under as a junior minister in the 1834–5 and 1841–6 Governments, that began to modify some of his harsher views. Gladstone later admitted that he was often confused in his political thinking during this early period. This explains his uncertainty about what to do following the split in the Conservative Party in 1846. Although an obvious Peelite in terms of his respect for Peel's memory, he made no consistent effort to rebuild a Conservative-Peelite party.

When did Gladstone first make a political impact?

It was as Chancellor of the Exchequer, first in Aberdeen's Coalition (1852–5), and then in Palmerston's Government (1859–65), that Gladstone made his first great practical contribution to British politics. The budgets he introduced in these years reorganised the public finance system and by removing many of the trade tariffs and regulations helped consolidate Britain's position as a free-trading nation. Such measures showed that he had accepted fundamental Liberal economic principles. They confirmed that Gladstone's decision in 1859 to accept office under Palmerston, a man whom he had previously viewed with as much distaste as he had Disraeli, meant that he could now be counted as a Liberal.

What were the great causes that Gladstone took up?

ACTIVITY

As you read through the sections on Gladstone, use the list of Liberal Principles on the right as a check list to measure how closely his actions conformed to them.

LIBERAL PRINCIPLES

▼ free trade
▼ low taxation
▼ cutting out of wasteful public expenditure
▼ reform of state institutions to make them more efficient
▼ minimum state interference in the rights of the individual
▼ representation of the rights of the nonconformists
▼ avoidance of unnecessary wars and foreign entanglements

Such was Gladstone's stature in his new party that within a decade of joining it in 1859 he had risen to the leadership. In 1868 he became Prime Minister for the first time. By then he was already in his sixtieth year. Yet his remarkable political life was to run for another quarter of a century. Three outstanding issues preoccupied him in that period: his leadership of the Liberal reforming ministry of 1868–74; his great moral campaign against the Turkish atrocities and Beaconsfieldism; and his valiant but unsuccessful struggle to settle the Anglo-Irish Question. Ireland was, indeed, to shape the rest of his political life. He sought again to fulfil the promise he had first made in 1868, that he would 'pacify Ireland'. It was a promise that was to change the course of British politics. Gladstone's perseverance in bringing in Irish Home Rule Bills in 1886 and 1893, in the face of opposition from the Conservatives, the House of Lords, and half his own Party, was an act of impressive personal courage, but it split the Liberal Party and allowed the Conservatives, during that period generally known as Unionists, to dominate British politics for a generation.

2 Disraeli and the Second Reform Act, 1867

We noted in Chapter 2 (page 38) that the First Reform Act of 1832 had established the principle that Parliament was prepared to reform the electoral system to make it more closely reflect the distribution of the population. By the 1860s strong pressure had grown inside and outside Parliament for further changes on these lines. Both parties accepted that reform had to come. The question was which of them would be responsible for introducing it – the Liberals or the Conservatives? Disraeli was a realist. He calculated that if reform was unavoidable then it would be better if the Conservatives introduced it. This would put them in a position to control and limit its effects. So, when Gladstone put forward a Reform Bill in 1866, Disraeli immediately launched an attack upon it. He was able to use the support of anti-reform rebels among the Liberals to outvote Gladstone's proposal. This defeat led to the government's resigna-

ISSUE
Was Disraeli's Reform Bill intended as a genuine extension of democracy?

ACTIVITY

Look at Figure 21. What point is the cartoonist making? In the light of what you have learned about Disraeli, how accurate is the cartoonist being?

tion and the return to office of the Conservatives. Disraeli, as Chancellor of the Exchequer in the new ministry, then proceeded to introduce his own Reform Bill in 1867.

THE DERBY, 1867. DIZZY WINS WITH "REFORM BILL."

Mr. Punch. "DON'T BE TOO SURE; WAIT TILL HE'S *WEIGHED.*"

Figure 21 Disraeli, portrayed as a jockey, steers his mount to the head of the parliamentary race, in a *Punch* cartoon, 1867.

Main Terms of the Second Reform Act, 1867

in the boroughs:
– vote extended to all male householders and lodgers paying £10 a year and to 'compounders', i.e. tenants who did not pay full rates but shared costs with their landlords;

in the counties:
– vote extended to male £12 leaseholders;
– boroughs of less than 10,000 lost one seat;
– 45 seats redistributed to counties and the larger towns.

The effect of the Act was to double the electorate from 1.1 million to over 2 million and to give the vote for the first time to large numbers of working men.

To allay Tory fears that reform was going too far Disraeli described his Bill as being wholly in keeping with 'the manners, the customs, the laws, the traditions of the people'. He stressed that the franchise was not a basic right of all citizens but a privilege that was attached to the ownership of property; that was why it was being extended only to direct ratepayers. Yet despite defining this as a principle, Disraeli showed himself perfectly prepared to accept a radical amendment which widened the franchise to include some half-million 'compounders', those who were not direct rate payers. The reason for Disraeli's apparent abandonment of principle was that he saw a major advantage for the Conservatives in an extension of the vote to the compounders. Although it would certainly increase the number of middle-class and working-class voters in the boroughs (who were expected mainly to vote Liberal), the amended 1867 Bill would more than compensate for this by strengthening the Conservative vote in the county constituencies. In the words of the historian, Maurice Cowling, Disraeli 'was prepared to let Radicals have their way in the boroughs, so long as he had his in the counties'.

Disraeli's introduction of reform in 1867 was a bold move since he could not know for sure how the new electors would vote. He was gambling that the majority would support the Conservatives. It was once said of him that, just as a sculptor perceives his finished creation in a block of rough marble, so he perceived the importance of the working-class voter in future English politics. Modern scholars tend to think this an exaggeration; they see Disraeli's appreciation of the need to enfranchise the working class as a question of opportunism rather than long-term perception. They regard Disraeli's major achievement in winning over large sections of the middle class to the Conservatives as being of greater significance. Despite his love of aristocracy, Disraeli understood that it was the middle class who mattered. They were the possessors of the wealth created by the industrial revolution. Now that they had the vote, they were the most influential stratum in politics and society.

Notwithstanding Disraeli's success in outwitting the Liberals over reform in 1867, he did not reap the rewards immediately. In 1868, in the first general election after the Second Reform Act, the Conservatives were defeated and Gladstone became Prime Minister at the head of a Liberal government.

How important was Disraeli's achievement over the second Reform Act?

ACTIVITY

Contemporaries described Disraeli's Reform Bill as 'a leap in the dark'. What do you think they meant by this? How fitting a description do you find it?

ISSUES
Did this ministry mark 'the high tide of Liberalism'?
Were the reforms that it introduced an attack upon the traditional character of the nation?

3 Gladstone's First Ministry, 1868–74

Gladstone's first government proved to be one of the great reforming ministries in modern British history. It is sometimes referred to as 'the high tide of Liberalism'. During its seven years in office it introduced an unprecedentedly wide range of reforms which affected nearly all the major institutions in the state. Gladstone also attempted to deal with the Irish question by a set of major reforms (see page 131).

The Major Reforms, 1868–74

The Army	– the practice of selling commissions to the highest bidder was abolished. Promotion was to be based on merit: – recruitment to be encouraged by reducing enlistment from twelve years to six, with six years in the reserve; – the infantry was completely reorganised on a county basis. The reforms were the work of the War Secretary, Edward Cardwell and were Britain's response to the growth of Prussian military power in Europe.
Education	The Education Act of 1870, introduced by W.E. Forster, aimed at establishing a national system of elementary education (see page 102).
University Reform	In 1871 religious tests were removed, allowing Nonconformists to enter Oxford and Cambridge on the same terms as Anglicans.
Trade Unions	The Trade Union Act of 1871 granted the unions new legal rights and protection of funds. The Criminal Law Amendment Act 1871 outlawed picketing (see page 181).
Licensing Laws, 1872	Restrictions were imposed on the opening hours of public houses.
Civil Service Reform, 1871	Entrance to the civil service and promotion within it were to be decided by open competitive examination.
The Ballot Act, 1872	This ended the previous system of open voting by a show of hands. Voting was now to be in secret; the voter would enter a booth and record his preference by marking a cross on a ballot slip against the name of his chosen candidate.
The Law	The Judicature Act of 1873 began the reorganisation of the central court system with the aim of streamlining and speeding up the notoriously slow trial and appeal procedures.

ACTIVITY

The list of major reforms may not seem very striking to a modern reader used to the idea of extensive government activity, but at the time the changes were viewed by many contemporaries as intrusive and dangerous. Why do you think this was? List the individual measures and say who would have benefited and who would have lost by them. The following paragraphs in the main text will help you do this.

Progressive though the reforms between 1868 and 1874 were, they angered those who felt their position was being undermined. On the labour relations front, the credit gained by the Liberals for the Trade Union Act of 1871, which gave the unions extended legal rights, was lost by the accompanying Criminal Law Amendment Act, which made picketing illegal. Similar loss of government popularity followed the University Test Act, which ended formal discrimination against Dissenters at Oxford and Cambridge, the Civil Service reforms which introduced open competitive examinations and promotion on merit, and the law reforms, which aimed to streamline the legal system. Traditionalists and those who had enjoyed privileges under the old systems felt directly threatened by the intended changes. Forster's Education Act offended both Anglicans and Nonconformists; the latter group were particularly important since it was from the Nonconformists that the Liberal Party had previously drawn some of its strongest supporters. The Ballot Act also had its critics who claimed that the introduction of secret balloting would enable electors in Ireland to vote in defiance of their landlord's wishes by returning pro-Home Rule MPs. Cardwell's army reforms which were also based on the principle of promotion on merit aroused the anger of the officer class which resented the attack upon its privileges. The attempt in the Licensing Act to lessen the harmful social effects of uncontrolled drinking was condemned by the liquor trade as an assault on the freedom of Englishmen. In the House of Lords, the Bishop of Peterborough declared that 'it would be better that England should be free than that England should be sober'.

All this anger and resentment combined to suggest that Gladstone's Liberal government was attempting to introduce some form of social revolution by undermining the nation's traditional institutions. However modern scholars, while acknowledging the achievements of the 1868–74 Liberal Ministry, dismiss the idea that it represented a comprehensive Gladstonian plan for changing society. They tend to see the reforms as a set of separate reactions to particu-

Why did the Liberal reforms meet strong opposition?

GLADSTONE'S LIBERAL PRINCIPLES – 'PEACE, RETRENCHMENT AND REFORM'

▼ **Peace** included the belief that Britain should avoid war by embracing the concepts of internationalism and anti-imperialism.

▼ **Retrenchment** was the idea of saving public money by tightly controlling central-government expenditure.

▼ **Reform** allowed for necessary changes to be introduced by government. But, since the chief characteristic of the older variety of Liberalism was its emphasis on individual freedom, it restricted government-directed reform to the redress of outstanding grievances. This meant that its approach to reform was piecemeal and not an integrated programme.

How justified were the criticisms of the Liberal reforms?

lar problems rather than a piece of systematic planning. They also stress that the Liberal government was far from a united force. It is true that Gladstone described it as 'one of the best instruments for government that ever was constructed', but as it ran its course he found it increasingly difficult to hold it together. Colin Matthew remarks that 'Gladstone had spent much of his administration in conflict with his colleagues and with groups in his party both "left" and "right"'. The Liberals far from being a single party with a single policy were made up of a variety of groups with a variety of different policies. The party is best understood as an uneasy coalition formed from the remnants of the Whigs and the Peelites. Gladstone himself in 1874 identified three serious weaknesses in the Liberal Party:

(a) It has had no present public *cause* upon which it is agreed.
(b) It has serious & conscientious divisions of opinion.
(c) The habit of making a career by & upon constant active opposition to the bulk of the party, & its leaders, has acquired a dangerous predominance among a portion of its members.

Source F From Gladstone's diary entry, March 1874.

The Liberals' difficulties were eagerly seized upon by Disraeli who greatly amused himself at the government's expense:

As I sat opposite the Treasury Bench the Ministers reminded me of one of those marine landscapes not very uncommon on the coasts of South America. You behold a range of exhausted volcanoes. Not a flame flickers on a single pallid crest. But the situation is still dangerous. There are occasional earthquakes, and ever and anon the dark rumbling of the sea.

Source G From a speech by Disraeli in the House of Commons, 1873.

Figure 22 A cartoon of 1873 shows Disraeli enjoying himself 'roasting' Gladstone's government. Each of the figures on the spit would be recognisable to contemporaries as representing a leading member or supporter of Gladstone's government..

ACTIVITY

Using Gladstone's diary entry, Disraeli's verbal mockery, and the cartoon in Figure 22 as starting points, suggest reasons why the 1868–74 ministry met mounting difficulties as it ran its course.

---

4 Disraeli's Reshaping of the Conservative Party, 1868–74

ISSUE

How far was the Conservative recovery after 1868 due to Disraeli's formulation of new party principles?

The internal difficulties which afflicted Gladstone's government and the fears that its reform programme created proved a godsend to Disraeli. While in opposition between 1868 and 1974 he cleverly exploited the anxieties that Gladstone's measures had aroused by portraying the Liberal government as being intent on destroying the interests of the propertied, commercial and industrial classes.

Typical of Disraeli's approach was his assertion that:

> The tone and tendency of Liberalism cannot be long concealed. It is to attack the institutions of the country under the name of Reform, and to make war on the manners and customs of the people of the country under the pretext of Progress.

Source H From a speech at Crystal Palace, June 1872.

He attacked Gladstone personally, characterising him as an irresponsible radical who was undermining the nation. But Disraeli's tactic was not simply to oppose. He put equal effort into presenting the Conservatives as the party the electorate could trust. In the period 1868–74 Disraeli projected an image of the Conservatives as 'the National Party'. He travelled widely in England making a number of what would now be called keynote speeches in which he set out Conservative policy. He described the Party as having three principal objectives:

Q What was new about Disraeli's style of attack on Liberalism?

▼ to defend the nation's traditional institutions
▼ to preserve and enlarge the British Empire
▼ to 'elevate the condition of the people' [to introduce social reform]

These policies were intended to show that the Conservatives were not a single class party, but could represent the middle classes and the newly enfranchised working-class voters as well as the landed class from whom the Tories had traditionally drawn their support. The tone and style of Disraeli's speeches are illustrated by the following extracts:

> What is the Tory Party unless it represents national feeling? If it does not represent national feeling, Toryism is nothing. It does not depend upon hereditary coteries of exclusive nobles. It does not attempt power by attracting to itself the spurious force which may accidentally arise from advocating cosmopolitan principles or talking cosmopolitan jargon. The Tory Party is nothing unless it can represent and uphold the institutions of the country.

Source I From a speech by Disraeli at the Mansion House, London, 1867.

ACTIVITY

Read the two extracts from Disraeli's speeches and then state in your own words what you understand Disraeli's three 'great objects of the Tory party' to have been. How, in Disraeli's judgment, did these help to make the Conservatives 'a National party'?

Source J From a speech by Disraeli at Crystal Palace, June 1872.

> Gentlemen, I have referred to what I look upon as the first object of the Tory party – namely, to maintain the institutions of the country, and reviewing what has occurred, and referring to the present temper of the times upon these subjects, I think that the Tory party, or, as I will venture to call it, the National party, has everything to encourage it. I think that the nation, tested by many and severe trials, has arrived at the first duty of England to maintain its institutions, because to them we principally ascribe the power and prosperity of the country.
>
> Gentlemen, another great object of the Tory party, and one not inferior to the maintenance of the Empire, or the upholding of our institutions, is the elevation of the condition of the people. What is the opinion of the great Liberal Party on this subject? A leading member denounced it as a 'policy of sewage'. Well, it may be a 'policy of sewage' to a Liberal Member of Parliament. But to one of the labouring multitude of England, who has found fever to be one of the members of his household, who has, year after year, seen stricken down the children of his loins, it is not a policy of sewage but a question of life and death.

5 The Conservatives in Office, 1874–80

ISSUES

How far was this government a fulfilment of Disraeli's ideas of 'Tory Democracy'?
Was the Conservative reform programme simply a continuation of what Gladstone's Liberal government had begun?

The effectiveness of Disraeli's campaign in capturing support for his party was shown in 1874 when the Liberals, already weakened by their own internal divisions, were heavily defeated at the general election. Characteristically, Gladstone spoke of his Government's having been 'borne down on a torrent of gin and beer', a reference to the unpopularity of the licensing laws. Disraeli became Prime Minister at the head of a Conservative government with a large majority in the Commons, He now had the opportunity to put into practice the policies he had so vigorously advanced. The government which he led for the next six years was to prove the equal of its Liberal predecessor in legislative achievement. Social reform figured prominently in the Conservative government's programme.

Chief Reform Measures, 1874–80

Factory Act, 1874	– protected female workers and limited hours of work to 56, thus establishing the ten hour day;
Artisans' Dwellings Act, 1875	– empowered local authorities to undertake slum clearance and the building of housing estates;
Sale of Food and Drugs Acts, 1875	– forbade the adulteration of foodstuffs;
Public Health Act, 1875	– codified over 100 regulatory statutes, thus implementing Disraeli's 'policy of sewage';
Employers and Workmen Act, 1875	– ended the anomaly by which workers who broke their contract could be charged as criminals and imprisoned whereas employers who did the same could only be sued for damages. The 1875 Act laid down that breach of contract was a civil offence whether committed by employers or employees;
Conspiracy and Protection of Property Act, 1875	– recognised the right of unions to picket peacefully;
Education Act, 1876	– made primary school attendance compulsory;
Merchant Shipping Act, 1876	– required ship owners to conform to statutory safety standards, e.g. by not loading vessels above a safety mark, called the Plimsoll line after Samuel Plimsoll, the outstanding agitator for the rights of merchant seamen, who introduced the Bill;
Agricultural Enclosure Act, 1876	– prohibited private enclosure of common land unless it was for the public good, e.g. the creation of public parks.

The reforms look very impressive. Yet it should be pointed out that a number of the measures, such as the Artisans' Dwellings Act, were permissive rather than obligatory, that is local authorities were encouraged to implement them but were not legally required to do so. It was also the case that, as with the Whig reforms of the 1830s (see page 44), some of the measures were forced on the government by the pressure of individual MPs. The outstanding example was Samuel Plimsoll's achievement in pressing the government to accept his Merchant Shipping Bill. What is particularly notable is that Disraeli himself played little part in the preparation of the various reforms. He left his ministers to do that.

However, later commentators have suggested that Disraeli's lack of personal involvement in the drafting of the reforms was unimportant. The key point is that he saw the necessity of his government's honouring the promise he had consistently made while in opposition to 'elevate the condition of the people'. It was evidence of his conviction that a modern party had to be seen to respond to the needs of a growing electorate. Ian Machin, one of his modern biographers, points out that in all that Disraeli did, 'the furthering of his party and of his own political fortunes was paramount. He had a genuine wish to carry out certain reforms but only if and when they assisted his political objectives'.

Disraeli's record on social reform tends to give him a very modern look and there have been attempts to portray him as an early supporter of 'one nation Conservatism'. What those who suggest this have in mind is the idea that since Disraeli, particularly in his novels, regretted the division of Britain into two nations, the rich and the poor, this qualifies him as a social healer whose aim was to reduce class differences and to promote economic equality.

How modern was Disraeli?

But there is a counter argument that suggests that it would be unhistorical to ascribe to Disraeli values and ideas that belong to a later time. No matter how modern he might seem, Disraeli was not a believer in the welfare state. As with Peel before him, he was prepared to introduce reform when the case for it was irresistible and therefore politically necessary. His approach was pragmatic not systematic. Another important consideration is that the Liberal and Conservative governments followed domestic reform policies that were remarkably similar. The personal rivalry between Disraeli and Gladstone has tended to obscure this, but the fact was that there was little to choose between the social-reform records of the two parties when in office. They differed in detail but not in substance. Although Disraeli attacked Gladstone's 1868–74 ministry as extremist, it is noticeable that the measures then introduced by the succeeding Conservative government were in many ways a continuation of what the Liberals had begun.

Was there any difference of principle between the Liberal reforms of 1868–74 and those of the Conservatives, 1874–80?

But if the similarities between the social policies of the parties was so marked, why was it that the Liberals and Conservatives developed as distinct and opposed political groups? The explanation is that the major division between the parties was not over domestic policies but over foreign and imperial affairs. This is sometimes referred to as the distinction between high and low politics; between the politics concerned with major moral or international issues and the down-to-earth politics relating to the improvement of social conditions at home. The great clash between Gladstone and Disraeli was over high politics. Disraeli and Gladstone came to personify wholly contrary attitudes towards the question of Britain's role in the world at large.

Following the Liberal defeat in 1874 Gladstone resigned as Prime Minister and, in 1875, as leader of the Liberal Party. He said that he 'deeply desired an interval between Parliament and the grave'. However in 1876 he came out of retirement in order to denounce the Turkish atrocities (see page 226 for the details of these). This developed into a fierce attack on 'Beaconsfieldism', Gladstone's term for what he regarded as the immorality of Disraeli's foreign and imperial policies. Gladstone's onslaught came to a climax in one of the great episodes in modern British politics – the election campaign in 1879 in the Midlothian constituency in Scotland.

6 Gladstone's Midlothian Campaign, 1879

In one typical week in Midlothian Gladstone made nine separate speeches. These were major set pieces, delivered to huge crowds numbering between 2,500 and 20,000. His audiences, often standing in pouring rain, listened transfixed to speeches which lasted for up to two hours. The Conservative newspapers accused him of cheapening politics by playing to the gallery. John Morley, Gladstone's contemporary and first major biographer, described the extraordinary performance of the seventy-year-old statesman:

> he took care to address all these multitudes of weavers, farmers, villagers, artisans, just as he would have addressed the House of Commons, – with the same breadth and accuracy of knowledge, the same sincerity of interest, the same scruple in right reasoning, and the same appeal to the gravity of public life.

Source K From *The Life of W.E. Gladstone* by John Morley, 1903.

What is particularly interesting about Midlothian to the historian is that it is one of the first examples in modern politics of the use of populism. Gladstone believed that a special bond had developed between himself and the British electorate. Richard Shannon writes that Gladstone made 'a holy drama' of Midlothian: 'He was appealing over the heads of the [upper and middle] classes to the virtuous masses'.

The success of the Midlothian campaign made Gladstone once again the undisputed leader of the Liberal Party. This was soon followed by his return to office as Prime Minister in 1880. A year later Disraeli died thus bringing to a close their bitter rivalry. Each leader had given his party a personal character that had helped to shape the two–party system in British politics.

ACTIVITY

Having read the preceding paragraphs, show that you understand the difference between high and low politics by defining the separate terms in your own words.

ISSUE

In what sense was the Midlothian campaign an example of Gladstone's populism?

'THE PEOPLE'S WILLIAM'

It was Gladstone's attempt to represent the feelings and hopes of the electorate in a personal sense that earned him the popular title of 'the people's William'. He had developed a belief in the basic moral worth of the British people; his instinct, he said, was always 'to back the masses against the classes'. He reflected: 'In 1880, Midlothian leading the way, the nation nobly answered to the call of justice and broadly recognised the brotherhood of man. It was the nation, not the classes'.

7 Gladstone's Later Ministries: 1880–5, 1886, and 1892–4

The last three ministries which Gladstone led were all dominated by the Irish question (see pages 131–36) but other important issues did arise.

ISSUE
Why did this government achieve relatively little on the domestic front?

a) The Ministry of 1880–5

Gladstone's personal commitment to parliamentary reform was evident in the major domestic measures of his 1880–85 administration: electoral reform.

Main Terms of the Third Reform Act, 1884 and the Redistribution Act, 1885

▼ qualifications for voting were to be the same in the boroughs and the counties – those who occupied land or property with an annual value of £10 or more were entitled to vote – this meant the extension of the franchise to all county householders;

▼ the Acts also established the principle that electoral reform had to be accompanied by a redistribution of parliamentary seats – 138 seats were redistributed;

▼ between them the Acts saw the electorate rise from 3 to 5 million;

▼ two out of three adult males now had the vote.

But this second ministry did not achieve the legislative success of his first. The truth was that Gladstone was preoccupied with Ireland. He also experienced particular difficulties over foreign affairs. In 1882 he felt compelled to order the British occupation of Egypt, a move which appeared to contradict his declared anti-imperialism. In 1885 his prestige was severely damaged when he was blamed by many for the death in the Sudan in 1885 of the British military hero, General Gordon (see page 241).

ISSUE
Why were these ministries so short-lived?

b) Gladstone's Third and Fourth Ministries, 1886 and 1892–4

Gladstone's 1886 government fell when it failed to push though the first Home Rule Bill for Ireland (see page 135). He devoted his fourth and last minstry of 1892–4 to the same task; he was able to steer a second Home Rule Bill through the Commons, only to have it rejected by the Lords (see page 136). In 1894, in his eighty-sixth year, half blind and seriously deaf, he finally retired from the fray.

c) Gladstone's Role as Party leader

ISSUE
Did Gladstone outlive his value to the Liberal Party?

Gladstone was more than simply a prime minister and party leader; he became a moral force in British public life. The outstanding figure of his time, he had a profound effect on the development of British politics. Yet it was not always a progressive influence. As he grew older he often confessed to feeling out of touch with the spirit of the age. He felt that his own deeply religious beliefs put him at variance with the Liberal Party. This raises an interesting paradox. Although, as the term 'the People's William' indicated, Gladstone was able to identify himself with the people, in many respects his own interests and attitudes detached him from the ordinary concerns of politics. During the last twenty-five years of his political life, two great crusades – the Eastern Question and Ireland – pre-occupied his time. Magnificent though he was in fighting these, his obsession with them obliged him to neglect issues which many of his fellow Liberals regarded as more pressing. At this stage, the Liberal Party was faced with a crisis of identity; what in an increasingly industrialised and democratic age did Liberalism represent?

For the traditional Whigs within the Party, the answer was the preservation of the character and constitution of England, objectives which were little different from traditional Conservatism. For the radicals, the answer was that the Liberal Party should be tackling the pressing social problems of the day, poverty, ill-health and urban squalor. Radical Liberals such as Joseph Chamberlain viewed Gladstone's struggle over Ireland as an unnecessary distraction from these vital concerns. The Liberal dilemma had been clearly expressed in 1885 in an exchange between Gladstone and Joseph Chamberlain following the issuing by the latter of his 'Unauthorised Programme' (see page 198), a radical challenge to the official Liberal policy. Chamberlain spoke of:

> Squalid homes, unhealthy dwellings, overcrowding; these are the causes of the crime and immorality of great cities. They are the direct result of a system which postpones the good of the community to the interest of individuals, which loses sight altogether of the obligations of property in a servile adulation of its rights.

Source L From a speech by Chamberlain in 1885.

Gladstone responded by saying:

> The [radical] Liberalism of today is far from being good. Its pet idea is what they call construction – that is to say, taking into the hands of the state the business of the individual man.

Source M From a letter by Gladstone to Lord Acton, 11 February 1885.

ACTIVITY

Use Sources L and M to describe and explain the differences between Chamberlain and Gladstone over the role of government and the policies to be followed by the Liberal Party.

Summary of Politics and Parties 2 – Disraeli and Gladstone

Year	Disraeli	Gladstone	Major Issues
1832		entered parliament as a Tory; opposed Reform Bill	Whig reforms
1835		served in Peel's 1834–5 government	Peel's Tamworth Manifesto
1837	entered Parliament as a radical Conservative		beginning of Peel's 1841–6 free-trade ministry
1841	joined Young England		
1843		President of the Board of Trade	
1844–47	trilogy of his major novels published		
1846	attacked Peel over Corn Laws		Repeal of the Corn Laws
1850–51		agitated against Neapolitan tyranny	
1852	Chancellor of the Exchequer under Derby	Chancellor of the Exchequer under Aberdeen	
1854–56			Crimean War
1858–9	Chancellor of the Exchequer under Derby		
1859		became Chancellor of the Exchequer in Palmerston's Whig-Liberal Government	
1867	piloted Second Reform Bill through Parliament	opposed Disraeli's Reform Bill	the Second Reform Act
1868	became PM for the first time	became leader of the Liberal Party	
1868–74	began modernisation of his Party by redefining Conservative principles	his first ministry – 'the high tide of Liberalism'	wide-ranging Liberal reforms and Irish policy aroused resententment among vested interests
1874	won major election victory and led a Conservative reforming ministry, 1874–80		
1875		resigned as Liberal leader and retired from politics	

Year	Disraeli	Gladstone	Major Issues
1876	became Lord Beaconsfield	came out of retirement to attack Turkish atrocities in the Balkans	parliament and nation divided over the Russo-Turkish question
1878	brought back 'peace with honour' from Congress of Berlin		
1879		resumed as Liberal leader and launched his Midlothian campaign	bitter dispute over 'the evils of Beaconsfieldism'
1880	defeated in general election	began his second ministry 1880–5; won major election victory over Beaconsfieldism	
1881	died		
1882		ordered the British occupation of Egypt	Anglo-Irish question became particularly divisive
1884		introduced the Third Reform Act	
1885		resigned as PM	
1886		undertook his third ministry introduced the Home Rule Bill – this was defeated in the Commons	Home Rule created deep divisions among the Liberals. Chamberlain left the Party in protest against Gladstone's limited concept of Liberalism
1892		began his fourth and last ministry	Ireland dominates
1893		introduced his second Home Rule Bill – defeated in the Lords	
1894		resigned as PM and finally retired from politics	
1898		died	

▼ Working on Conservatism and Liberalism

An effective way of analysing the politics of this period is to follow
the swing of the pendulum during the Gladstone years:

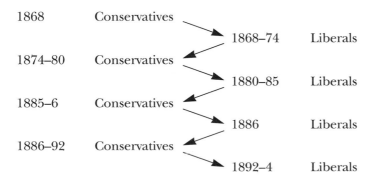

1868	Conservatives
	1868–74 Liberals
1874–80	Conservatives
	1880–85 Liberals
1885–6	Conservatives
	1886 Liberals
1886–92	Conservatives
	1892–4 Liberals

Using the diagram as a framework, try to explain each change of ministry in terms of government weakness or opposition strength. To take an example, the 1874 change could be put in these terms:

Government weaknesses	Opposition strengths
1. the wide ranging reforms since 1868 (e.g. civil service, education, law courts, army, universities, trade unions, Ballot Act, licensing laws – plus Gladstone's Irish measures) had offended the vested interests concerned and made the government unpopular.	1. Disraeli's skilled campaign since the early 70s had rejuvenated the Conservatives.
2. Gladstone and his Cabinet had grown weary in office and were losing their administrative touch. Disraeli's jibe about 'exhausted volcanoes' (see page 68) could be quoted here to good effect.	2. His reformulation of Conservative principles – defence of the nation's institutions, imperialism, and social reform – had a wide appeal.
3. the serious split that had occurred within the government ranks.	3. Disraeli had cleverly played on the fears of the propertied and commercial classes, suggesting that Gladstone was intent on social revolution.

With the above as an example it should be possible for you to examine each of the changes of government so that you develop a comprehensive understanding of the main political issues in the period between 1867 and 1894.

Answering extended writing and essay questions on Conservatism and Liberalism

You will be familiar now with the way we break down essay questions into their types. The following list shows the style of questions you are likely to encounter on the topic of Conservatism and Liberalism.

On this occasion let us consider number 6, the type of question that asks you to make a comparison. 'Were Gladstone's last three ministries less successful than his first?' We suggested on page 51 that success should always be judged against problems and aims. That notion is helpful here. Briefly set out the problems confronting, and the aims of, Gladstone and the Liberals in each of the four ministries, 1868–74, 1880–5, 1886, and 1892–4, and then suggest how far

Type of Issue	Examples of typical questions
1 causes/reasons/motives	Why did Disraeli decide to introduce the Second Reform Bill in 1867?
2 course of events	Trace the growth of political rivalry between Disraeli and Gladstone in the period 1867 to 1881.
3 consequences/results/effects	Consider the view that the Second Reform Act of 1867 was a victory not for radicalism but for conservatism.
4 success/failure	How far did Disraeli succeed in his aim of making the Conservatives the 'national' Party?
5 significance/importance	'In the final analysis what Disraeli and Gladstone did was less important than what they were.' Discuss.
6 comparison	Were Gladstone's last three ministries less successful than his first?
7 right/wrong (moral/ethical judgments)	'In pursuing great moral causes Gladstone made the error of ignoring the nation's economic and social difficulties.' How acceptable is this view?

the problems were overcome and the aims achieved. Jot down brief notes to prove to yourself that you have enough material at your disposal. If in doubt read back over pages 66–75 of this chapter. Ask yourself in what ways the aims of the first ministry differed from those of the last three. The sheer number and range of reforms which were introduced in the 1868–74 period were highly impressive. You could refer here to the ministry's being the 'high tide of Liberalism'. Yet did this mean that the ministry was therefore a major political success? Here you might feel it appropriate to emphasise the widespread resentment that the 1868–74 reform programme aroused. You could also argue that this ministry exhausted the Liberal Party's reforming aims. It had gone as far as it could go. Hence during the last three ministries the government contemplated a much smaller reform programme. Does that provide grounds for claiming that they were as successful according to their more limited aims as the first ministry had been according to its larger ones? Then there is the key consideration relating to Gladstone's own personal approach to government. When Gladstone came out of retirement in 1876 his main concern was not domestic politics but the great moral causes of the Eastern Question and Ireland. It is well worth your considering how this might alter the way the success of his later ministries should be assessed.

Answering source-based questions on Disraeli and Gladstone

Read Sources I and J on page 70. They were addresses in which Disraeli defined the role of the Conservative Party. When you have re-read them, consider the following questions which will test your understanding of the material. On this occasion the questions are accompanied by a set of responses which are intended as a guide to how you might tackle particular types of question.

▼ QUESTIONS ON SOURCES

1. Explain the meaning of the following term as it appears in the Mansion House speech.
   'hereditary coteries of exclusive nobles' (line 3) **[2 marks]**
2. In the two speeches Disraeli frequently uses the phrase 'the institutions of the country'. What did he mean by this? **[6 marks]**
3. How far can an understanding of Disraeli's Conservatism be drawn from these extracts? **[6 marks]**

Suggested response to question 1

Disraeli does not consider that the Tory Party is any longer simply a privileged group of landed magnates, wielding power by right of birth and responsible to no one but themselves.

Suggested response to question 2

The English institutions that Disraeli revered were: the Established Church, which provided a moral framework for society; the House of Lords, which expressed the virtues of the aristocratic hereditary principle; the authority of the JPs in the counties, which guaranteed the rule of law; and above all, the Crown, which symbolised the nation's identity.

Suggested response to question 3

In his Mansion House address, Disraeli points out how the Conservative Party had both enlarged the rights of the English people and strengthened the institutions of the country. This, indeed, formed the basis of what came to be termed Tory Democracy. Of equal weight in Conservative policy, as Disraeli put it in his Crystal Palace speech, was the commitment to 'the elevation of the condition of the people'; this promise of social reform was a calculated appeal to the newly-enfranchised working-class voter. Interestingly, these two aspects of policy were interlocking; imperialism was to prove as attractive as social reform to the bulk of the working class in the last quarter of the century.

Further Reading

Books in the 'Access to History' series

Whigs, Radicals and Liberals 1815–1914 by Duncan Watts has two informative chapters on Gladstone (pages 53–81). The same author studies Disraeli's politics in *Tories, Conservatives and Unionists 1815–1914* (pages 80–115). The 1867 and 1884 Reform Acts are analysed in *Government and Reform 1815–1918* by Robert Pearce and Roger Stearn (pages 53–81) The Second Reform Act is also covered in *Labour and Reform Working-Class Movements 1815–1914* by Clive Behagg, pages 81–92.

General

A particularly helpful text is *Why Tory Governments Fell, 1783–1997* edited by Anthony Seldon (Opus, 1997). Among the many biographies of Disraeli the modern classic is *Disraeli* by Robert Blake (Eyre & Spottiswoode, 1966). The same author has written a fascinating essay, *Gladstone, Disraeli and the Queen* (Clarendon Press, 1993). Four up-to-date biographies which students would find particularly provocative and interesting are *Disraeli* by John K. Walton (Routledge, 1990), *Disraeli* by John Vincent (OUP, 1990), *Disraeli* by Ian Machin (Longman, 1995), and *Disraeli* by Paul Smith (CUP, 1996). Studies of him as a literary and social figure are provided in *Disraeli* by Sarah Bradford (Stein and Day, 1983) and in *Disraeli: a Biography* by Stanley Weintraub (Hamish Hamilton, 1993). An outstanding analysis of Disraeli's politics is *The Age of Disraeli 1868–81: the Rise of Tory Democracy* by Richard Shannon (Longman, 1992). Matching Robert's Blake study of Disraeli in its scholarship and readability is *Gladstone* by Roy Jenkins (Macmillan, 1995). The leading Gladstone authority is H.C.G. Matthew, the editor of Gladstone's diaries. His *Gladstone 1809–74* (OUP, 1988) and *Gladstone 1874–98* (OUP, 1995) are a must. An absorbing study which takes a strongly critical view of Gladstone's politics is *Gladstone Heroic Minister 1865–1898* by Richard Shannon (Allen Lane, 1999). Other recommended biographies from the large number now available are: *Gladstone* by Philip Magnus (John Murray, 1954), *Gladstone* by E.J. Feuchtwanger (Allen Lane, 1975) and *William Ewart Gladstone* by Agatha Ramm (University of Cardiff Press, 1989). An excellent set of essays, introducing some of the latest research on Gladstone, is to be found in *Gladstone* edited by Peter J. Jagger (Hambledon Press, 1998). Gladstone's development as a populist politician is the subject of *Liberty, Retrenchment and Reform Popular Liberalism in the Age of Gladstone, 1860–1880* by Eugenio F. Biagini (CUP, 1992) and *Liberal Politics in the Age of Gladstone and Rosebery* by D.A. Hamer (OUP, 1972). There are informative chapters giving up-to-date assessments of Disraeli and Gladstone in *Modern British Statesmen 1867–1945* edited by Richard Kelly and John Cantrell (Manchester UP, 1997). Helpful documentary studies are *Gladstone, Disraeli and Later Victorian Politics* by Paul Adelman (Longman, 1970) and *Gladstone and Disraeli* by Michael Lynch (Hodder & Stoughton, 1991).

SOCIAL POLICY IN NINETEENTH-CENTURY BRITAIN

In Chapter 1 you were introduced to the main economic developments that occurred in Nineteenth-Century Britain. In this chapter you will be studying the social problems these developments created and how government and Parliament tried to deal with them. To help you do this four major problems have been selected – poverty, public health, factory conditions and education. There were many other social problems, of course, and many of these appear in other chapters, but the four selected ones provide clear examples of the pressures for and against social reform in this period. Although you may be interested in finding out about only one or two of the topics, it would help your understanding of each of them if you discover what they have in common and the way in which they illustrate the various attitudes towards reform in industrial Britain.

Introduction

Steadily through the nineteenth century, government extended its authority into areas which previously had not been considered its responsibility. This expansion of activity often met strong resistance from those who believed in the principle of *laisser faire*, and asserted that no matter how well-intentioned a government might be, it had no right to encroach on individual liberties.

It was this debate over how far government should intervene in economic matters that complicated the response of the authorities to the great social issues studied in this chapter. The big questions they had to answer were:

▼ How were they to react to the increase in poverty that accompanied the growth of population and industry?

▼ Should they regulate working conditions in the factories?

▼ Should they try to direct the economy or let it take its own course?

▼ How responsible were they for the welfare of ordinary people and how far were they entitled to interfere in their lives?

LAISSER-FAIRE

Best translated as 'leave alone' or 'do not interfere', *laisser-faire* was a concept associated with the free-trade ideas of Adam Smith (see page 13) who had argued that the government should play a minimal role in economic and social matters. Individuals should be left free to make their own decisions regarding their living and working conditions.

When considering whether action was needed over a particular social problem, Parliament normally appointed a select committee or a special commission to investigate. Experts in the relevant field were called to serve on these bodies or to give evidence to them. This enabled hard facts to be gathered. The completed reports were usually bound in blue leather covers. This gave the name 'blue books' to the information on which Parliament then relied when preparing its legislation. A pattern developed:

problem identified
|
committee/commission investigations
|
blue book report
|
Parliamentary Bill.

Nearly all the major social reform measures of the period went through this process. It marked an important aspect of the modernisation of government.

1 Dealing with Poverty

ISSUES
Why did the question of poverty arouse so much public concern during the first three decades of the nineteenth century? How far was the reformed Poor Law based on the notion that poverty was the fault of the poor?

a) Attempts Made before the Nineteenth Century

From the mid-sixteenth century onwards, the authorities in England had become increasingly concerned about the problem of **poverty**. It was so central an issue that it was often referred to as 'the condition of England' question. Until the nineteenth century the way chosen to deal with the problem was to make the locality (the parish) in which the poor (normally referred to as 'paupers') lived responsible for finding answers. Levies, known as the poor rate, were raised from the better-off members of the parish in order to provide funds to help those in need. However, what is noticeable about the response of the local authorities was that they did not think simply in terms of providing relief. They drew a distinction between indigence and poverty, between those who could not help being poor and those who were in a position to improve their lot if only they so chose.

It was the thought that many paupers were responsible for their own poverty that led the authorities to regard such persons as the 'undeserving poor', who therefore required not assistance but punishment. In Elizabethan times severe penalties were imposed on 'sturdy beggars' who, instead of seeking the work of which they were capable, opted to live off the parish by relying on handouts.

Major Poor Relief Measures Introduced before the Nineteenth Century

▼ **1601** the Elizabethan Poor Law instructed each parish to raise a poor rate from those owning property in the area. This money was to be used to help deserving paupers and to find work for the able-bodied;

▼ **1782** Gilbert's Act laid down that able-bodied paupers were not to be taken into parish 'work-houses' but were to be given 'outdoor relief' payments if work could not be found for them;

▼ **1795** the Speenhamland system, which took its name from the Berkshire village where it was first introduced, was a relief scheme based on the price of bread. If a pauper family's income fell below the level at which it could afford to buy enough bread to feed itself, it received a subsidy from the local poor rate to make up the difference. The Speenhamland system, which was primarily aimed at helping agricultural labourers, was adopted in many of the southern counties of England.

Table 6 The Speenhamland system.

cost of a gallon loaf (4 kilos)	labourer's wage subsidised to reach	allowance for his wife	allowance for each child
5p	15p per week	7.5p per week	7.5p per week
5.5p	16p per week	8p per week	8p per week
6p	17p per week	8.5p per week	8.5p per week
6.5p	18p per week	9p per week	9p per week

(Original figures converted into decimal currency)

ACTIVITY

In the light of the facts and figures given in Section 1a, explain why the various attempts to deal with the poor had proved inadequate by the early nineteenth century. Among the points you should consider are the growth and movement of the population and the attitude of the ratepayers and employers towards relief schemes. Table 7, showing the cost of the poor rate, offers some clues.

b) The Response to Poverty in the Nineteenth Century

By the early nineteenth century, the population of industrial towns and cities was increasing so rapidly that the existing parish poor relief systems simply could not cope with the swelling numbers of the poor. On the land, agricultural workers suffered badly in the economic recession and the decline in cottage industries that followed the ending of the Napoleonic wars in 1815 (see page 29). The

POVERTY
The condition of those people who did not have means of supporting themselves except by what they could earn through working. Poverty, therefore, was the natural condition of most people and was the incentive that turned them into workers and responsible citizens.

INDIGENCE

The misfortune workers found themselves suffering when they could not find paid employment or when the wages they received for working were too low to meet their needs. It followed that poverty was avoidable by the worker's efforts whereas indigence was not. To put it in simple terms: the indigent were those who wanted to work but could not, the poor were those who could work but did not.

Table 7 Cost of the poor rate in England, 1785–1851.

1785	£2,000,000
1801	£4,000,000
1812	£6,000,000
1831	£7,000,000
1851	£5,000,000

Source A From *A Treatise on the Wealth, Power and Resources of the British Empire*, by Patrick Colquhoun, published in 1814.

ACTIVITY

Having read Source A, attempt the following task:
Put into your own words what you think Colquhoun meant by saying, 'It is indigence, and not poverty, which constitutes the chief burden to which civil society is exposed.'

government began to feel that it had to create a national system for dealing with the problem of pauperism. It was the notion that many of the poor chose to be poor that inspired the official response towards poverty at this time. This attitude was powerfully expressed in a book by Patrick Colquhoun, a London magistrate whose work brought him into daily contact with the effects of poverty:

> Poverty is a most necessary ingredient in society without which nations and communities could not exist in a state of civilisation. It is the lot of man. *It is the source of wealth*, since without poverty there could be no labour; there could be *no riches, no refinement, no comfort*, and no benefit to those who may be possessed of wealth; inasmuch as without a large proportion of poverty, surplus labour could never be rendered productive in procuring either the conveniences or luxuries of life.
>
> It is indigence, therefore, and not poverty, which constitutes the chief burden to which civil society is exposed. It is the state of any one who is destitute of the means of subsistence, and is unable to procure it by labour to the extent nature requires. The natural source of subsistence is the labour of the individual; while that remains with him he is denominated *poor*; when it fails, in whole or in part, he becomes **indigent**. But it may happen, and does indeed frequently happen in civil life, that a man may have ability to labour and cannot obtain it. The great desideratum [need], therefore, is to prop up poverty by judicious arrangements at those critical periods, when it is in danger of descending into indigence.

Colquhoun's ideas had much in common with one of the powerful influences of the time – **utilitarianism**. The social and economic problems that industrialisation created in Britain produced a number of responses. Some of these, such as humanitarianism are discussed later (see page 97), but the one that most profoundly affected attitudes towards poverty was utilitarianism (also known as Benthamism). This was an approach that judged everything in terms of its utility or usefulness. When examining any of Britain's institutions, such as the Law, Parliament, or the Church, utilitarians asked a simple question – Does it work? If the answer was no, then the system or organisation under consideration had either to be changed to make it work more effectively or abolished altogether. Utilitarianism became a powerful influence among the civil servants responsible for drafting schemes of reform. It was particularly strong among those officials who sat on the Royal Commission set up by Parliament in 1832 to consider plans for the reform of the Poor Law. Guided by its dedicated and tireless secretary, Edwin

Chadwick, the Commission drafted a report whose proposals became the basis for the Poor Law Amendment Act of 1834. Chadwick took utilitarianism as his guide.

Historians now accept that Chadwick's Report had many weaknesses as a piece of social science but they do not question the great impact it made at the time. It started from the conviction that the existing Poor Law was inefficient and costly, its biggest flaw being its provision of outdoor relief. This, the Report argued, was a direct encouragement to idleness. A clear distinction was drawn between poverty and indigence. Only indigence would qualify for relief from public funds. This relief would no longer be given in direct form as a money payment; instead, charity for the indigent poor would be provided by placing them in parish workhouses. In order to deter idleness among the able-bodied, conditions in these workhouses were to be deliberately made worse than those of the lowest-paid of employed labourers. This would be an incentive to the poor to seek work, even of the most menial kind, thus ending the scandal and waste which occurred when the pauper received relief greater in amount than that earned by the most depressed of independent labourers. The key passages in Chadwick's Report read:

> The most pressing of the evils which we have described are those connected with the relief of the Able-bodied. In no part of Europe except England has it been thought fit that the provision, whether compulsory or voluntary, should be applied to more than the relief of *indigence*, the state of a person unable to labour, or unable to obtain, in return for his labour, the means of subsistence. It has never been deemed expedient that the provision should extend to the relief of *poverty*; that is the state of one who, in order to obtain a mere subsistence, is forced to have recourse to labour.
>
> The first principle is that his situation on the whole shall not be made really or apparently as eligible as the situation of the independent labourer of the lowest class. In proportion as the condition of any pauper class is elevated above the condition of independent labourers, the condition of the independent class is depressed; their industry is impaired, their employment becomes unsteady, and its remuneration in wages is diminished. Such persons, therefore, are under the strongest inducements to quit the less eligible class of labourers, and enter the more eligible class of paupers. The converse [the opposite] is the case when the pauper class is placed in its proper position, below the condition of the independent labourer. Every penny bestowed, that tends to render the position of the pauper more eligible than that of the independent labourer, is a bounty on indolence and vice.

UTILITARIANISM

This was a body of ideas associated with the philosopher, Jeremy Bentham, who believed that human beings acted out of self interest in accordance with the pleasure–pain principle. He argued that what motivated them was the desire to avoid pain and to seek pleasure. It followed, therefore, that to be successful a social policy had to offer either reward or punishment. If people knew that a certain course of action would make them suffer they would avoid it, but if they thought it would bring them advantages they would pursue it. Consequently, social reform, to be at its most useful or utilitarian, should be based on the pleasure–pain concept. In this way it would achieve 'the greatest happiness of the greatest number'.

Source B Adapted from the Report of the Commissioners on the Poor Law, presented to Parliament in 1834.

ISSUE

How did the utilitarian principle influence the amended Poor Law?

c) The Poor Law Amendment Act, 1834

Main Points of the Poor Law Amendment Act, 1834

▼ outdoor relief for the able-bodied to be abolished;

▼ parishes to be grouped into unions under the authority of Boards of Poor Law Guardians;

▼ workhouses to be set up in each union;

▼ conditions in the workhouses to be made 'less eligible' (harsher) than that of the lowest paid worker so as to discourage the idle poor from entering them;

▼ Poor Law Commissioners, based in London, were to supervise the working of the scheme and maintain national standards.

'Less eligibility' became the guiding concept behind the operation of the revised Poor Law. It followed logically from the Report's belief that every penny spent improving conditions for the pauper over those of the independent labourer encouraged 'indolence and vice'. With only minor modifications, the Poor Law as amended in 1834 remained in operation until after the First World War. It aroused great bitterness among its major victims – the old who could no longer earn their living, widows left destitute by their husband's death, the mentally or physically disabled, and orphaned or abandoned children. It was these unfortunates rather than the indolent able-bodied who became the inmates of the workhouse. Those who ran these places were only too willing to make conditions so prison-like and miserable that they would deter all but the most desperate from entering. Workhouse regulations imposed strict segregation between the sexes, parting husbands and wives, and between parents and children. A rule of silence applied for most of the day, food was minimal and of the poorest kind, clothing was coarse and uniform, and work was arduous and repetitive. Yet in the weekly religious service which the inmates were obliged to attend they were urged to regard the charity they were receiving as the gift of a loving god and of generous ratepayers. It was little wonder that fear and hatred of the workhouse became widespread among the working classes and underlay many of the social protest movements of the century.

Not all workhouses were equally bad; there were humane guardians and managers. Nor was there a uniform response to the requirements of the Poor Law Amendment Act. In some areas local opposition to the abolition of outdoor relief was so great that the authorities chose to continue it rather than risk riots. Such was the scale of evasion of the new system that, in 1850, out of one million paupers, only 110,000 were inmates of the workhouses. But in the workhouses the broad picture was one of misery created by a too rigid enforcement of the 'less eligibility' principle. It was not until the introduction of old age pensions in 1909 and National Insurance in 1911 (see pages 208 and 210) that a more compassionate treatment of poverty was formally introduced.

Modern research has tended to emphasise the failings of the New Poor Law in its attempt to deal with pauperism. A representative of this viewpoint is the historian, Pamela Horn:

Once established, the basic philosophy of the poor relief system persisted almost until the end of the century. The stigma [shame] of pauperism was inculcated from an early stage, and only those who could manage in no other way resorted to Poor Law assistance. So while the 1834 Act may have fostered self-dependence – it boosted friendly society [working-class self-help associations] membership, for example – it failed to recognize the genuine needs of the poor.

Source C From Pamela Horn, *The Rural World*, Hutchinson 1980.

Figure 23 Contemporary drawing of the dormitory in the Marylebone Workhouse in 1847, from the *Illustrated London News*. This particular workhouse and the one in Figure 24 came to regarded by the Poor-Law authorities as model examples of the successful implementation of the 'less eligibility' principle.

Figure 24 Meal-time at the St. Pancras Workhouse, 1900.

ACTIVITY

Study Figures 23 and 24, and then answer the following questions:
1. Why are there so many religious texts on the walls and ceilings in Figure 23?
2. Why is it that there are no partitions and so little space between the individual bed-boxes in this dormitory?
3. Suggest reasons to explain why in Figure 24 there appear to be:
    ▼ so few young women present
    ▼ no men present
    ▼ no conversations taking place
    ▼ hardly any differences in style of clothing worn.
4. How useful are these visual sources to the historian who is analysing the operation of the Poor Law?
5. What other types of evidence would this historian need to study in order to get a fuller picture?

ISSUE
Why, despite the obvious need, did it take so long to achieve advances in public health provision?

2 Public Health

The following is a description of the River Aire, the main source of drinking water to the city of Leeds, in 1841:

It is charged [filled] with the contents of about 200 water closets and similar places, a great number of common drains, the drainings from dunghills, the Infirmary (dead leeches, poultices for patients, etc.), slaughter houses, chemical soap, gas, dung, dyehouses and manufactories, spent blue and black dye, pig manure, old urine wash, with all sorts of decomposed animal and vegetable substances from an extent of drainage, amounting to about 30,000,000 gallons per annum of the mass of filth with which the river is loaded.

Source D From *The Leeds Intelligencer*, a local newspaper, 1841.

Figure 25 'A Court for King Cholera', *Punch* cartoon of 1864, depicting the slum conditions that encouraged disease to spread.

ACTIVITY

Read the extract from the *Leeds Intelligencer* and study Figure 25. What public health hazards would be likely to exist in conditions such as those shown and described in the sources?

Such conditions were not untypical of the cities and urban areas of Britain in the mid-nineteenth century. They help to explain why the population of Britain was vulnerable to epidemic disease. The increase in the numbers of people living in Britain and their concentration in the insanitary slums of towns and cities provided conditions in which ill-health flourished. Between 1830 and 1870 there were four major outbreaks of typhoid which caused thousands of deaths on each occasion. In 1848 there was a particularly severe outbreak of cholera in London. The greatest friend of such disease was dirt and its greatest enemy was cleanliness. As medical knowledge increased through the century, increasing emphasis began to be placed upon the need for improved public hygiene, the key to which was the availability of clean water. Both contagious disease (the type spread by bodily contact) and infectious disease (the type spread by germs in the air or in water) could not be effectively combated unless sanitation was improved. This could be done only by an integrated and concerted public health programme. It was the battle to achieve this that makes up the story of public health reform in the nineteenth century.

Diseases

The major epidemic diseases of the Victorian years, which caused serious ill-health and in the worst cases brought death:

cholera	an intestinal infection causing violent vomiting and diarrhoea
diphtheria	a throat infection causing a leathery membrane to block the victim's air passages
pneumonia	inflammation of the lungs, resulting from bacterial infection
scarlet fever	a throat infection accompanied by a livid skin rash
small pox	the most contagious of all diseases, marked by disfiguring eruptions on the face
tuberculosis	a wasting disease particularly affecting the lungs
typhoid	a severe stomach infection transmitted by polluted water. One of its most notable victims was Prince Albert who was thought to have caught it from the drains at Windsor Castle
typhus	similar in its effects to typhoid, transmitted by lice
whooping cough	an infection of the lungs and throat, especially prevalent among children. It took its name from the rasping sounds it produced from its victims as they struggled to breathe

---

ACTIVITY

Drawing on the information given earlier in this section, explain why epidemic disease was so constant a threat in the nineteenth century.

Edwin Chadwick proved as commanding an influence on the public-health question as he had been on the issue of poverty. His Report on the Sanitary Conditions of the Labouring Population, published in 1842, was a landmark document which prepared the way for a succession of health measures that began with the Public Health Act of 1848. The shocking evidence his report presented of the foul conditions in which so many people lived was an overwhelming argument for reform on a national scale. The following are brief extracts from the Report:

> Dr Duncan reports on Liverpool: There is beneath the dayroom a cellar, let off either by the landlord or tenant of the house, to a more improvident class of labourers: which cellar, in almost all cases, is small and damp, and often crowded with inhabitants to excess. These cellars are the source of many diseases, particularly catarrh, rheumatic affections, and typhus.

Dr Howard reports on Manchester: Whole streets in these quarters are unpaved and without drains or main-sewers, are worn into deep ruts and holes, in which water constantly stagnates, and are so covered with refuse and excrement as to be almost impassable from depth of mud, and intolerable from stench.

Mr Baker reports on Leeds: In one *cul-de-sac* there are 34 houses and in ordinary times, there dwell in these houses 340 persons but as these houses are many of them receiving houses [lodgings] for itinerant labourers at least twice that number are congregated. The name of this place is the Boot and Shoe Yard, in Kirkgate, a location from whence the Commissioners removed, in the days of the cholera, 75 cart-loads of manure, which had been untouched for years, and where there now exists a surface of human excrement of very considerable extent, to which these impure and unventilated dwellings are additionally exposed. The property is said to pay the best annual interest of any cottage property in the borough.

Mr Wood of Manchester contrasts the expectation of life in town and countryside:

	Average Age of Death	
	In Manchester	In Rutlandshire
Professional persons and gentry	38	52
Tradesmen, farmers and graziers	20	41
Mechanics and labourers	17	38

Source E From the *Report on the Sanitary Conditions of the Labouring Population of Great Britain,* presented to Parliament in 1842.

Historians are quick to stress that the various public health acts did not always produce immediate results. London and Scotland were not included in the 1848 Act which, in any case, did not force the councils to promote health schemes; it only gave them the authority to do so if they chose. It was not until 1875 that certain measures became compulsory. Local people often opposed reforms if they thought the laying on of water and the cleaning of the streets would raise the rates they paid. They felt a sense of injustice that as ratepayers they had to foot the bill for facilities from which everybody benefited.

A complaint from the ratepayers:

Shall the town obtain money by a tax upon a few and appropriate it for the benefit of the many – and that tax interminable without those few who find the money having any direct control over its expenditure or any possible means of having it repaid?

Source F From the *Leeds Intelligencer,* 23 October 1836.

DEVELOPMENT OF PUBLIC HEALTH

1842 Chadwick's vivid Report on the Sanitary Conditions of the Labouring Population of Great Britain published, alerting Parliament to the grim conditions in towns and cities;

1848 cholera outbreak prompted the passing of Public Health Act:
– central Board of Health established
– local boards of health to be set up when one tenth of the ratepayers requested it or when the death rate rose above 23 per thousand of the local population
– these to be responsible for water supplies and sewerage;

1868 the Torrens Act entitled local councils to undertake the clearance of insanitary dwellings;

1871 Local Government Board created with authority to oversee health policies of local councils;

1875 Artisans Dwelling Act permitted councils to clear slums and build new housing estates;

1875 Public Health Act was a compulsory measure that required councils to appoint a Medical Officer of Health and to provide water supplies, sewerage and public lavatories.

Businesses, such as private water companies, were reluctant to see changes introduced which might threaten their established position as suppliers. In 1844 Edwin Chadwick complained to a fellow social reformer:

> Frequently interested parties are seated at the Boards of Guardians who are ready to stop anything which may lead to expenditure for the proper repair of the dwellings of the labouring classes. Where measures of drainage are proposed and the works carried out by Commissioners of Sewers are found to be defective a cry is raised nothing must be done for fear of offending the Commissioners. When additional supplies of water are called for one cry raised is 'Oh the interest of the companies is too powerful to be touched.'
>
> **Source G** From a letter by Edwin Chadwick to Lord Ashley (also known as Lord Shaftesbury), April 1844.

Figure 26 'The City Narcissus, or, the Alderman Enamoured of his Dirty Appearance'. A *Punch* cartoon of 1849, ridiculing the refusal of some local councils to clean up their towns. (Narcissus was a character in Greek mythology who fell in love with his own reflection.).

EDWIN CHADWICK (1800–90)

-Profile-

A modern biography of Chadwick is sub-titled 'England's Prussian Minister', a reference to the cold efficiency and thoroughness with which he did his work. It is certainly true that Chadwick lacked warmth and had difficulty in inspiring affection. But perhaps these were ideal weaknesses in someone who was a natural administrator in what has been called 'the heroic age of the civil servant'. For the truth was that Chadwick was at his best in the formal atmosphere of committees and public enquiries. He was what today would be called a workaholic. He loved statistics and his appetite for administrative work was extraordinary. He has been described as a one-man lobby or pressure group. His daughter wrote of him:

> To understand him one must remember that he belonged to a generation which was working its way out of the barbarism of former ages. The Reformers of those days were so much absorbed in the tasks they had undertaken that they had hardly any thoughts for the minor details of social or domestic life.
>
> **Source H** From a letter by Marion Chadwick to Mrs Aubrey Richardson, 1928.

Chadwick took great pride in having defined the less-eligibility principle which he made central to his Poor Law Report. Two powerful instincts motivated him – orderliness and morality. He believed that the social reforms that he devoted his life to promoting would create a better world because it would be an orderly one. Order was at the core of civilisation. His powerful moral sense was especially evident in his 1842 Report on Britain's sanitary conditions in which he pointed out the connection between poverty, poor public health and social disorder. During the fifty years of his working life, between 1828 and the 1870s, there was barely a day when he did not serve on a committee. During that time he wrote or co-authored 250 official reports, many of them the length of books. More than any other single person he was responsible for creating the notion of a modern, incorruptible, public service.

His will made a fitting summary of the causes which had consumed him. He left £47,000 to help finance 'the chief objects to which I have devoted myself for the advancement of sanitary science and the physical training of the nation'. He also left annual prizes and medals to be awarded to the following:

1800 born in Manchester;

1817 –23 trained as a lawyer;

1830 –32 worked as Jeremy Bentham's secretary and nursed him during his last illness;

1833 became Royal Commissioner to enquire into child labour; became secretary of the Poor law Commission;

1834 presented his Report of the Poor Law Enquiry;

1836 contributed to the preparation of the Civil Births, Marriages and Deaths Registration Act;

1836 –39 worked as commissioner examining ways of establishing local police forces;

1842 presented his Report on the Sanitary conditions of the Labouring Poor;

1848 appointed Commissioner on the General Board of Health;

1848 –54 engaged in a fierce battle with the water companies;

the sanitary authority which shall have obtained the greatest reduction in the death rate of the population by the application of the separate system of drainage.

the manager of a poor law district who could show the largest proportion of scholars got into productive industry.

the commander and medical health officer who showed the greatest reduction of death-rate whilst in command.

Source I From the will of Edwin Chadwick, quoted in *The Life and Times of Sir Edwin Chadwick* by S E Finer, 1952.

1855 responsible for setting up a Commission to enquire into sanitary conditions in the Crimea;

1860 & 70s his utilitarian ideas shaped the modern Civil Service;

1871 designed a sewerage system for Cawnpore in India;

1890 died.

Although corruption and blindness to the health needs of the community continued throughout the century, the 1848 Public Health Act and those that followed were clearly important stages in the development of public awareness. It became increasingly difficult for councils which dragged their feet to justify their resistance to necessary improvements. Table 8, which indicates the significant drop in the death rate relating to infectious diseases during the last part of the nineteenth century, is an important measure of the beneficial effects that public health reforms had begun to achieve.

Table 8 Deaths in percentages from various causes, 1850–70, 1900.

	1850–70	1900
infectious and contagious diseases	32%	10%
respiratory diseases	17%	17%
heart failure	9%	20%
infant mortality	25%	24%
cancer	4%	5%
accidents	3%	3%
other	10%	21%

What should be noted about Table 8 is how imprecise the categories were. The understanding of disease was still very rudimentary. Cancer, for example, was probably much more prevalent than the figures suggest. It was simply that the condition was not diagnosed as readily as it would be today.

ACTIVITY

As indicated by the visual and written sources in section 2, people at the time were made aware of the danger of tolerating insanitary conditions. Why, then, did it take so long in the nineteenth century for the proper steps to be taken to protect public health?

3 Factory Reform

The first moves towards regulating conditions in the workplace concerned the protection of women and children. The exploitation of these groups of workers was not new. It long predated the industrial revolution, but what the machine age did was to increase the opportunities for their mistreatment. Women and children were essential workers in the textile industries where their slighter build and lighter weight made them vital for tasks such as the cleaning of fluff from the looms and the replacing of empty bobbins while the machinery was still running. In mines, too, children could often wriggle into seams and crevices that were too narrow for men to negotiate.

Since women and children were such a vital link in the pattern of factory production, it followed that if government took steps to limit their work this would fundamentally affect the whole labour pattern. That is why there was often a resistance to reform among workers themselves. Large numbers of families had become dependent on the earnings of wives and children. They could not afford to lose such income. But as evidence began to be gathered about the often desperate conditions in factories and mines, the authorities were pushed towards action.

Prominent among those demanding reform were two prominent Tory churchmen, Michael Sadler, himself a factory owner, and Richard Oastler. They were **humanitarians** who were disturbed by the grim working conditions which industrialisation had brought, being particularly appalled by the suffering of children. A public letter Oastler wrote in 1830 dramatically highlighted the issue and led to a fierce debate between proponents and opponents of factory reform:

> Thousands of little children, both male and female, but principally female, from seven to fourteen years of age, are daily compelled to labour from six o'clock in the morning to seven in the evening, with only – Britons, blush while you read it! – with only thirty minutes allowed for eating and recreation. Poor infants! ye are indeed sacrificed at the shrine of avarice [greed], without even the solace of the Negro slave; ye are no more than he is, free agents; ye are compelled to work as long as the necessity of your needy parents may require, or the cold-blooded avarice of your worse than barbarian masters may demand!

ISSUES
What was the importance of female and child labour in industrial Britain? Why was the State reform of working conditions resisted for so long?

HUMANITARIANISM
An attitude that stood in marked contrast to utilitarianism. It judged things not by their usefulness but by how human beings were affected by them. It was particularly strong among evangelical Christians, such as Ashley and Wilberforce, who took seriously the biblical precept that charity and compassion were the highest virtues. In practical terms, humanitarianism was concerned with the relief of suffering. It was a major influence in the campaigns against negro slavery and child labour.

Source J From Richard Oastler's letter to the *Leeds Mercury*, 1830.

The manufacturers responded by pointing out the disastrous results that would follow if children were to be prevented from working

FACTORY REFORM

1819 Factory Act prohibited the employment of children under 9 – children between 9 and 12 to work only 12 hours a day. The Act applied only to cotton mills;

1833 Factory Act laid down that in textile factories:
– children under 9 not to be employed
– those between 9 and 13 to work no more than nine hours a day
– those between 13 and 18 to work no more than twelve hours a day

1842 Mines Act:
– abolished female labour in mines
– boys under 10 prohibited from working underground
– inspectors appointed to implement the measures;

1844 Ashley's Factory Act:
– children under 13 limited to 6½ hours work per day
– young persons under 18 and females to work no more than 12 hours a day;

1847 Fielden's Factory Act:
– established the 10-hour day for female and young male workers;

1850 Grey's Factory Act gave factory inspectors greater powers;

1864 'Climbing Boys Act' forbade chimney sweeps to use children under 16;

1878 Consolidating Act brought all factories and workshop regulations into one national code;

1909 Trade Boards Act brought small workshops (sweatshops), under the same regulations as factories.

such long hours:

> A law which will shorten the hours of labour, or limit the age of children employed in worsted [a type of woollen cloth] mills, will produce the following effect. It will cause a reduction in wages of this class especially those who have large young families, who in many cases are the main support of their parents. It will raise the price of goods to the consumers, which will affect the home trade considerably. It will produce the most serious effects upon the prosperity of this district, by helping the manufacturers of foreign nations, our trade with whom depends upon the cheap terms on which we supply them with goods. It will throw many children out of employment.
>
> **Source K** From a letter by a group of employers to the *Leeds Mercury*, 1831.

ACTIVITY

It is important for historical balance that you try to see both sides of the argument.
▼ What, according to the manufacturers' letter, would be the harmful effects of a reduction in the working hours of children employed in the factories?
▼ How convincing do you find their arguments?
▼ Is there any other information that you think it necessary to have before forming your opinion?
Having studied section 3, describe the main ways in which Oastler and Sadler differed from Chadwick in their approach to the social problems of the day?

The passion and conviction with which Oastler presented his case played its part in persuading Parliament to appoint a commission of enquiry into factory conditions. Chaired by Michael Sadler, the Commission produced a report that strongly supported the claims that Oastler had made. What is particularly notable about all this is how greatly government and Parliament depended on reports of this kind for their knowledge of what life was actually like in the industrial areas of Britain. For most of the nineteenth century the majority of MPs remained men of landed wealth whose experience of urban working conditions was very limited. It was the information supplied by reports such as Sadler's that opened their eyes. The following were some of the key findings of the Commission:

1st. That the children employed in all the principal branches of manufacture throughout the Kingdom work during the same number of hours as the adults.

2nd. That the effects of labour during such hours are, in a great number of cases,

Permanent deterioration of the physical condition;

The production of disease often wholly irremediable; and

The partial or entire exclusion (by reason of excessive fatigue) from the means of obtaining adequate education and acquiring useful habits, or of profiting from those means when afforded.

3rd. That at the age when children suffer those injuries from the labour they undergo, they are not free agents, but are let out to hire, the wages they earn being received and appropriated by their parents and guardians.

We are therefore of the opinion that a case is made out for the interference of the Legislature on behalf of the children employed in factories.

Source L From the *First Report of the Factory Commissioners*, presented to Parliament in 1833

Parliament was sufficiently moved by these recommendations to introduce a major Factory Act, restricting the hours of work of children in textile mills, in the same year. This was the first in series of such measures over the next seventy years. Each of them involved a battle between reformers and employers, but in every case the argument was essentially the same as that between Oastler and the Yorkshire manufacturers in the early 1830s. Both sides claimed to be concerned with protecting the interests of the workers; their disagreement was over how this could be best achieved.

a)

Figure 27a and *b* Children at work in the mines (from the Parliamentary Commission's Report on Employment of Children in Mines, 1842). In the days before adequate photographs, strong reliance was placed on drawings such as these as a way of conveying the reality of the conditions being discussed. Many MPs found themselves moved and angered by what they were shown.

b)

ACTIVITY

Having studied the sources in section 3, suggest which of the following you think would be most likely to influence public attitudes towards child labour: Oastler's letter, the drawings accompanying the Select Committee's Report in Figures 27a & b, or the written descriptions in the Factory Commissioners' Report.

ISSUES
What motives inspired the educational reform movement in the nineteenth century?
Were the religious bodies more of a help or a hindrance to the development of a national system of education?

4 Education

With the exception of Scotland, which could boast a school in most of its villages, there was no formal education available to the mass of the population in Britain in 1830. The few schools that did exist were provided by rival Christian groups. The Anglican Church, which had been the official state religion since England had broken away from the Roman Catholic Church at the time of the Reformation in the sixteenth century, had created the National Society for the Education of the Poor in Accordance with the Principles of the Established Church (known as the National Society). As its full name suggests, the main aim of the National Society was a religious one. It had been set up to compete with the Nonconformist churches, those Protestant denominations that did not accept Anglicanism, in the struggle to gain converts. The Nonconformists had already provided a number of voluntary schools, (i.e. schools paid for by their own voluntary subscriptions and organised by them). Thus any scheme for expanding education would come up against the problem of the Anglican-Nonconformist competition.

The Nonconformist argument:

> The [Anglican] Church has no more claim for exclusive pecuniary [financial] aid from the State or for any pecuniary aid at all, than is possessed by any other of those many corporations with which our country abounds. To call upon Parliament to vote any money for the exclusive support of the Church of England is to call upon Parliament to do what is unjust. The taxes are collected from persons of all religions and cannot be fairly expended for the exclusive maintenance of one.

Source M From a letter by W.F. Hook, a Leeds clergyman, to the Anglican Bishop of St. David's, 1846.

The Anglican position:

> The late Report on the state of education in our great towns had showed that the [Anglican] Church had done nearly everything there. It had established good schools, and carried them on quietly and unostentatiously for years. If anybody desired to know which religious body was the most earnest in the cause of education, let him consult any one of the Reports of the Committee of Council, and he would see how Churchmen had laboured, what large sums they had expended, and how many schools they had maintained.

Source N From a speech by Robert Montagu, the Conservative spokesman on Education, in the House of Commons, 1870.

Figure 28 'Who shall educate? or, Our babes in the wood', a *Punch* cartoon of 1853, showing the duel between Anglicanism and Nonconformity.

Put into your own words the main Anglican and Nonconformist arguments on education as expressed in Sources M and N. Why, as illustrated in Figure 28, did both denominations obstruct the introduction of a national system of education?

Q Why did education become a major political and social issue?

Despite the religious difficulties, there was by the middle of the nineteenth century broad acceptance that education was so important that it had to be organised on a national basis. The industrial age demanded it. Factories could be neither fully productive nor safe unless the workers had the ability to read notices and instructions, write simple messages and make basic mathematical calculations. There was also a growing conviction that the extension of the vote to increasing numbers of the working classes meant that it was important to raise their educational level. Robert Lowe, a Liberal politician, said at the time of the passing of the second Reform in 1867 that it was now 'absolutely necessary to compel our new masters to learn their letters'.

The first major step towards a national system of schooling came three years later, in 1870, with an Education Bill introduced by W.E. Forster, the Vice-President of the Privy Council Committee for Education. Forster's great problem was that he could not start from scratch. He had to co-operate with the Anglicans and Nonconformists whose existing schools he needed as the basis of the universal system of elementary education he planned. His aim, therefore, was to achieve a balancing act. On one side was the National Education Union, the voice of the Established Church, which claimed that educational reform must include government financing of the existing Anglican voluntary schools. On the other was the National Education League, the representative body of the Nonconformists, which also wanted a national system of schooling but which fiercely opposed the notion of state funds being used to promote the teaching of Anglican doctrines. Forster's compromise was that voluntary schools were to remain and were to be publicly financed. Complementing these would be newly established schools, run by locally elected school boards, in which there would be no denominational instruction. Forster had hoped that both sides would be content with having got at least part of what they wanted. But in the event both were angered by the concessions made to the other.

Although the 1870 Bill was by no means a perfect measure it did establish the principle of a national system of elementary schooling, paid for from the public purse. All subsequent measures built upon the foundations laid by Forster's Act. In 1902, under the Conservative government of Arthur Balfour, the principle of state education was extended into the secondary area. But the religious problem had not gone away. The Nonconformists again bitterly resisted 'Church on the rates', their dismissive term for the upkeep of Anglican schools at the ratepayers expense, which they saw as the most objectionable part of Balfour's Act. What all this again demonstrated was that there had scarcely been a single social reform in Britain in the nineteenth century which had not been opposed by some interest group which believed its position was being threatened by the change.

Table 9 Amounts allocated by government to education, 1833–1910.

1833	£20,000
1840	£170,000
1850	£370,000
1860	£1,270,000
1870	£1,620,000
1880	£4,000,000
1890	£5,800,000
1900	£12,200,000
1910	£17,900,000

Table 10 Increase in the number of school places, 1870–86.

1870	3.5 million children needing education – places for 1,878,000
1876	4 million children needing education – places for 3,500,000
1886	5 million children needing education – places for 4,500,000

ACTIVITY

To help consolidate your ideas on education reform, a question worth asking yourself is – Why did it take so long to achieve a national system of education in the nineteenth century? The long-running rivalry between the Anglicans and Nonconformists is obviously a main part of the answer, but the other details and statistics given in section 4 should also be examined to see what clues they offer.

DEVELOPMENT OF THE EDUCATIONAL SYSTEM

by 1811 The National Society (Anglican) and the British and Foreign Society (Nonconformist) had begun to compete in setting up schools;

1833 first annual government grant (£20,000) for education;

1839 Cabinet Committee appointed to monitor spending on education;

1858 Newcastle Commission reported on inadequate provision of education;

1862 Education Department of Privy Council recommended 'payment by results';

1870 Forster's Education Act:
– existing voluntary schools still to be supported
– school boards to be elected by local ratepayers responsible for administering new schools which would provide non-denominational religious education;

1876 Sandon's Act penalised parents who kept their children from school;

1880 Mundella's Act made schooling compulsory for children below 13;

1891 government grant made education free in all elementary schools;

1899 school leaving age fixed at 12;

1902 Balfour's Act:
– school boards replaced by 144 Local Education Authorities (LEAs) run by the County and County Borough Councils.

Summary of Social Policy in Nineteenth-Century Britain

Year	Poverty	Public Health	Factory Reform	Education
1795	Speenhamland system of outdoor relief widely adopted in the south			
1819			Factory Act limited the employment of children in cotton mills	
1832	Royal Commission under Edwin Chadwick set up to examine the working of the Poor Law		Sadler's Select Committee on child labour recommended reform	
1833	Chadwick presented his Report – strongly utilitarian in its recommendations		Factory Act further restricted the hours of work of children and young persons in textile mills	first annual government grant for education of £20,000
1834	Poor Law Amendment Act introduced – outdoor relief abolished – indoor relief to be provided by parish workhouse according to harsh less eligibility principle			
1839				Cabinet Committee appointed to monitor spending of education grant
1842		Chadwick's Report on the Sanitary Conditions of the Labouring Population of Great Britain published	Mines Act abolished female labour in mines – boys under 10 prohibited from working underground – inspectors appointed	
1844			Ashley's Factory Act – children under 13 limited to $6\frac{1}{2}$ hours work per day – young persons under 18 and females to work no more than 12 hours a day	
1847			Fielden's Factory Act – established the 10-hour day for females and young males	

Year	Poverty	Public Health	Factory Reform	Education
1848		Public Health Act created Central Board and local boards of Health		
1850			Grey's Factory Act gave factory inspectors greater powers of enforcement	
1858				Newcastle Commission reported on inadequate provision of education in Britain
1862				Education Department of Privy Council produced a Revised Code aimed at improving school standards
1864			'Climbing Boys Act' forbade chimney sweeps to employ children under 16	
1867			Factories and Workshops Act extended previous legislation to all manufacturing industries	
1868		the Torrens Act entitled local councils to clear insanitary dwellings		
1869				Education League demanded broad extension of state education
1870				Forster's Education Act – set up board schools alongside existing religious voluntary schools – board schools to be funded from local rates – boards empowered to make school attendance compulsory

Year	Poverty	Public Health	Factory Reform	Education
1871		Local Government Board created to oversee health policies of local councils		
1875		Artisans Dwelling Act permitted councils to clear slums and build new houses; Public Health Act required councils to appoint a Medical Officer of Health and to provide water supplies		
1876				Sandon's Act penalised parents who kept their children from school
1878			Consolidating Act brought all factories and workshop regulations into one national code	
1880				Mundella's Act made schooling compulsory for children under 13
1891				government grant made education free in all elementary schools
1902				Balfour's Act – School Boards replaced by council LEAs
1907		medical examinations in schools made compulsory		
1908	Old Age Pensions Act passed: non-contributory pensions of 5s (25p) a week were provided at the at the of 70		Trade Boards Act brought sweatshops under the same regulations as factories	
1911	National Insurance Act			

▼ Working on Social Policy in Nineteenth-Century Britain

The 'Points to Consider' at the start of the chapter suggested that social reform in the nineteenth century can be best understood as a battle between supporters and opponents of change. An effective way of making notes on the material introduced in the chapter would be for you to draw up two columns: arguments for – arguments against. Under each heading you could list brief appropriate references to each of the four categories of reform you are studying. An example might be:

FACTORY REFORM	
Arguments for	**Arguments against**
Christian duty to relieve suffering of the workers, particularly women and children	government had no right to regulate industry
Oastler's view – grim conditions in the factories like those of slavery	economic argument – shortening of hours and restrictions on female and child labour workers would cut family incomes and interfere with the pattern of factory life
practical argument – Factories such as Robert Owen's and Michael Sadler's showed that child labour was not necessary	– employers profits would fall and male workers would be laid off

Compile similar models for poverty, public health, and education. Try not to let your own opinions stop you seeing the strength of the arguments of the time. We live in an age when it is widely accepted that it is not merely the right but the duty of government to remedy social ills. However, it took a long time for that view to take hold in the nineteenth century. Ask yourself whether those who, for example in the area of public health, opposed schemes for drainage and pure water supplies were merely being selfish when they said that such things were matters for decision by private citizens, not imposition by national or local governments. It would be interesting here to look back at the arguments about parliamentary reform (pages 38–42) and the notion of losing and winning sides in history. It is relevant to recall the striking phrase of the social historian E.P. Thompson. He warned against our being too influenced by 'the condescension of posterity'. He meant by this that we should not neglect considering ideas and attitudes in the past simply because they are no longer fashionable. Historical balance requires that we try to understand all sides of an argument, even when we find them objectionable.

Answering extended writing and essay questions on Social Policy in Nineteenth-Century Britain

You will be familiar now with the way we break down essay questions into their types. The following list shows the style of questions you are likely to encounter on the topic of social reform.

Type of Issue	Examples of typical questions
1 causes/reasons/motives	Why had social reform become such a demanding issue by the 1830s?
2 course of events	Trace the development of public health reform in the nineteenth century.
3 consequences/results/effects	'Its cure for poverty proved worse than the disease.' Examine this view of the effects of the Poor Law Amendment Act of 1834.
4 success/failure	How successful was Edwin Chadwick as a social reformer?
5 significance/importance	Assess the importance of the Forster's Education Act of 1870.
6 comparison	Which was the more influential in bringing about social reform in the nineteenth century: utilitarianism or humanitarianism?
7 right/wrong (moral/ethical judgments)	'In attempting to achieve reform they exceeded their legitimate authority.' Consider this view of the role of government and Parliament in social affairs in the nineteenth century.

On this occasion, let us consider number 3, the type of question that asks you to make judgments about results and effects. The first point you will notice is that it is based upon a quotation. Don't shy away in horror. Questions about quotes are not necessarily more difficult than direct questions. Indeed, their particular form can make them easier to handle since the quotation provides a very strong clue as to what the questioner wants from you. As always, look for the key words in the question. Here the vital ones are 'cure', 'poverty', 'worse', and 'disease'. Note how the questioner uses figurative language, comparing poverty to a medical condition. This invites you to consider whether poverty was cured or made worse by the treatment laid down in the Poor Law Amendment Act (PLAA).

Suggested response

Begin by defining the problem of poverty in the early nineteenth century. This could be done by showing how the existing poor law and other schemes, such as Speenhamland, had proved inadequate in the face of rapid population growth and destitution, particularly in the industrial and urban areas. It would impress the examiner if you were to make the point that contemporary social observers often drew a distinction between poverty and indigence. The utilitarians – a brief definition of utilitarianism would help here – who were the main influence in shaping the PLAA were convinced that while poverty was natural and unavoidable, indigence could be cured by the appropriate measures. A brief quotation of your own choice from Colquhoun or from Chadwick's report would add weight to your argument. A good example from page 86 of this chapter is 'It is indigence and not poverty which constitutes the chief burden to which civil society is exposed.' It is worth memorising a stock of short punchy quotations on key topics.

Having set up your answer in this way, now go on to describe the main clauses in the PLAA. The application of the less eligibility principle, the abolition of outdoor relief, the severe regime to be followed in the workhouses: these should feature prominently in your description as they define the intentions of the reformers.

You are now in a strong position to discuss whether such measures did produce a cure for poverty. Some points you might like to consider are: Did the workhouse prove only too successful in making life deliberately hard for the inmates as the terror with which it was regarded by the working classes throughout the century made plain? Instead of catching the idle poor did it not ensnare the unfortunates – the orphaned, the sick, the widowed, the infirm, the aged? Here you could extend the questioner's metaphor by saying that the PLAA dealt with the symptoms not the causes of the disease and that that was its major weakness. However, it would show some awareness and subtlety on your part if you were to emphasise that, while one has to generalise in answering this question, the effects of the PLAA were different in different parts of the country. Some areas enforced the PLAA more rigorously than others; some chose to ignore it altogether.

Answering source-based questions on Social Policy in Nineteenth-Century Britain

For this exercise we have selected passages that have already appeared in this chapter. Locate them by their references, re-read them, and then answer the questions that appear here.

Source D	a description in 1841 of the River Aire, the main source of drinking water for the people of Leeds (page 91)
Source E	expert witnesses give evidence for Edwin Chadwick's inquiry into the Sanitary Conditions of the Labouring Population (pages 92–93)
Source F	A leader from the *Leeds Intelligencer*, 23 October 1836 (page 93)
Source G	Edwin Chadwick complains to a fellow social reformer, Lord Ashley (also known as the Earl of Shaftesbury), about the obstructive attitude of the water companies (page 94)
Figure 26	'The City Narcissus, or, the Alderman Enamoured of his Dirty Appearance' (page 94)

▼ QUESTIONS ON SOURCES

1. What do Source D and Figure 26 have in common in regard to their expressed attitude to public health? **[6 marks]**
2. Which offers the greater insight into the character of the opposition to public-health reform, Source F or Source G? Explain your answer. **[7 marks]**
3. Using the evidence in Source E and your own knowledge, explain the significance of Chadwick's Report on the Sanitary Conditions of the Labouring Population. **[12 marks]**

Points to note about the questions

Question 1 This a straightforward question of the type you have met before in earlier chapters (for example, see page 25). It asks you to locate the similarities in two sources. One is a written description, the other a provocative cartoon, but in both cases you are being asked about the attitude they convey. In your answer stress how the stark description of the polluted River Aire complements and justifies the scorn that infuses the *Punch* cartoon.

Question 2 This is a more difficult question. Here you are being asked to judge the relative value of two sources. You will gain little credit from simply restating what is in the sources. Your task is to make a judgment. It does not matter which one you choose and you are entitled to sit on the fence and say that they are equally valuable. But you must explain the reasons for your choice, not merely describe what the sources contain. Is a private letter more valuable as a historical document than a published newspaper leader? What particular insight does each one offer? It may be that you think that the views of Chadwick, the outstanding figure in the whole social reform question, are necessarily of more importance than the opinion of a provincial newspaper. This is certainly a justifiable point of view. But it could equally well be argued that to have the resentment of the ratepayers who had to foot the bill for public health improvements so clearly expressed makes source C particularly enlightening.

Question 3 You have not met this style of question so far in this book. Its essential difference from the others you have worked on is that it asks for a combined approach. You are required both to analyse the document and to bring in your own knowledge in order to judge the significance of the source. In this type of two-part question you are not told how much attention you should pay to each part, but as a rule of thumb it is best to play safe by giving each a roughly equal treatment. There is a great deal of very valuable information packed into source B. Chadwick's report gives the findings of four highly informed experts who provide illuminating accounts of the appalling conditions in the industrial cities of Liverpool, Manchester, and Leeds. In addition there is simple set of figures of comparative death rates in industrial Manchester and rural Rutland. Even if you had no prior knowledge, your reading of this extract would provide you with facts and figures that would take you right into the heart of the issue of public health provision.

Having made those points, you are now in a position to develop them by bringing your own knowledge to bear. You will know from your reading of the earlier sections that the significance of Chadwick's report was that it provided powerful evidence of the need for systematic and properly organised reform. Chadwick's meticulous approach to the accumulation of detail was resented by the vested interests precisely because it was so thorough. Modern analysis can now fault Chadwick's reports because they did not measure up to the scientific standards of today's techniques of information gathering. But no historian would dispute that in their time they were remarkable documents which helped to lay the basis for subsequent social research. What Chadwick did was to show the connection between poverty, poor public health and social disorder. After Chadwick's report on sanitary conditions, things could never be the same. It would, of course, involve a long struggle against determined resistance before his findings were fully acted upon. But the report from which source B is taken helped set in motion a vital process of investigative social analysis in Victorian Britain.

Further Reading

Books in the 'Access to History' series

A helpful introduction to the problem of poverty is to be found in *Poverty and Welfare* by Peter Murray. *Whigs, Radicals and Liberals 1815–1914* by Duncan Watts deals with the Poor Law (pages 35–39) and factory reform (pages 33–34). The same topics are covered in *Labour and Reform Working-Class Movements 1815–1914* by Clive Behagg, pages 44–48. Public health reform figures in *Government and Reform 1815–1918* by Robert Pearce and Roger Stearn (pages 89–91) while education is analysed in *The Changing Role of Women 1815–1914* by Paula Bartley (Chapter 3) and *Religion Society and Reform* by Andrina Stiles (Chapter 3).

General

The Age of Reform, 1820–50 and *The Edwardian Age*, both by Vyvyen Brendon (in the Hodder & Stoughton 'History at Source' series, 1994 and 1996) cover the four themes of this chapter. Another useful book in the same series is *Chartists and Chartism* by Joe Finn, 1992, which deals with poverty). *The Years of Expansion Britain 1815–1914* edited by Michael Scott-Baumann (Hodder & Stoughton, 1994) provides a case study of the Poor Law in action and examines factory and public health reform. There are excellent analyses of all the four themes of this chapter in *The Evolution of the British Welfare State* by Derek Fraser (Macmillan, 1978) and in two studies by J.F.C. Harrison, *Early Victorian Britain* (Fontana, 1988) and *Late Victorian Britain* (Fontana, 1990). An important study of motives behind reform is *Endangered Lives, Public Health in Victorian Britain* by A. Wohl (Dent, 1990). Asa Briggs, one of the outstanding authorities on British social history, deals with the reforms of the period in *The Age of Improvement 1783–1867* (Longman, 1959) and in *Victorian Cities* (Penguin, 1963). Other important studies are *The People and the British Economy 1830–1914* by Roderick Floud (OUP, 1998), *The Forging of the Modern State: Early Industrial Britain 1783–1870* by Eric Evans (Longman, 1983), *British Economic and Social History 1700–1982* by C.P. Hill (Arnold, 1985) and *Victorian Social Reform* by Eric Midwinter (Longman, 1982). There are useful chapters in *The Shaping of the Welfare State* by R.C. Birch (Longman, 1976). Also strongly recommended is *The Poor Law in Nineteenth Century England and Wales* by A. Digby (Historical Association, 1982). An excellent brief survey of educational reform is provided in *Elementary Education in the Nineteenth Century* by Gillian Sutherland (Historical Association, 1971). A classic study of the outstanding reformer of the age is *The Life and Times of Sir Edwin Chadwick* by S.E. Finer (Methuen, 1952). A particularly useful article is 'The New Poor Law' by J. Garrard (in *New Perspectives*, March 1997).

THE ANGLO-IRISH QUESTION

CHAPTER 5

POINTS TO CONSIDER

In this chapter you will be studying one of the most important long-running controversies in nineteenth-century British history – Anglo-Irish relations. It is a big and often complicated topic. You will need to take it step by step. To help you do this the chapter has been divided into eleven parts – an Introduction and ten numbered sections. Whether or not you are studying the complete topic, it is vital that you begin by working on the Introduction because this sets out the framework into which the ten following sections fit. The ability to set your knowledge in a rounded context is a considerable advantage when studying any topic in history, but with Anglo-Irish relations it is of particular importance.

Introduction

The term, the Anglo-Irish question, refers to the difficult and often bitter relations that had existed between England and Ireland since the twelfth century and which became intensified in the nineteenth century. As the hyphen between the words suggests, the Anglo-Irish question was a two-way affair. Historians now emphasise that it has to be studied from both the English and Irish viewpoints. This was not always the case. In England in the nineteenth century the standard way of referring to Irish affairs was to speak and write of 'the Irish question' or the 'Irish problem'. Behind such expressions lay two ideas – that Ireland was important only insofar as it impinged upon England and that England's difficulties with Ireland were the fault of the Irish. Of course, not all English people held this notion but it was certainly the predominant view in government and Parliament. Most modern historians now make a deliberate effort to avoid taking sides in this way. They aim at balance. In 1971, an Irish scholar, Patrick O'Farrell, wrote a book entitled *Ireland's English Question* – a neat way of showing how the angle of approach can be altered.

One historian waggishly remarked that anybody who understood the Irish question was not fully informed. Another observed that the trouble with the Irish question was that, by the time the English had

Figure 29 Map of Ireland in the nineteenth century (with small insert showing the entire United Kingdom).

found an answer to it, the Irish had changed the question. These witticisms do point to the difficulty that faces the student of Irish history. Because of its complexity and highly controversial nature, modern Irish history presents historians with particularly difficult problems of interpretation. The aim of this chapter is to provide a balanced analysis of the many issues that made up the Anglo-Irish question by looking at what happened from the viewpoint of both the Irish and the English participants.

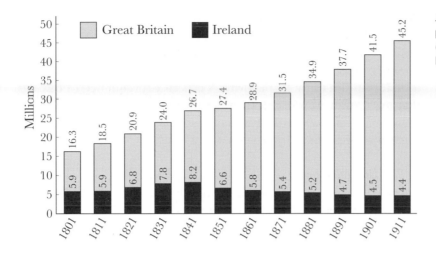

1 The Rebellion of 1798

ISSUES
Why did it happen? How far was it provoked by the actions of the English government?

At the end of the eighteenth century the prevailing attitude of the Irish towards the English was one of such distrust that in 1798 Ireland broke out into open rebellion. To understand why this occurred it is helpful to look at both the long-term and the more immediate causes of an event which the British subsequently referred to as a rebellion, and the Irish as a rising.

a) The Long-term Causes

i) The English occupation of Ireland

Anglo-Irish hostility went back to the twelfth century. At that time Ireland was not one nation, but was composed of different tribes led by kings or chieftains who were at constant war with each other. In 1170 one of those kings, in an effort to subdue his rivals, invited English troops to come to Ireland to assist him. Having arrived, the English forces stayed to assert the authority of the English king over Ireland. By no means the whole of the island or all the tribes were brought under immediate control, but the extension of English authority over the next four centuries led most Irish people to regard themselves as being under English occupation.

ii) Religion

Relations were further embittered in the sixteenth century when England underwent a religious Reformation which led it to reject the Roman Catholic Papacy and adopt Protestant Anglicanism as the

TITHES

Tithes were an annual tax of one tenth on earnings or produce and were raised for the upkeep of the Irish Church and clergy. Since they were levied on a population most of whom were Catholic for the maintenance of a Protestant Church, the tithes had been a constant source of bitterness since they had first been imposed in late-Tudor times.

official religion of the nation. However, most of Ireland remained Catholic. The result of this was that the official established Church in Ireland (the Anglican Church) represented only the Protestant minority (7 per cent) of the population but was paid for by **tithes** levied from the Catholic majority. A crucial consequence of this was that the Catholicism of the Irish became an important part of their identity as a nation in their struggle against what they regarded as English oppression.

iii) The plantation policy

English governments from the time of Elizabeth I (1558–1603) onwards strengthened their hold on Ireland by dispossessing the native Irish of their land and granting it to loyal Protestants who came over from England and Scotland. The majority of the Scottish Protestants (Presbyterians) settled in Ulster. A bitter and bloody Catholic rising against the plantation policy in 1641 was brutally suppressed and the policy was continued by the governments of the Interregnum (1649–60). During this period Oliver Cromwell undertook such a savage suppression of Irish resistance that by the 1660s 80 per cent of the Catholic Irish had been deprived of their land.

iv) The penal laws

In 1690 the defeat in Ireland of James II, the last Catholic monarch of the three separate kingdoms of England (including Wales), Scotland and Ireland, by William III consolidated the grip of the Protestant land owners. Their supremacy was reinforced by the penal laws, a series of severe legal restrictions imposed on the Catholics, who were effectively deprived of the rights of citizenship.

Source A From the Autobiography of Wolfe Tone, leader of the 1798 Rising.

> In Ireland, a conquered and oppressed and insulted country, the name of England and her power is universally odious.

v) Economic problems

To these political and religious restraints on the Irish Catholics were added heavy economic burdens. The plantation policy had created a situation in which the majority of estates were owned by Englishmen who seldom lived in Ireland and who regarded their property merely as a source of income, little of which they reinvested to improve the conditions of their tenants. Even in good years the poverty-stricken peasants were hard pressed to feed their families and pay their rents. In bad years they could do neither and faced eviction and destitution. In addition, the peasants had become dependent on the potato as their staple diet. While the potato was nutritious and had sustained the rapidly-expanding Irish peasantry, it was very prone to destruction by disease. Potato blight was a frequent occurrence in Ireland and caused acute hunger.

vi) The Government of Ireland

The English government controlled Ireland by a pro-English administration in Dublin whose chief concern was not efficient government in the service of the Irish people but the preservation of the privileges of the Protestant minority and the absentee landlords. In practice, Ireland was governed more as a colony whose role was to serve the needs of England, than as an integral part of the United Kingdom.

Thus by the end of the eighteenth century the Irish peasantry had a collection of fears and grievances. A memorable definition and summary of these was given by Benjamin Disraeli:

> A dense population in extreme distress inhabits an island where there is an Established Church which is not their Church. Over them rules a territorial aristocracy the richest of whom live in distant capitals. Thus you have a starving population, an absentee aristocracy, and an alien Church, and in addition the weakest executive in the world. That is the Irish question.

Source B From a speech by Disraeli in the Commons, 1844.

ACTIVITY

To make sure you have understood the analysis so far, take Disraeli's description of the Irish question problem and divide it into its essential points by reference to his key words. A likely break down would be: 'starving population' – 'absentee aristocracy' – 'alien Church' – 'weakest executive'. Then, drawing on the information provided in paragraphs i to vi above, use your own words to illustrate his categories.

---

b) Short-term Causes of the 1798 rising

i) The influence of the American and French Revolutions

Events abroad in the late eighteenth century had a powerful influence on Irish affairs. The radical ideas of the American revolution, summed up in the Declaration of Independence (1776) that all peoples had the right to 'life, liberty and the pursuit of happiness', had a particular appeal for the Irish. The French Revolution, which began in 1789, was greeted with similar enthusiasm. The proclaimed ideals of 'liberty, equality, and fraternity' struck a resonant chord with the Irish.

ULSTER PRESBYTERIANISM

The majority of settlers in Ulster since the sixteenth century had been Presbyterians of Scottish descent. Presbyterianism was a particularly severe form of Christian nonconformity which had predestination as its main belief. Presbyterians had a particular hatred of 'Popery' (Catholicism) which they regarded as a mixture of superstitious practices and subservience to an ungodly pope in Rome.

ii) The Society of United Irishmen

In 1791 the Society of United Irishmen (SUI) was formed. This movement looked forward to the day when Ireland would become a self-governing democratic republic. Led by Wolfe Tone, a Protestant lawyer from Dublin, the SUI was non-sectarian (both Catholics and Protestants were welcome within it). This co-operation was exceptional. It contrasted sharply with the prevailing rivalry between Catholics and Protestants which in Ulster took the form of violent clashes between the Catholic 'Defenders' and the Presbyterian 'Peep O'Day Boys'.

iii) English fears of French intervention in Ireland

The disorder in Ireland was a great worry to the English government. By 1793 England was at war with revolutionary France and feared the French would use Ireland as a 'backdoor' to England. In the hope of reducing Irish unrest, the government offered the Irish Catholics an electoral reform that would allow them to vote though not stand for Parliament. But the plan failed to win support among the Catholics. It also aroused the anger of the Ulster Protestants, who believed their position was threatened by this concession to 'Popery'. Their response was to form the Orange Society in 1795, dedicated to the maintenance of Protestant supremacy.

c) Immediate Causes: 1796–8

▼ The Insurrection Act of 1796 imposed tight controls and heavy penalties on the Irish.

▼ The English government ordered the arrest of the Irish leaders and the suspension of Habeas Corpus, the law protecting citizens against arbitrary arrest (see page 33), but troubles intensified.

▼ Wolfe Tone tried unsuccessfully to organise a French landing in Ireland.

d) The Rising, 1798

The rebellion broke out in May in Leinster and then spread to Wexford and Ulster. Protestant opinion was split between the Orangemen, who helped suppress the rising, and the SUI. As a result, the rising faltered badly in the north while gaining considerable support in the south. There the Irish nationalists took revenge on the Protestants for Orange repression in Ulster. In general terms, the rising was a violent but ill-organised affair and the English forces, backed by the Orangemen, had little difficulty in crushing it. The defeated rebels were brutally treated with the result that Irish bitterness increased. Thus the new century opened with Anglo-Irish relations at a very low ebb. The Irish nationalists had been beaten but their sense of grievance had deepened. It was this that fashioned the attitude of the Irish towards their own situation and towards England, which they regarded as the chief source of their woes.

ACTIVITY

Test your grasp of section 1 by answering the question, 'What were the causes of the Irish Rebellion of 1798?' Remember that questions about causes are essentially asking you why something happened, and that each of the points you make should in effect be saying 'because'.

Points to consider in your answer:
▼ long-standing grievances of the Irish.
▼ the influence of the American and French Revolutions on Irish attitudes.
▼ the mistaken attempts of the British government to pacify Irish nationalist feelings.
▼ Catholic–Orange rivalry.
▼ Renewed British oppression.
▼ French interference in Ireland.

---

2 The Act of Union, 1800–1

> **ISSUE**
> Was the Act a betrayal of Ireland by the English government?

The 1798 rising was a decisive event in Anglo-Irish history. It convinced the English government that Ireland must be brought under tighter control. England could not risk a French-style revolution occurring in Ireland. The method decided on was a union between the two countries under which direct rule from Westminster would be imposed on Ireland. In order to make this change acceptable to the Irish, William Pitt, the Prime Minister, proposed that union should be accompanied by Catholic Emancipation – the extension to the Catholic population of full civil rights.

Accordingly, in 1800 the British government pushed through the Act of Union, which became law in the following year. The Act ended the separate Irish Parliament and formally made Ireland part of Great Britain. The official name of the newly extended state was the United Kingdom of Great Britain and Ireland, although it continued to be referred to as Britain or even England. Catholics duly looked for emancipation as the government's part of the bargain. Pitt felt morally committed to it and expected George III to grant it. However, the cabinet was split on the question, which gave the King an excuse for refusing to give his assent to the measure. Pitt resigned in protest.

As a short-term expedient the Act of Union met British needs. The threat of a French invasion from the west had been removed and the Protestant supremacy in Ireland had been confirmed. But the long-term costs were heavy. To the Irish the Union had been yet another betrayal; the English government had used the Union to subject Ireland to further suppression. The issue of the Union was to cast its shadow over the Anglo-Irish political scene for the next 120 years.

ACTIVITY

Test your understanding of section 2 by answering the following question: Why was the Act of Union passed in 1800?

Suggested line of response:

▼ One obvious part of the answer is that the English government and Parliament wanted the Union as a means of quelling the troubles in Ireland and strengthening a vulnerable point of attack from France.

▼ But as much attention needs to be paid to the reasons for the Irish acceptance of the measure. Here mention should be made of the bribe of emancipation which aroused the political as well as the religious hopes of the Catholic Irish.

▼ It would also be relevant to draw attention to the attitudes of George III, Pitt and his Cabinet towards the emancipation issue.

▼ It is important to emphasise that the Act of Union was very much the result of short-term thinking.

ISSUE

How far was the emancipation movement a reaction by the Irish to what they regarded as England's 'betrayal' over the Union?

3 Catholic Emancipation

The breaking by the English government of its promise to grant emancipation made Catholic relief the dominant issue in Irish politics for a generation. The outstanding figure who emerged to lead the Catholic emancipation movement was Daniel O'Connell, who was to dominate Irish politics in the first half of the nineteenth century and became popularly known as 'the great liberator'. By the 1820s he had founded the Catholic Association. This was financed by the 'Catholic rent', money collected by the parish clergy from their congregations. So alarmed were the authorities by the rapid growth of the Association that in 1825 they tried to suppress it. However, O'Connell simply changed the name of the Association to preserve its legal status.

In 1828 Daniel O'Connell stood in a by-election in County Clare against Vesey Fitzgerald, a local Protestant landlord. Fitzgerald was popular among his tenants and sympathised with the demand for Catholic emancipation. After a campaign that excited a fanatical response in Catholic Ireland, O'Connell duly won the election, a result which, as he had hoped, greatly embarrassed the Duke of Wellington's government. Rather than face the risk of civil war in Ireland, Wellington supported the introduction of a Catholic Relief Bill granting Catholic emancipation. It was passed and became law in 1829 (see page 37).

> **Q**
>
> Why do you think O'Connell chose to challenge Fitzgerald? What special significance would a victory over him have?

KEY DATES

1798 the Irish Rebellion was easily and savagely suppressed;

1800 the Act of Union ended Ireland's separate Parliament;

1803 Robert Emmet was executed after leading an unsuccessful rising;

1823 Daniel O'Connell's Catholic Association founded;

1825 O'Connell changed the name of the Association to avoid prosecution;

1828 O'Connell won the County Clare election;

1829 Catholic Emancipation Act passed.

ACTIVITY

Consider the question, 'Why was O'Connell able to achieve Catholic Emancipation in 1829?'

Key points to develop:
▼ the power of O'Connell's personality and leadership
▼ the scale of the demand in Ireland for Emancipation
▼ the significance of the great tactical victory at County Clare
▼ the British government's wish to remove the risk of a civil war breaking out in Ireland.

---

4 Daniel O'Connell – the Great Liberator

Having gained Catholic Emancipation, O'Connell turned his attention to obtaining further concessions from the British government. Repeal of the Act of Union remained O'Connell's ultimate aim, but he concentrated first on organising the Irish MPs at Westminster into a lobby group to press for further internal reforms in Ireland. Among their demands were:
▼ the disestablishment of the Irish Church
▼ the extension of the 1832 Reform Act to Ireland (see page 38)
▼ the ending of the tithe system.

> **ISSUE**
> Did O'Connell's achievements merit the popular title he was given?

O'Connell's policy between 1835 and 1840 was to 'test the Union', meaning to see whether the link between the two countries could be used to bring direct benefits to Ireland. But he was disappointed with the results. Despite some gains, such as the Tithe Commutation Act, being forced from Parliament in the 1830s by O'Connell and his MPs, the legislation for Ireland largely failed to meet nationalist hopes. The Irish became more than ever convinced that the Union was a sham. One radical group, Young Ireland, asserted that force was the only means by which the hated Union could be broken.

> ## TITHE COMMUTATION ACT, 1838
> This Act made the tithe payable on property, not earnings or produce. In theory this eased the burden on the Irish peasant since the tithe was now to be paid by the landowner directly to the clergy. However, the Act did not prevent the landlords passing on the cost of the new tithe to their tenants in the form of higher rents.

YOUNG IRELAND
A movement of radical Irish nationalists, founded in 1841, in opposition to the moderate methods of O'Connell's Repeal Association. Its belief in violent agitation led it to break away completely from O'Connell in 1846.

ACTIVITY

Having read the profile of O'Connell, consider whether he deserved the title 'the great liberator'

O'Connell struggled to retain his political leadership among the Irish by creating the Repeal Association to organise mass protest along lines similar to those of the successful Catholic Association of the 1820s. 'Monster' meetings, demanding an end to the Union, became common. But the Repeal movement met the implacable opposition of the Conservative leader, Sir Robert Peel, who was Prime Minister from 1841 to 1846. In October 1843, he prohibited a monster meeting planned to be held at Clontarf. Rather than call the government's bluff by going ahead with the meeting, O'Connell backed down and cancelled it. Despite this, he was convicted of conspiracy and imprisoned for a year. During his imprisonment much of his popular support evaporated. In his last years O'Connell was terminally ill and could no longer inspire as he had in the past. By the time of his death in 1847 the leadership of Irish nationalism had been largely taken over by Young Ireland.

ISSUE
How far was the scale of the disaster the fault of the British government?

5 The Great Famine

By the 1840s the Irish economy was in a very weak condition. Over 60 per cent of the rapidly growing population lived in the countryside on plots of less than one acre, on which they grew potatoes and perhaps kept a pig. Despite its obvious inefficiency, the system had managed to sustain the population. But the position was precarious. Should there be a serious or sustained failure of the potato harvest there were no alternative food supplies available to see the Irish peasants through a bad period.

It was the arrival from Europe in 1845 of a virulent fungus, *phythophthera infestans*, which turned the potato crop in Ireland to inedible slime and created the Great Famine. Disease had frequently

DANIEL O'CONNELL (1775–1847)

-Profile-

All who heard O'Connell speak, friends and enemies, paid tribute to his powers of oratory. Some of the flavour of this can still be detected even in cold print:

> Are we to be trampled under foot? Cromwell, the only Britishman who ever possessed Ireland, sent 80,000 Irishmen to work as slaves beneath the ungenial sun of the Indies. Peel and Wellington may be second Cromwells. They may try to enact Cromwell's massacre of the women of Wexford. But by God they never shall. [tremendous cheering and waving of handkerchiefs by the ladies] Remember that deed. When Cromwell entered the town, 300 inoffensive women of all ages and classes were collected around the cross of Christ, erected in the Bull Ring. They prayed to heaven for mercy. They prayed to the British for humanity and Cromwell slaughtered them. [cries of 'Oh! Oh!' and a great sensation and many ladies screaming with terror] But there is no danger to the women of Ireland, for the men of Ireland would die to the last in their defence. [wild cheering, the entire company on its feet] We were a paltry remnant in Cromwell's time. We are nine million now!

Source C From a speech by O'Connell at a monster meeting in 1843.

O'Connell was capable of showing and arousing both great affection and deep hatred. He was a constant target for attacks by the Tories and Conservatives. Disraeli once described him as 'the hired instrument of the Papacy [whose] mission is to destroy your Protestant society'. O'Connell gave as good as he got. His denunciation of Disraeli in a public speech in 1835 was an extraordinary mixture of racism and religious prejudice:

> Disraeli is a living lie; I can find no harsher words in the British language by which to convey the utter abhorrence I entertain for such a reptile. He possesses all the necessary requisites of perfidy, selfishness, depravity, and want of principle. His name shows that he is of Jewish origin. I do not use it as a term of reproach; there are many most respectable Jews. But there are, as in every other people, some of the lowest and most disgusting grade of moral turpitude; and of those I look upon Mr Disraeli as the worst. He has just the qualities of the impenitent thief on the cross.

Source D From a speech by O'Connell as reported in *The Courier*, May 1835.

1775 born in county Kerry into one of the few prosperous Irish Catholic families;

1792 educated abroad and at Lincoln's Inn in London;

1798 became a barrister in Irish courts where his eloquence soon made him famous – supported the SUI but opposed the 1798 Rising;

1809 his first public speech was an attack on the Union;

1823 founded the Catholic Association;

1828 won the County Clare election;

1830 entered the Commons as the first Catholic MP in modern history;

1830 –47 represented Irish Catholic opinion on all the major Anglo-Irish questions of the day;

1841 –42 Lord Mayor of Dublin;

1844 imprisoned for his organisation of monster meetings;

1847 died.

ravaged the potato harvest before. What was deadly about the blight of the mid-1840s was that it repeated itself in three successive years, 1845, 1846, and 1847. The disaster was so great that it was probably beyond the resources of any government in that era to remedy. Nonetheless, the reaction of the British administration appeared to make things worse.

a) The Government's Response to the Famine

i) Negative

British officials were slow to act. Part of the reason was that they were strongly influenced by the dominant economic theory of the day, *laissez-faire*, which emphasised minimum government interference in the working of the principle of supply and demand (see page 83). A further constraint on their actions was the new Poor Law, whose ban on outdoor relief discouraged the immediate distribution of aid. Government policy seemed more concerned with avoiding an increase in public expenditure, than with the alleviation of suffering.

ii) Positive

Once government and Parliament awoke to the scale of the hunger in Ireland, measures were rushed through in an attempt to reduce the misery. The repeal of the Corn Laws in 1846 was in part a belated but misguided attempt to increase the flow of foodstuffs to Ireland. In 1847 Parliament passed the 'Act for the Temporary Relief of Destitute Persons'. As its popular title 'the Soup Kitchen Act' suggested, this measure was an attempt to deliver food directly to the starving.

Q

Why did the Government's measures not lead to a lessening of hunger in Ireland?

When the government grain depots were opened in December 1846 stocks went on sale at the market price plus 5 per cent. But the starving peasants simply did not have the money to buy the available grain. What was needed was a massive relief effort to distribute supplies either freely or at very low cost. However, the authorities had neither the means nor the inclination to organise such a programme. The fact was that what would now be called the infrastructure simply did not exist in Ireland in the middle of the nineteenth century to enable the necessary welfare schemes to operate. The organisations that there were at the time, such as the Board of Works, broke down under the strain. Individuals and organisations made great efforts to provide aid. Queen Victoria made a personal donation that amounted to over one million pounds when converted into today's values. However, it was all too little too late. The predominant Irish perception was that the severity of the famine was the product of British indifference and landlord obstinacy.

Figure 31 A contemporary print depicting the failure of the potato crop in 1845.

NOTICE.

ROSCOMMON UNION.

Notice is hereby given, that the State of the Poor House, both from Excessive Numbers and Sickness, makes it absolutely necessary for the Guardians to proclaim the utter impossibility to admit any more persons until further notice.

The Guardians have on two occasions given a small portion of Bread to disappointed applicants; but after this Notice, it can never be done again, such expenditure being illegal, and possibly may not be allowed by the Auditor of the Poor Law Commissioners.

By Order of the Guardians,

JOHN CORR, Clerk of the Union.

January 9th, 1847.

L. W. LENNON, PRINTER AND STATIONER, ROSCOMMON.

Figure 32 A public notice published in 1847 declaring that the local workhouse had been overwhelmed by the famine and could no longer provide any form of relief. Such notices were common in the famine areas.

What were the lasting effects of the famine?

Table 11 Number of recorded deaths in Ireland, 1843–52.

Recorded Deaths	
1843	70,499
1844	75,055
1845	86,000
1846	122,899
1847	249,335
1848	208,252
1849	240,797
1850	164,093
1851	96,798
1852	80,112

Table 12 The population of Ireland, 1841–71.

Population of Ireland	
1841	8,175,000
1851	6,552,000
1861	5,799,000
1871	4,412,000

The Famine caused a dramatic drop in the population of Ireland. By 1850 nearly a million deaths from starvation and disease had occurred. In the same period (1846–50) a further million people emigrated, beginning a process that was to last well into the next century. By 1900 Ireland's population stood at four million compared with the eight million it had been in 1840. Ireland entered a period of long-term economic decline as a result of the Famine. However, modern research emphasises that the Famine did not so much create new problems as magnify existing ones. That is to say, the Irish economy with its overpopulation and inefficient use of land was already heading towards collapse. Appalling though the Famine was in terms of human suffering, it did have some positive results: it stimulated population relocation, emigration, and eventually better land use.

ACTIVITY

You will not be surprised to learn that the Famine remains probably the single most controversial event in Anglo-Irish relations. The more extreme Irish nationalists, insist that the Famine represents an act of genocide by the British government. It is worth asking yourself if is there any truth in that charge.

Points to consider:
▼ Did the British government deliberately refuse to offer help until it was too late or does the lack of action have other explanations?
▼ How important was *laisser-faire* in determining the British response?
▼ Did the limited welfare and transport systems of the mid-nineteenth century make it impossible for any government to respond adequately?
▼ How big a culprit was the Irish Poor Law Amendment Act?
▼ How far were the Irish peasants the authors of their own misfortune?

ISSUE
How successful were the Fenians in achieving their aims?

6 Fenianism and the Land League

a) Fenianism

One immediate consequence of Irish bitterness over the government's handling of the Famine was the Young Ireland rebellion in 1848, led by Smith O'Brien. Although this was a desperate and badly-planned affair that was easily subdued, it was an early illustration of the militant Irish nationalism that was to develop in the second half of the century. This took its most violent form in the Irish Republican Brotherhood (the **Fenian** movement).

KEY DATES

1845 failure of potato harvests
–47 created the Great Famine;
1846 Corn Laws repealed;
1847 Temporary Relief Act
passed;
1848 Smith O'Brien led
unsuccessful Young Ireland
rising;
1858 Fenian (Irish Republican
Brotherhood) movement
founded;
1858 Fenianism established in
USA;
1867 Fenians launched bomb
attacks in London and
Manchester.

FENIANISM

This movement, which took its name from 'Fianna', the warriors of Irish legend, came into being in 1858. Its aim was to drive the British out of Ireland by force. In the 1860s the failure of the Fenians to stimulate a major rising in Ireland, led to their campaign being carried to the British mainland for the first time. In 1867 Fenian bombs caused the deaths of civilians and policemen in Manchester and London.

Figure 33 The Fenian bomb attack on Clerkenwell prison in London in 1867, which blew down an outer wall, killing thirty civilians.

b) The Land League

This organisation, which was founded in 1879, aimed at breaking the grip of the landlords as the first move towards full independence for Ireland. From the first, the Land League adopted radical activist methods against the British and the landowners. In Ireland evictions of tenants for failure to pay rent were countered by retaliatory outrages in which the property and possessions of the landlords were attacked. The architect of this aggressive policy of rent resistance was the League's first President, Charles Stewart Parnell, who was to become as outstanding an Irish leader in the second half of the century as O'Connell had been in the first.

Parnell introduces the boycott:

BOYCOTT

The word 'boycott' came into the language after Captain Boycott, a land agent in County Mayo, became one of the early victims of the ostracism Parnell advocated.

Source E From a speech by Parnell in County Clare, 1880.

When a man takes a farm from which another has been evicted you must shun him on the roadside when you meet him – you must shun him in the streets of the town – you must shun him in the shop – you must shun him in the fair-green and in the market place, and even in the place of worship, by leaving him alone, by putting him into a moral Coventry, by isolating him from the rest of his country as if he were the leper of old – you must show him your detestation of the crime he has committed. If you do this, you may depend on it there will be no man so full of avarice – so lost to shame – as to dare the public opinion of all the right-thinking men in the county and transgress your unwritten code of laws.

Figure 34 The famine meant that large numbers of tenants could not pay their rents. Eviction invariably followed.

Figure 35 Land League Cruelty – a Unionist depiction of the violent methods of the Land League.

Figure 36 'Landlordism on the Horns of a Dilemma' – a Land League cartoon suggesting that its 'Plan of Campaign' was successful in forcing landlords into the impossible position of having to choose between coercion and conciliation.

ACTIVITY

The visual sources, Figures 34, 35 and 36, are all taken from published prints of the time.
▼ How effective do you find them?
▼ What techniques are used to convey their message?
▼ Are they superior to written accounts in portraying the violence associated with the Land League?
▼ Compare them with the passage above in which Parnell advocates boycotting and with the following account by an outside observer.
▼ How reliable do you consider the drawings and writings to be as evidence of Land League activities?

A French visitor describes the effects of Land League coercion:

On the dusty road before us slowly walked five cows in rather an emaciated condition. Those beasts strike me by an odd appearance which I am unable to make out at first. When I am close I see what it is: *they have no tails.* The absence of that ornament gives the poor animals the awkward and most absurd look.

I turn to my guide who is laughing in his sleeve.

'Look at their master!', he whispers in a low voice.

'Well?'

'The cows have no tails, and the man has no ears.'

It is true. The unlucky wretch vainly endeavoured to hide his head, as round as a cheese, under the battered hat; he did not succeed in hiding his deformity.

'By Jove! who arranged you in this guise, you and your cows' I said to the poor devil. He made a few grimaces before explaining. He told me that the Moonlighters had come with a razor to cut his ears, a week after having cut off the tails of his cows as a warning. 'And what could have been the motive of such cowardly, barbarous mutilation?'

He had accepted work on a *boycotted* farm, though the League had expressly forbidden it; in other words he was what the Irish call a 'land-grabber'.

Source F Ireland's Disease: the English in Ireland by Paschal Grousset, 1888.

ACTIVITY

If you have opportunity to work with other students, it would be a useful exercise if one or more of you were to assume the role of members of the Land League and defend yourself against the charge of engaging in violence in the Irish countryside.

▼ Imagine you are making a defence plea in court. What arguments would you put forward to justify boycotting and the use of physical intimidation?

▼ Alternatively, you might care to take the role of a prosecutor attacking the League.

▼ Some members of the group could act as magistrates or judges and try to give a summing up.

▼ Since the magistrates in Ireland were invariably landlords appointed to the bench by the government, it is worth asking yourselves how impartial they were likely to have been at this time.

7 Gladstone and Parnell

The relationship between Gladstone and Parnell was a critical one in Irish affairs. Both men wanted a satisfactory settlement of the Irish question but how they interpreted 'satisfactory' was very different. On becoming Prime Minister in 1868, Gladstone, the leader of the Liberal Party, declared that 'the state of Ireland after seven hundred years of our tutelage is an intolerable disgrace'. He set himself the task of remedying that situation.

THE UPAS TREE

Gladstone likened the problems of Ireland to the legendary upas tree whose poisoned boughs were said to spread corruption. He identified the toxic branches in Ireland as the Church, land, and education. He believed that, if the outstanding Irish grievances relating to these issues were to be 'lopped off' by legislation, Ireland would enjoy a 'national content'. Accordingly, his government introduced measures for the disestablishment of the Irish Church (1869), the protection of tenants against arbitrary eviction (1870) and the creation of a new Irish university that Catholics could attend (1873).

Despite Gladstone's good intentions the reforms he attempted during his first administration (1868–74) failed to stem the rising tide of evictions and the violent reactions. Whatever their individual merits, his measures did not satisfy Irish demands. One reason was that they were simply regarded by nationalists as evidence of what could be forced from a reluctant British government by violent agitation.

Parnellism

Although he was a landowner and a Protestant, Charles Stewart Parnell was motivated by an abiding detestation of the English. He believed that once Ireland was given back its own Parliament, it would be able to solve its own problems. He devised a two-line strategy for pressurising the British government: in Ireland the tenants were to wage a campaign of rent-strikes and boycotts against the landlords, while at Westminster the Irish MPs were to follow a programme of persistent obstruction of parliamentary business. Initially he used the Land League as the main instrument for agitation; then in 1882 he founded the National League with the declared aim of achieving 'national self-government'. He declared in 1880 that he would not be content until he had 'destroyed the last link which keeps Ireland bound to England'.

ISSUE

Who came nearer to resolving the crisis – the Liberal leader or the Irish leader?

KEY DATES

1868 Gladstone began his first ministry having resolved 'to pacify [bring peace to] Ireland';
1869 Irish Church disestablished;
1870 Gladstone's First Irish Land Act;
1870 Home Rule movement founded in Ireland by Isaac Butt;
1873 Gladstone's Irish University Bill defeated;
1875 Charles Stewart Parnell elected to Parliament;
1877 Parnell became President of the Home Rule Confederation;
1879 Irish National Land League founded – 'land war' began;
1880 Gladstone formed his second ministry;
1880 Parnell became Chairman of the Irish Parliamentary Party;
1880 boycotting campaign started;
1881 coercion acts introduced;
1881 Gladstone's Second Land Act introduced the '3 Fs';
1881 Parnell arrested for conspiracy;
1882 Kilmainham Treaty;
1882 Phoenix Park murders;
1885 Gladstone lost office – Irish MPs held balance in Commons;
1885 Gladstone's conversion to Home Rule leaked.

By the time of Gladstone's second ministry (1880–85) the situation in Ireland had deteriorated still further. The Land League had become increasingly disruptive and aggressive in its methods. Gladstone tried to counter the League by using a mixture of coercion and concession (stick and carrot). For example, Parnell was first imprisoned and then released under the terms of the so-called Kilmainham Treaty.

Figure 37 Contemporary illustration of the 'Phoenix Park murders': The situation in Ireland took a dramatic turn in 1882 when Gladstone's nephew, Lord Frederick Cavendish, the newly-appointed Chief Secretary for Ireland, was murdered along with the Under Secretary, Thomas Burke, in Phoenix Park Dublin. The assassins were the 'Invincibles', an off-shoot of the Irish Republican Brotherhood.

THE KILMAINHAM TREATY

In 1881 Parnell was held in Kilmainham Gaol, Dublin, on charges of seditious conspiracy. Gladstone was not against tough measures where necessary, but he preferred conciliation and accepted the offer of Joseph Chamberlain, the leading radical in the Liberal Party, to negotiate some form of unofficial agreement with Parnell, whereby the Irish Leader would be released on condition that he then used his influence to lessen the violence in Ireland. This informal agreement was known as the Kilmainham Treaty.

ACTIVITY

What do you think were the main differences between Gladstone and Parnell in their interpretations of the Anglo-Irish question? The boxed sections on the Upas Tree, Parnellism and the Kilmainham Treaty will point you in the right direction.

Year	Families evicted	Agrarian outrages
1878	980	301
1879	1,238	863
1880	2,110	2,585
1881	3,415	4,439
1882	5,201	3,433
1883	3,643	870
1884	4,188	762
1885	3,127	944
1886	3,781	1,056
1887	3,869	883
1888	1,609	660

Table 13 The scale of the Land War.

ACTIVITY

What story does Table 13 tell? How complete a picture of the land war does it give? What other type of evidence would you need to examine in order to judge the value of these statistics?

Despite the severe disorder in Ireland, Gladstone still clung to the notion that if the particular grievances of the Irish could be settled it would still be possible to achieve peace. That was what underlay his Second Land Act of 1881 in which he attempted to extend 'the three Fs' – fixity of tenure, fair rents and free sale – to the Irish peasantry. Gladstone's hopes even survived the assassination of his nephew, Lord Frederick Cavendish, the Irish Secretary. But as the troubles continued, Gladstone was drawn to the conclusion that nothing short of home rule could resolve the Irish question.

ACTIVITY

It is worth pondering an apparent paradox. How was it that Parnell, a Protestant landowner, should have led a movement that was violently anti-landlord in policy and overwhelmingly Catholic in membership?

Points to consider:
▼ the cross-currents that made up Irish nationalism
▼ the religious divisions did not always match the political ones
▼ to be Protestant did not always mean being pro-British
▼ not all landlords lacked sympathy with the plight of the peasants.

ISSUES

Why was Gladstone unable to achieve Home Rule for Ireland?

Who came closer to resolving the Irish question in the generation after 1868 – the Liberals or the Conservatives?

Why did Gladstone introduce Home Rule when he did?

DILKE'S RETIREMENT

Dilke was forced to withdraw from public life when a spectacular divorce case in which he was involved in 1885 ruined his reputation by providing lurid details of his three-in-a-bed-romps with his mistress and a servant girl.

8   Home Rule

Gladstone knew that Home Rule would be unacceptable to both the Whig right and the Radical left of the Liberal Party. Initially, therefore, he hoped that there could be a joint Liberal-Conservative introduction of such a measure. He was also willing to support the Conservatives if they chose to introduce it as their own answer to the Irish Question. But his plans were destroyed in December 1885 when his son, Herbert, unintentionally leaked to the press the news that his father was a convert to Home Rule. Salisbury's Conservatives considered that this public revelation of Gladstone's conversion let them off the deadly Home Rule hook. Soon after they resigned office and handed what they regarded as the 'poisoned chalice' of the Irish crisis back to Gladstone. What added to his difficulties at this critical point was the loss of the services of Sir Charles Dilke, one of the leading radicals among the Liberals. Gladstone had hoped that Dilke would bring the radical wing of the party round to support Home Rule. But Dilke's sudden retirement from politics ended this hope. Nevertheless, Gladstone went ahead, even at the cost of splitting his own party. In 1886 he introduced his First Home Rule Bill, only for it to be defeated in the House of Commons. Ninety Liberals joined the Conservatives in voting against it.

Despite the failure of his 1886 Bill, Gladstone remained dedicated to the eventual achievement of Home Rule. He hoped that with the support of Parnell's Irish MPs, who in numbers held the parliamentary balance between the Liberals and the Conservatives, he would still be able to secure its passage. What destroyed the chance of this occurring was the break up of the Irish Nationalist Party in 1890, following another scandalous divorce case, this time involving no less a figure than Parnell.

The Fall of Parnell

It was not his public but his private life that proved Parnell's political undoing. For some years he had had a sexual liaison with Kitty O'Shea, wife of Captain O'Shea, one of his party's MPs. This was one of those Victorian 'known secrets' that did not become a scandal unless it was openly admitted and became public knowledge. This duly happened in 1890 when Parnell was cited as co-respondent by O'Shea in a divorce action against his wife. Parnell made no attempt to defend himself. A majority of the Irish Nationalist MPs voted against Parnell's remaining their leader. For a time Parnell tried to carry on, but his cause was now a hopeless one. He died shortly afterwards, in 1891.

Gladstone made no public comment on the scandal, but he calculated that there was little future in co-operating with Parnell now that the Irish leader had lost the support of his Irish nationalist party. He also feared that if he were to continue his political relationship with an admitted adulterer, the Nonconformists, a major support group of the Liberals, might desert his Party. Nevertheless, despite the loss of Parnell, Gladstone pressed on with his plans for Home Rule. He interpreted the widespread support that the Irish Nationalists had gained in all the elections since the Third Reform Bill (1884) came into force, as imposing a moral duty on Parliament to grant Home rule. Accordingly, in 1893, during his last administration (1892–4), he introduced his Second Home Rule Bill. It passed narrowly through the Commons, but was heavily defeated by the Unionist-controlled House of Lords.

ACTIVITY

Ensure you understand the events covered in this section by thinking through answers to the following questions:

▼ Which approach was better suited to the times – Parnell's aggressive agitation or Gladstone's attempt to create an 'Irish content' through selective reform?

▼ Why did both men fail to achieve their full objectives?

---

9 The Ulster Question

For reasons which dated back to the enforced Elizabethan and Cromwellian land settlements, the northern Irish province of **Ulster** was peopled predominantly by Protestants of English and Scottish origin (see page 116). They rejected any suggestion that the whole of Ireland should be separated from Britain, since this would, in their eyes, lead to the inevitable subjection of their province to the rule of an oppressive Catholic majority. The fears of Protestant Ulster were expressed in the slogan, 'Home Rule means Rome rule'.

ULSTER

Ulster, where the majority of the population was Presbyterian, was the most industrially advanced region in Ireland. This made nationalists determined that the area should remain part of the nation should Ireland ever be granted Home Rule or independence. Clearly Ulster Unionism and Irish nationalist separatism were wholly incompatible.

KEY DATES

1885 Gladstone lost the services of the radical Sir Charles Dilke; Herbert Gladstone's indiscretion pushed Gladstone into Home Rule;

1886 Gladstone returned to office; Gladstone's First Home Rule Bill defeated in the Commons; Liberal Party split over policy of Home Rule for Ireland;

1886 Land League began 'Plan of Campaign';

1887 'Parnellism and Crime' series published in The Times;

1889 Charges against Parnell shown to have been based on forgeries;

1890 Parnell declared to be a guilty party in the O'Shea divorce case – Gladstone announced he could no longer co-operate with Parnell – Irish MPs abandoned Parnell;

1891 Parnell died;

1893 Gladstone's second Home Rule Bill rejected by the Lords.

ISSUE
Why was Ulster so bitterly opposed to Home Rule?

'ULSTER WILL FIGHT AND ULSTER WILL BE RIGHT'

This became a highly effective rallying cry of the Unionists. The force of the slogan was that if Home Rule were passed, the Unionists claimed the right to resist even if that led to civil war in Ireland.

WYNDHAM'S LAND ACT

In 1902, £100 million was provided by the government to buy out the landlords and enable the peasants to purchase the land that then became available. Within six years a quarter of a million tenants had bought their own farms.

It was their defence of the right of Ulster to remain part of the United Kingdom that turned the overwhelming majority of the Conservative Party and a large number of Liberals into 'Unionists'. The Tory radicals, led by Randolph Churchill, played 'the orange card' (i.e. supported the Protestant Orangemen) by taking up the Unionist cause.

The political result of the Liberal split over Gladstone's Home Rule Bill was that the Conservatives (Unionists) were in office for a generation after 1886. The Conservatives were clear in their aims. They rejected Home Rule because it undermined the unity of the United Kingdom and betrayed Ulster. However, short of Home Rule, they were prepared to introduce measures to improve conditions in Ireland. Arthur Balfour, Irish Chief Secretary (1887–91) and Prime Minister (1902–5) expressed the essential approach of the Conservative governments through his policy of 'killing Home Rule by kindness'. Although the Irish branded him 'bloody Balfour', a reference to the various coercive measures he adopted, his aim was to administer Irish affairs with a balance between firmness and reform. A major example of the latter was Wyndham's Land Act which may be regarded as having ended the land question in Ireland by making it possible for tenants in Ireland to buy the land they farmed. However, by that time land was no longer the outstanding question affecting Anglo-Irish relations. It had been superseded by the Home Rule movement and the drive towards Irish independence.

ACTIVITY

Anglo-Irish relations in the Home Rule era are complex. Try to draw your ideas together and clarify them by tackling the following question:
Which party had the more realistic approach to the Anglo-Irish question, the Liberals or the Conservatives?

ISSUE
Did the Bill create more problems than it solved?

10 The Third Home Rule Bill, 1912–14

The period following the failure of Gladstone's Home Bills had been one of relative calm in Ireland, but by 1910 the situation had again become dangerously volatile. Although severely damaged by their split over the Parnell scandal in 1890, the Irish Nationalist MPs in the Commons had continued to function as a party. They gained a sudden increase in influence after the two general elections in 1910, which left the Liberal Government dependent on them for its parliamentary majority. Such were the growing tensions in Ireland that Asquith's Liberal Government turned again to Home Rule as the only solution. In 1912, in a Commons evenly split between Liberals and Unionists, the government relied on the 84 Irish nationalists, led by John Redmond, to force through the Third Home Rule Bill. Since the Conservatives' customary ability to veto measures passed by the Commons had been curtailed by the reform of the House of Lords in 1911, there was now nothing to stop Home Rule from eventually becoming law (see page 215).

The Parliament Act of 1911

This laid down that any Bill passed by the Commons in three successive sessions should become law even if it had been defeated in the Lords on each occasion.

Sinn Fein

In 1908 a number of nationalist groups in Ireland came together under the banner of Sinn Fein ('Ourselves Alone'), a political party which claimed, as the Fenians had, that Ireland was a free nation temporarily enslaved by the British. It sought the creation of a *Dail* (Parliament) to rule Ireland in the name of its people. According to its chief spokesman, Arthur Griffith, Sinn Fein's aim was to break both the political and the economic stranglehold Britain had over Ireland. Griffith opposed the Third Reform Bill in 1912 on the grounds that it did not go far enough in advancing Ireland's independence.

KEY DATES

1908 Radical nationalist groups amalgamated to form Sinn Fein;

1910 Two elections left Irish MPs holding the balance in the Commons;
Edward Carson elected Chairman of the Irish Unionist Party;

1911 Parliament Act ended the Lords' absolute veto;

1912 Commons passed the Third Home Rule Bill;

1913 Lords rejected the Home Rule Bill;
Ulster Volunteer Force formed (Unionists);
Irish Volunteers formed (Nationalists);

1914 Curragh mutiny;
Britain declared war on Germany;
Home Rule Act suspended until the end of the war.

The Ulster Protestants reacted to the Home Rule Bill by swearing to the Covenant. This was a document that pledged those who signed it to use 'all means which may be found necessary' to resist home rule for Ireland. The Covenanters claimed that the Liberal Government had no electoral mandate for Home Rule. Led by Edward Carson, they prepared to fight to prevent what they regarded as the subjection of Protestant Ulster to the Catholic south. Andrew Bonar Law, the Conservative leader, added fuel to the flames when he declared, 'I can imagine no length of resistance to which Ulster will go, which I shall not be ready to support'. By the summer of 1914 Ireland had split into two armed camps, nationalist Irish Volunteers confronting Carson's Ulster Volunteer Force. Civil war seemed imminent.

Asquith managed to defuse the situation by calling a constitutional conference in June 1914. Reluctantly both sides agreed to

Why was Ireland on the verge of civil war in 1914?

THE CURRAGH MUTINY, 1914

A number of British officers, stationed at the Curragh army base in southern Ireland, who were sympathetic to the Ulster Protestants, resigned their commissions to avoid being sent north against the Ulster Volunteers. Technically this was not a mutiny since their resignations meant they were no longer in the army, but in the tense atmosphere the word was seized on by the press to show how dangerous the Irish situation had become.

Figure 38 'Enrol under the Green flag', a 1914 Nationalist poster calling on Irish patriots to enlist in the Irish National Volunteers, a counter army to the Ulster Defence Volunteers.

Figure 39 Ulster-Unionist postcard: the Solemn League and Covenant. Claims vary, but it is likely that over 250,000 Unionists signed this Covenant.

consider a form of compromise: Ireland would be partitioned between the Catholic south, which would be granted Home Rule, and the Protestant north which would remain part of the United Kingdom. In July 1914, with war against Germany imminent, it was further agreed that the Home Rule Bill would be suspended for the duration of the conflict. This produced a temporary easing of the situation, but it was clear that the issue was far from solved. After 1914 Ireland was destined to undergo still greater turmoil before anything approaching a genuine settlement was reached.

ACTIVITY

Having studied section 10, say whom you regard as the more to blame for the bitterness of the divisions over the third Home Rule Bill: the Ulster Unionists or the Irish nationalists?

Summary of The Anglo-Irish Question

Date	Issues	Organisations	Aims
1798	the Irish rising	the SUI	end British control
1800–1	the Union	British government	made Ireland part of the UK
1823–9	Catholic Emancipation	the Catholic Association	civil rights for Catholics
1830s & 40s	reform in Ireland	the Repeal Association	win concessions and repeal the Union
1850s & 60s	Britain's control of Ireland	Young Ireland; the Fenians	end British occupation
1870s to 90s	the land	the Land League	break power of the landlords
1880s & 90s	ending of the Union	Home Rule Confederation	home rule for Ireland
1880s & 90s	retention of the Union	Irish Unionist Party Conservative and Unionist Party	keep Ulster within the UK
1870s to 1914	full separation from the UK	Irish Nationalist Party and Sinn Fein	Irish independence

▼ Working on The Anglo-Irish Question

Having studied this chapter make sure that you have a grasp of the Anglo-Irish question by setting down what you regard as its essential features.

Then take the ten sections in the chapter and ask yourself in relation to each one which of the three basic issues – politics, land and religion – was the most dominant or operative. It may often be the case that more than one, or that indeed all three issues, applied in particular instances. For example, the conflict over Home Rule appears to have all the ingredients mixed into it. There is a basic question that will help you steer your way:

Why did it prove impossible to achieve a lasting settlement of the Anglo-Irish question between 1798 and 1914?

Keep this question in mind as you explain the issues and list the reasons why problems persisted despite the many attempts to resolve them.

Answering extended writing and essay questions on The Anglo-Irish Question

You will be familiar now with the way we break down essay questions into their types. The following list shows the style of questions you are likely to encounter on the topic of Anglo-Irish relations.

Type of Issue	Examples of typical questions
1 causes/reasons/motives	Was it bad luck or bad judgement that prevented Gladstone from achieving Home Rule for Ireland?
2 course of events	Trace the efforts made by Gladstone between 1868 and 1885 to provide a solution to the Irish question.
3 consequences/results/ effects	Why did the arrival of potato blight in Ireland in 1845 lead to such catastrophic social consequences?
4 success/failure	How accurate is it to say that the Irish Rising in 1798 was 'a total failure'?
5 significance/importance	Why did the victory of Daniel O'Connell's in the County Clare election of 1828 prove so significant?
6 comparison	Who came closer to resolving the Irish question between 1868 and 1914, the Liberals or the Conservatives?
7 right/wrong (moral/ ethical judgements)	'The right measure introduced at the wrong time': How acceptable is this verdict on the Home Rule Bill of 1912?

Let us examine question 1, the type that asks you to examine the reasons why a particular policy failed:

▼ identify key terms – 'bad luck', 'bad judgement'
▼ identify target objective – a balanced assessment of Gladstone's Irish policy.

Suggested line of response
One view of Gladstone is that his Irish policy was both perceptive and courageous. After twenty-five years of trying to provide particular reforms for particular problems, he came to realise that Ireland was fundamentally a political question and therefore could be settled only by a political answer. He concluded that, no matter what the difficulties, a just settlement of the Irish question must be pursued by means of home rule. A contrary view is that his approach was basically flawed since he never fully understood what the Irish people wanted. His persistence for a quarter of a century in trying various solutions hardened attitudes on all sides and made an eventual solu-

tion even more difficult to achieve. The conclusion, therefore is that he was guilty of bad judgement.

The counter argument put forward by those who admire Gladstone's approach is that such a conclusion overlooks how close he came to success. This is where bad luck came in. Ponder the following queries. Had the news of his conversion to Home Rule not leaked out in 1885, had Dilke not been destroyed by sexual scandal in the same year, and had the news of Parnell's involvement in the O'Shea divorce case not broken in 1890, perhaps Home Rule would have been carried by either a Conservative or a Liberal government or by the two parties acting together. This is speculation, of course; we cannot know for certain. But by raising the issue of bad luck, the question invites you to speculate. So you are entitled to consider the balance of probabilities and then judge whether bad judgement or bad luck is the more fitting description.

Answering source-based questions on The Anglo-Irish Question

I come back to the great question of national self-government for Ireland. No man has the right to say to his country, 'Thus far shalt thou go and no further', and we have never attempted to fix the *ne plus ultra* [the final limit] to the progress of Ireland's nationhood, and we never shall.

Source G From a speech by Parnell in Cork, January 1885.

About local government for Ireland, the ideas which more and more establish themselves in my mind are such as these.

Until we have seriously responsible bodies to deal with us in Ireland, every plan we frame comes to Irishmen, say what we may, as a British plan. As such it is probably condemned. At best it is a one-sided bargain, which binds us, not them.

In truth I should say, that for the Ireland of today, the first question is the rectification of the relations between landlord and tenant. The next is to relieve Great Britain from the enormous weight of the government of Ireland unaided by the people, and from the hopeless contradiction in which we stand while we give a Parliamentary representation, hardly effective for anything but mischief without the local institutions of self-government which it presupposes, and on which alone it can have a sound and healthy basis.

Source H From a letter by Gladstone to a member of his Cabinet, April 1882.

▼ QUESTIONS ON SOURCES G AND H

1. Using your own knowledge and the evidence in the source H, explain what Gladstone means by saying that 'every plan we frame comes to Irishmen ... as a British plan'. **[5 marks]**

2. Explain the difference in tone and style between the two sources. **[5 marks]**

3. Using your own knowledge and the evidence in these sources, examine the view that there was an unbridgeable gap between Gladstone and Parnell in their interpretation of Home Rule. **[10 marks]**

Points to note about the questions

Question 1

Use your own knowledge *and* the evidence in the source.

Explain here means put into your own words.

The 5-mark allocation suggests a substantial treatment rather than just a few words in response.

Question 2

Here you have to call on your own knowledge.

What sort of language and vocabulary are used?

Bear in mind one is a public speech, the other an official letter.

What audiences were being addressed?

How does this influence the style and tone of each?

Question 3

Again, you must use your own knowledge and the evidence.

Do the sources confirm or contradict what you already know?

Is 'unbridgeable' too strong, given that the two leaders cooperated over a substantial period of time?

Gladstone's views evolved over time. Does not his recognition in Source H of England's responsibility for Ireland's plight, suggest that he might have been willing in time to bridge the gap? Or was Parnell's passionate nationalism, as expressed in Source G, so strong as to be incompatible with Gladstone's measured approach?

Further Reading

Books in the 'Access to History' series

Britain and the Irish Question 1800–1922 by Paul Adelman is a detailed study of the themes covered in this chapter. You should find it very helpful as a source of additional information on each of the issues dealt with in this chapter. Further analysis is provided in Chapters 4–6 of *Tories, Conservatives and Unionists 1815–1914*, and in Chapters 5 & 6 of *Whigs, Radicals and Liberals 1815–1914*, both books by Duncan Watts.

General

One of the outstanding books covering the whole period is *Modern Ireland 1600–1760* by R.F. Foster (Penguin, 1988). Another very good text with attractive visual illustrations is *Ireland, a History* by Robert Kee (Weidenfeld and Nicholson, 1978). An important set of sources with linking commentary is provided by *Ireland and England 1798–1992* by Joe Finn (Hodder & Stoughton, 1995). *The Year of Liberty* by Thomas Packenham (Methuen, 1985) is a very lively account of the 1798 Rising. Recommended studies of particular themes and persons include: *Daniel O'Connell* by Fergus O'Farrell (Gill and Macmillan, 1970), *The Liberator, Daniel O'Connell and the Irish Party, 1830–47* by Angus Macintyre (Hamish Hamilton, 1983), *The Irish Famine: an Illustrated History* by Helen Litton (Wolfhound Press, 1997). The classic book on this theme is *The Great Hunger* by Cecil Woodham-Smith (Hamish Hamilton, 1964). Strongly recommended texts are *Ireland and the Land Question* by M.J. Winstanley (Methuen, 1984) and *C.S. Parnell* by Paul Bew (Gill and Macmillan, 1991). Useful short studies are 'The Irish Question and British Politics 1868–1986' by D.G. Boyce in *British History in Perspective* (Historical Association, 1988), *Home Rule and the Irish Question* by Grenfell Morton (Longman, 1980) and 'Charles Stewart Parnell' in *Modern British Statesmen 1867–1945* edited by Richard Kelly and John Cantrell (Manchester University Press, 1997). Also helpful is the coverage of the Irish question in *Years of Expansion*, edited by Michael Scott-Baumann (Hodder & Stoughton, 1995). A slightly dated but very readable study is *Gladstone and the Irish Nation* by J.L. Hammond (republished with a modern introduction by M.R.D. Foot, Cass, 1984). The crisis in Ulster over the Home Rule Bill can be followed in *The Ulster Question in British Politics to 1914* by Patricia Jalland (Harvester Press, 1990). Helpful articles are: 'Gladstone and Ireland' by Alan Day, in *History Review*, Mar 1990, 'Gladstone's Irish Policy: Expediency or High Principle' by Edgar Feuchtwanger, in *Modern History Review*, Nov 1991, 'Britain and Ireland 1880–1921: Searching for the Scapegoat' by Christopher Collins, in *Modern History Review*, April 1991, 'Parnell and Home Rule' by Donald MacRaild, in *Modern History Review*, Feb 1993.

CHAPTER 6

BRITAIN AND THE WIDER WORLD – FOREIGN POLICY, 1815–65

POINTS TO CONSIDER

Britain's foreign relations can be conveniently examined by reference to the three outstanding Foreign Secretaries of the period: Castlereagh, Canning and Palmerston. Although Castlereagh and Canning differed sharply in character and had a strong personal dislike of each other, they adopted a broadly similar approach to foreign affairs. Canning, who followed Castlereagh as Foreign Secretary in 1822, continued the work that his predecessor had begun in 1812. The legacy that they left was in turn built upon by Palmerston who, with only minor breaks, directed British foreign policy for the whole of the period between 1830 and his death thirty-five years later. The aims they shared were the preservation of the balance of power in Europe, the detachment of Britain from military action in Europe unless it became absolutely necessary, and the protection of Britain's international commercial interests. All three foreign secretaries took the safeguarding of British interests as their guiding principle. Where they appear to differ is in their manner and style; in matters of policy they were largely consistent. You will see that the chapter is broken down into two main sections: Britain and the Congress system, and the Foreign Policy of Lord Palmerston, which is sub-divided into its main issues.

ISSUE

How far was Britain responsible for the failure of the Congress System?

1 Britain and the Congress System

a) The Role of Castlereagh

A direct way into an understanding of the British attitude towards Europe at the end of the Napoleonic Wars is to study the following two extracts:

The Holy Alliance

Conformable to the words of the Holy Scriptures, which command all men to consider each other as brethren, the Three contracting Monarchs [Alexander I of Russia, Francis I of Austria and Frederick William III of Prussia] will remain united by the bonds of a true and indissoluble fraternity, and considering each other as fellow countrymen, they will, on all occasions and in all places, lend each other aid and assistance; and, regarding themselves towards their subjects and armies as fathers of families, they will lead them, in the same spirit of fraternity with which they are animated, to protect Religion, Peace, and Justice.

ISSUE
Was Castlereagh's foreign policy anything more than the preservation of British interests?

Source A Article I of the Holy Alliance, 26 September 1815

The Quadruple Alliance

To facilitate and to secure the execution of the present [Vienna] Treaty, and to consolidate the connections which at the present moment so closely unite the four Sovereigns for the happiness of the World, the High Contracting Parties [Austria, Great Britain, Prussia and Russia] have agreed to renew their meetings at fixed periods, either under the immediate auspices of the Sovereigns themselves, or by their respective Ministers, for the purpose of consulting upon their common interests, and for the consideration of the measures which at each of these periods shall be considered the most salutary for the repose and prosperity of Nations, and for the maintenance of the Peace of Europe.

Source B Article VI of the Quadruple Alliance, 20 November 1815

The Congress of Vienna, 1815

This drew up the Treaty that formally ended the Napoleonic Wars. The continental victors, Prussia, Russia, and Austria, rewarded themselves by taking large areas of neighbouring territory, while Britain acquired a number of strategic possessions overseas. The French Bourbon monarchy was restored. The principles of nationalism and representative government were largely ignored in the redrawing of the map of Europe which was based on the principle of legitimacy. Thus the Vienna Treaty left a bitter legacy; it became the object of nationalists in Poland, Italy, Germany, Belgium and Norway to break the control of the despotic governments they had been placed under in 1815.

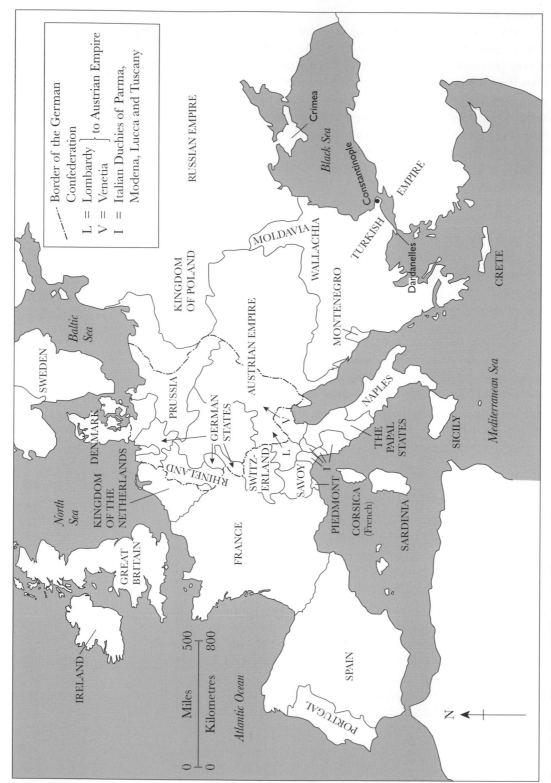

Figure 40 Map of Europe in 1815 after the Congress of Vienna.

The creator of the Holy Alliance was the Russian Tsar, Alexander I. His aim in the restored Europe of 1815 was to enlist the monarchs of Austria and Prussia in jointly re-affirming the principle of the **divine right** of princes to govern their peoples, a principle which had been undermined by the French Revolution. Article 1 was a religious justification for combined action against challenges to their authority. The commitment to 'lend each other aid and assistance' provided the pretext for a combined effort by the governments of Austria, Prussia and Russia to put down constitutionalism and liberalism, movements produced by the French Revolution and seen as the greatest threat to restored Europe after 1815.

By contrast, the Quadruple Alliance was concerned with creating a mechanism for preventing the recovery of France to the point where it could again threaten Europe. In this it reflected the influence of its creator, the British Foreign Secretary, Castlereagh, who saw a need for a regular means of consultation between the victors of the Napoleonic Wars as a safeguard of European peace. The Congress System was a logical extension of this aim. For Russia, Austria and Prussia, the Holy Alliance was their warrant for the suppression of internal opposition, carrying with it the right to intervene in the affairs of troubled member states. For Castlereagh, the Quadruple Alliance was a way of upholding the Vienna settlement; it was not a writ for interfering in the domestic affairs of Europe. He declined to commit Britain to the Holy Alliance which he dismissed as 'a piece of sublime mysticism and nonsense'. Given this basic difference of purpose between the two alliance systems, it was likely that Britain would prove the awkward partner in European relations after 1815.

And so it proved. Disturbed by outbreaks of revolution in Spain, Piedmont, Naples and Portugal, the Russian Tsar convened a Congress at Troppau. Since neither Britain nor France sent formal representatives, the meeting at Troppau was effectively a gathering of Holy Alliance members only. They were thus free to interpret the situation in Europe in their own reactionary way. The Protocol they issued proclaimed the right and intention of the Holy Alliance to use military force to put down revolutionary movements wherever they might occur in Europe.

> The Allied Powers agree to refuse recognition to changes brought about by illegal methods. When States where such changes have been made, cause by their proximity other countries to fear immediate danger, and when the Allied Powers can exercise effective and beneficial action towards them, they will employ, in order to bring them back to the bosom of the Alliance, first friendly representation, secondly measures of coercion, if the employment of such coercion is indispensable.

DIVINE RIGHT (ABSOLUTISM)

The notion that monarchs derive their right to govern their people directly from God. This gives them absolute authority and makes challenges to their power both illegal and sinful.

CASTLEREAGH AS FOREIGN SECRETARY, 1812–15

1812 –14 Britain drawn into war with USA which objected to British interference with American shipping;

1813 –14 Castlereagh played a major role in the forming of the Fourth Coalition between Britain, Russia and Prussia which led to the defeat and abdication of Napoleon;

1815 Castlereagh was instrumental in renewing the alliance against Napoleon after his escape from Elba again threatened Europe, allied diplomats acknowledged Castlereagh as the chief figure in the peace settlement drawn up at the Congress of Vienna and as 'father of the congress system'.

Source C The Troppau Protocol, October 1820.

THE REPRESENTATIVE PRINCIPLE

The concept which allows a greater participation by the governed in the running of their affairs, usually by means of an electoral system which enables the people to vote governments in or out of office.

Castlereagh rejected the claims in the Protocol. In 1820 he issued a public statement, known as the State Paper, indicating where Britain stood in regard to the question of European revolutions. In this he accepted that the current problems of those nations trying to reshape their constitutions 'upon the **Representative Principle**' were indeed formidable but their difficulties in no way justified interference from outside, no matter how benevolent the intention might appear.

> There can be no doubt of the general Danger which menaces the stability of all existing Governments from the Principles which are afloat, and from the circumstances that so many States of Europe are now employed in the difficult task of casting anew their Governments upon the Representative Principle; but the notion of limiting or regulating such Experiments, either by foreign Council or by foreign force, would be as dangerous to avow as it would be impossible to execute.
>
> In this Alliance as in all other human Arrangements, nothing is more likely to impair or even destroy its real utility, than any attempt to push its duties and obligations beyond the Sphere which its original Conception and understood Principles will warrant: It was an union for the Reconquest and liberation of the Continent of Europe from the Military Dominion of France. It never was, however, intended as an Union for the Superintendence of the Internal Affairs of other States.
>
> We shall be found in our place when actual danger menaces the System of Europe, but this Country cannot, and will not, act upon abstract and speculative Principles of Precaution.

Source D From Viscount Castlereagh's State Paper of 5 May 1820.

Castlereagh warned that the alliance system would collapse if it was pushed beyond its original objective. It had never been intended as a programme for international government or as a method of overseeing the internal affairs of other nations. The Quadruple Alliance had come into being in order to defeat French aggression. Castlereagh's approach was a practical one; he did not approve of the revolutionary principles that were circulating in parts of Europe, but he declined to commit Britain to a defence of 'abstract and speculative Principles of Precaution'. The British government and Parliament had approved of the Alliance in 1815 on particular grounds – the safeguarding of Europe against the menace of France. For Britain to support measures which went beyond that would be a breach of faith.

The Troppau Protocol and Castlereagh's State Paper clearly illustrate the fundamental difference of attitude between Britain and the

THE CONGRESS OF AIX-LA-CHAPELLE, 1818

Castlereagh persuaded the other powers to admit France to the Quadruple Alliance, thus making it a Quintuple Alliance.

Holy Alliance powers. For Austria and Russia, there was little distinction between the purposes of the Holy and the Quadruple Alliances; they had both been formulated as methods of securing the stability, political as well as military, of restored Europe. The essential purpose of meeting in regular congresses was to monitor movements that threatened the established order. The Troppau Protocol was a natural extension of this objective; the right of the Alliance members to act collectively to crush revolution was implicit in the original understanding.

Britain was the odd-man-out in all this. Personally responsible for the inauguration of the Congress System at the end of the French wars, Castlereagh had always interpreted its aim in a highly restrictive sense. He did not share the fear of revolution that animated the other powers; France had been the enemy and it was to guard against a resurgence of the French threat that he had formulated the Alliance system. But now with the expansion of the Quadruple into the Quintuple Alliance by the inclusion of France in 1818, Britain's essential objective had been achieved. Britain had no territorial interests in continental Europe; unless the balance of power in Europe was seriously disturbed, it had no need to become deeply involved in European matters.

b) The Role of Canning

George Canning's flamboyance made him appear very dissimilar to the dour Castlereagh from whom he took over. Yet it was the difference in their characters and personal styles rather than any real divergence of policy that provided the contrast in their conduct of foreign affairs. Modern scholars now stress that in essentials Canning continued the line established by Castlereagh. Any apparent changes were matters of detail and emphasis. One of the emphases was on support for **liberal movements**. Wherever possible, Canning gave them diplomatic, if not military, assistance. He instructed the Duke of Wellington whom he appointed as the British representative at the Congress of Verona not to join with the other powers in sanctioning intervention in Spain to crush the rebellion against the absolute monarchy there. He also moved swiftly in 1824–5 to recognise the independence of Spain's former colonies in South America. His motive was a commercial one. During the few years of the colonies' independence, their trade with Britain had increased fifteenfold. Any suggestion that the colonies might return to Spanish control was obviously not in British interests because the Spanish had attempted to restrict trade with their colonies to their own citizens.

It was over the issue of the Latin American colonies that Canning negotiated with President Monroe of the USA who was determined

THE CONGRESS OF TROPPAU, 1820 (TRANSFERRED TO LAIBACH, 1821)
Castlereagh declined to attend; he sent an observer instead, who conveyed the message that Britain would intervene on the continent only in the case of a rising against the restored French monarchy. It was at this Congress that the Holy Alliance issued its notorious Troppau Protocol.

THE CONGRESS OF VERONA, 1822
This was called to discuss the problem of revolutions in the Spanish colonies and in Greece. Castlereagh again refused to attend personally. It was while the Congress was in session that Canning became Foreign Secretary following Castlereagh's suicide.

THE CONGRESS OF ST. PETERSBURG, 1825
Britain did not attend what proved to be the last of the congresses. It produced little of note.

ISSUE
Were there any essential differences between Castlereagh's and Canning's foreign policies?

LIBERAL (CONSTITUTIONAL) MOVEMENTS

The general description given to those groups who struggled against absolutist regimes and pressed for the adoption of a constitution which allowed the people (at least, property owners) to play some part in choosing the government.

THE MONROE DOCTRINE

In 1823 President Monroe warned the European powers that any attempt on their part to encroach on the liberties of the newly independent republics in central or southern America would be interpreted by the USA as 'the manifestation of an unfriendly disposition to the United States'.

ACTIVITY

Drawing on what you have read so far in this chapter, write a brief comment on how appropriate you judge Canning's statement, 'every nation for itself and God for us all', to have been as an explanation for the limited success of the European alliance systems after 1815.

that the European powers should relinquish their claims in the western hemisphere. Although Canning would have preferred a joint Anglo–American declaration, he accepted the principle of the '**Monroe doctrine**' issued unilaterally by the Americans in 1823 and he gave formal British recognition to the republics of Buenos Aires (Argentina) Colombia and Mexico. In the Commons, Canning justified his action in a sentence that has gone into the history books. He announced grandly 'I have called the New World into existence to redress the balance of the old'. By blocking France and Russia, both of whom had considered sending forces to assist Spain to retake its Latin-American colonies, Canning effectively killed off what remained of the Congress System. The notion of the European nations acting in concert had been dealt a death blow. This was further emphasised by Canning's defence of the liberal King of Portugal who was in conflict with his reactionary brother. Canning's decision to dispatch warships and a force of 5,000 troops to Lisbon angered the French and Spanish who were backing the reactionaries, but it saved Portugal from absolutism.

Canning by choice would also have preferred to give unconditional support to the Greeks in their national struggle against Turkish control. The study of the classics which was central to the curriculum of the public schools and universities of the day gave the educated classes in Britain a love of Greece. But there was a conflicting interest. Canning was troubled by a fear, which disturbed all Britain's foreign statesmen throughout the nineteenth century, that any serious weakening of Turkey would encourage Russian expansionism. This for Britain was the essence of what was known as the Eastern Question. Canning's solution to the Greek dilemma at this point was to advance a compromise. He proposed that the Greeks should be granted self-government while at the same time remaining technically under Turkish authority. A treaty based on this proposal was signed in London in July 1827 by the British, French and Russians. Canning, however, died before seeing the outcome of his policy. Wellington who succeeded him, was faced by a rapid turn of events which involved an outbreak of war between Russia and Turkey which the former easily won. Wellington, judging that a semi-independent Greece would simply give Russia continual pretexts for interference, decided to grant full British recognition to Greece as a sovereign state.

Shortly before he died, Canning surveyed the international divisions and remarked, 'Things are getting back to a wholesome state again – every nation for itself and God for us all'. It was his way of describing the failure of the Congress System to reconcile the conflicting interests of the European nations.

2 Palmerston's Foreign Policy

a) Palmerston's Approach to Foreign Affairs

British foreign affairs in the middle years of the nineteenth century were dominated by Henry John Temple, third Viscount Palmerston. In all, he was responsible, either as Foreign Secretary or Prime Minister, for foreign policy for 26 years (1830–41, 1846–51, 1855–8, and 1859–65). An immediate idea of Palmerston's approach to the task of representing his nation can be drawn from the following extracts:

> I hold with respect to alliances, that England is a Power sufficiently strong, sufficiently powerful, to steer her own course, and not to tie herself as an unnecessary appendage to the policy of any other Government. I hold that the real policy of England – apart from questions which involve her own particular interests, political or commercial – is to be the champion of justice and right, pursuing that course with moderation and prudence. We have no eternal allies, and we have no perpetual enemies. Our interests are eternal and perpetual, and those interests it is our duty to follow. And if I might be allowed to express in one sentence the principle which I think ought to guide an English Minister, I would adopt the expression of Canning, and say that with every British Minister, the interests of England ought to be the shibboleth [defining characteristic] of his policy.

Source E Palmerston, speaking in the House of Commons, March 1848.

> Although events of the greatest importance have been passing in rapid succession in almost every part of Europe, the position of your Majesty's Government has been one rather of observation than of action, it being desirable that England should keep herself as free as possible from unnecessary engagements and entanglements.

Source F From a letter by Palmerston to Queen Victoria, April 1848.

ACTIVITY

Read the passages above and then write down your own version of what Palmerston's foreign-policy objectives were. You can check your description by comparing it with the points made in the following paragraphs.

PALMERSTON'S TITLE
Peers of the realm were usually debarred from becoming MPs in the House of Commons. However, the Act of Union of 1800 had exempted Irish peerages from this prohibition. Since Palmerston's title was an Irish one he was therefore entitled to sit in the Commons, which he did for 58 years.

What the extracts clearly illustrate is that Palmerston regarded Britain as strong enough not to require formal ties with other governments. The only enduring consideration was British interests. Other matters would be assessed in the light of circumstances. In 1865, nearing the end of his career, Palmerston re-affirmed that the guiding principle of his foreign policy had been the retention of the balance of power in Europe. Balance was protection; it allowed no one nation to become too powerful and thus threaten the security of its neighbours.

b) Palmerston's Personal Style

Palmerston approached foreign affairs as if they were very much his own personal concern. This frequently caused upsets at home and abroad. The Queen was seldom pleased with him and their relations were often strained. He had already been Foreign Secretary for seven years when Victoria came to the throne in 1837 and thereafter he tended either to patronise her or ignore her. The upright Prince Albert found Palmerston's style distasteful and influenced the Queen against him. The royal couple suspected that Palmerston was contemptuous of European royalty, including the British variety. What especially irked the Queen was Palmerston's habit of not consulting her before embarking on his courses of action. His recognition of the Second Republic of France in 1848 and his behaviour two years later over the Haynau incident were two particular examples of his off-hand manner. Palmerston went even further in regard to the Kossuth affair in 1851 by deliberately going against her wishes. The climax to this period of tension between the Court and the Foreign Secretary came later in that year when Palmerston, without reference to the Queen, formally recognised Louis Napoleon's seizure of power in France.

c) Palmerston's Foreign Policy in Action

How was Belgian independence achieved?

i) The Belgian Question, 1830–9

Under the terms of the Treaty of Vienna, the area which had been known as the Austrian Netherlands (modern-day Belgium) before the Napoleonic Wars had been given to Holland in the hope of forming a strong barrier to potential French expansion along the English Channel coast. However, the Belgians disliked this arrangement because they felt the Dutch treated them as second-class citizens. When Belgian agitation for independence gathered strength in 1830, Palmerston supported the Belgians in their struggle to break free of Dutch control. His diplomacy was instrumental in persuading the major powers to recognise and guarantee Belgian independence in 1839. In the process Palmerston successfully foiled French attempts to establish their own dominance over the area.

ii) Liberal movements in the 1830s

Palmerston used Britain's influence to prevent Austria and France from intervening in Italy to put down liberal anti-government risings. He also gave valuable diplomatic support to the young monarchs of Spain and Portugal who were trying to establish liberal constitutions in the face of the resistance of the reactionary forces they had ousted. He extended the same sympathy to the Polish nationalists in their attempt to break the Russian control over them, but since no British interest was at risk he was not prepared to go as far as giving direct military help to the Poles.

 What was Palmerston's attitude to liberalism abroad?

iii) The Opium War, 1839–42

By the 1830s, China, which had traditionally regarded itself as a superior culture, had begun to feel deep resentment at Western demands for unlimited trading rights. Matters reached a crisis in 1839 when the Emperor Daoguang ordered the seizure of all British-owned opium and forbade further Chinese trade with Britain. Palmerston supported the British merchants in their refusal to tolerate this interference with their highly lucrative trade. He ordered British warships to bombard Canton. Lacking the military power to resist, the Chinese were forced, in 1842, to sign the humiliating Treaty of Nanjing, in which they agreed to return the confiscated opium, to increase their imports of the drug and cede the port of Hong Kong to the British.

 Why did Britain become involved in war with China?

The Opium Trade

From the 1750s on, British merchants from India and Burma had established a flourishing opium trade with China. This brought excellent returns for the traders but drained China of its silver reserves and increased Chinese drug addiction to alarming proportions.

---

iv) The 1848 revolutions

1848 was a dramatic year in Europe. Taking their cue from the collapse of the monarchy of Louis-Philippe in France, nearly every country in Europe witnessed attempted revolutions against the existing regime. Palmerston showed a general sympathy for these liberal challenges to authority. He did nothing to help save Louis-Philippe and then, without gaining the Queen's approval, rushed to recognise the republic that replaced him. He secretly allowed weapons to be sent to the nationalists in Italy who were rebelling against Austrian control. Similarly, he supported the liberals in Spain and Portugal. His reasoning was that the victory of the rebels in these countries

 How did Palmerston respond to the 1848 revolutions?

would lessen the opportunity for powers like France and Austria to interfere.

His underlying aim throughout was to see the balance of power maintained in Europe. This is why he declined, with the exception of Italy, to support liberal movements within the Austrian Empire. He did not want Austria to be weakened since this would undermine its position in central Europe as a barrier to westward Russian expansion. This was very evident in his refusal to give aid to the Hungarian liberals in their struggle against Austrian domination, despite their desperate appeals. His natural inclination may have been to side with liberal movements abroad but he never allowed this to divert him from his central aim of preserving a balance of power in Europe.

v) The Don Pacifico Affair, 1850

Q What does the Don Pacifico Affair reveal about Palmerston's attitude towards British interests?

In 1847, Don Pacifico, a Portuguese Jew, had his property damaged during an anti-Semitic riot in Athens. Claiming that since he had been born in Gibraltar he had a right to British citizenship, he called on the British Government to support him in his demand for compensation from the Greek authorities. Don Pacifico's claims to British nationality were highly dubious and his estimate of damages suffered was grossly exaggerated, but Palmerston decided to back him fully. Ignoring French offers of mediation, Palmerston ordered the blockading of the port of Athens and the seizure of Greek shipping to the value of Pacifico's claim. A fierce row broke out in Parliament when the matter came up for debate in 1850. Cobden and Bright accused him of 'reckless diplomacy'. Palmerston, however, excelled himself in his response. In a four and a half hour speech he defended the whole of his foreign policy since 1830. His concluding statement, in which he justified his actions over the affair, perfectly illustrates his ability to capture the public mood. His words were soon being repeated approvingly throughout Britain in the drinking clubs of the rich and the taverns of the poor:

Source G From Palmerston's speech in the House of Commons, June 1850.

> As the Roman, in days of old, held himself free from indignity when he could say, *'Civis Romanus sum'* [I am a Roman citizen], so also a British subject, in whatever land he may be, shall feel confident that the watchful eye and the strong arm of England will protect him against injustice and wrong.

vi) The Haynau Affair, 1850

Q Were British interests genuinely involved in the Hayanau Affair?

General Haynau, an Austrian general, came on an official visit to England in 1850. Unfortunately for him his notorious reputation had preceded him. His record in suppressing the Hungarian revolution a year earlier, particularly his brutal treatment of women, had made him a hated figure in the eyes of the British public. While visiting a brewery in south London he was set upon by the workers. He was rescued but not before his clothes had been torn and his pride injured. Palmerston was quick to applaud the workers' action. The only pity, he said, was that they had not 'tossed him in a blanket, rolled him in the kennel, and then sent him home in a cab'. Rather than apologise and without consulting the Queen, Palmerston informed the Austrian embassy that it would have been better all round if the General had never left Austria. Palmerston's support of the brewery workers and his insulting of Haynau earned him great popular acclaim. Yet, considering that he had declined to give any positive backing to the Hungarian nationalists in their rebellion against Austrian control, his behaviour appears impulsive and illogical.

vii) The Kossuth Affair, 1850

The Hungarian rebel leader, Kossuth, who had led the nationalist rising against the Austrians which began in 1848, fled to London in 1851. Much to Austrian fury, Palmerston showed his sympathy for Kossuth and his cause by offering to receive him at the Foreign Office in London. This was in direct defiance of the Queen's express wishes.

> **Q** What light does the Kossuth Affair throw on Palmerston's relations with the Queen?

viii) The Second French Empire, 1851

In 1848, Louis-Napoleon Bonaparte, the nephew of the first Napoleon, had become President of the new French Republic. He longed to restore the glories of his uncle, and in 1851 he took power in a *coup d'état*; a year later he declared himself Emperor Napoleon III. At the time of the coup, Palmerston, judging that Louis-Napoleon was less of a threat to British interests than the French republicans, sent a telegram to congratulate him on his successful coming to power. This was too much for the Queen, who compelled Russell, the Prime Minister, to dismiss Palmerston.

> **Q** Why was Palmerston willing to accept Louis Napoleon's seizure of power?

ix) The Second China War, 1856–60

In 1856 a Hong Kong vessel, the *Arrow*, sailing under highly suspect British registration, was caught by the Chinese in an act of piracy; the crew were arrested and the ship was impounded. The British Consulate in Canton demanded the release of the ship and crew and a full apology for the affront to the British flag. Under threat, the Chinese authorities released the pirates but refused to apologise. The Governor of Hong Kong, reacted to this by ordering the shelling of Canton. The Cabinet in London were far from united in approving the Governor's actions but Palmerston, as Prime Minister, carried the majority with him when he argued that whatever the

> **Q** Why were there deep divisions in Britain over the Second China War?

justice of the original incident, Britain was honour bound to back her representatives in China.

When the matter came before the Commons early in 1857, Richard Cobden was prominent among an array of MPs who attacked the Government for sanctioning such arbitrary and immoral conduct. The modern mind is sympathetic towards Cobden's respect for Chinese culture and his distaste for the British defence of piracy. At the time, however, Palmerston, true to his concept of foreign policy as the preservation of British interests, responded to the vote of censure moved by Cobden by making it a simple question of whether Britain was prepared to defend her own subjects against Chinese brutality. As he had in the Don Pacifico affair, he appealed to the patriotism of the nation. Despite being out-voted in the Commons, Palmerston showed his uncanny knack of judging public opinion correctly by calling a snap election in 1859, which he won convincingly. By 1860 China's resistance had been broken and it was forced to sign another humiliating peace treaty in which it accepted Britain's demands and gave up further territory.

ISSUE
What was the Eastern Question?

THE BALANCE OF POWER

The traditional concept that no one European nation should be allowed to become so strong that it could be a threat to its neighbours. The maintenance of the balance of power was a constant object of British foreign policy throughout the nineteenth century.

x) The Eastern Question

The key factor in the Eastern Question was the condition of Turkey. At its height in earlier centuries the Turkish (Ottoman) Empire had been a mighty power. But by the nineteenth century it had become known as 'the sick man of Europe' whose death was thought to be imminent. What worried the European states was the effect Turkey's collapse would have on the **balance of power**. Britain's particular concern was that as Turkey declined, Russia would expand into the regions that the Turkish Empire had previously possessed. This would leave Russia in a position to threaten the land routes to India. Palmerston's approach to the issue was largely determined by the deep British distrust of Russia which he inherited and maintained. One of his first successes as Foreign Secretary was his outmanoeuvring of the Russians over the question of the Straits.

THE STRAITS QUESTION

In 1833, under the secret terms of the Treaty of Unkiar-Skelessi, Russia had gained a notable strategic advantage by persuading Turkey to close the Straits of the Dardanelles and the Bosphorus, which joined the Mediterranean and Black Seas, to all foreign warships except those of Russia. When Palmerston learned of the terms, he set in motion a subtle diplomacy that culminated in the major powers coming together to oblige Russia to sign the Straits Convention in 1841 which, by closing the Straits to all warships, cancelled out Russia's original gain.

Figure 41 Map of the eastern Mediterranean and Black Sea showing the strategic importance of the Straits.

xi) The Crimean War, 1854–6

Britain's sustained determination not to see the Straits fall under the control of Russia was always likely to cause trouble between the two nations. Russia considered that, since the Straits provided its only warm water outlet (i.e. a sea route which did not freeze up during the winter), it had a legitimate claim to influence in the region. From the British viewpoint Russia's mastery of the area would be the means by which it could both threaten Europe and apply a stranglehold over the routes to British India. Given this basic rivalry and the weakness of the Turkish Empire, a Russo–British war was always likely to break out. It was a question not of *if* but *when* war would occur. All that was needed was a serious diplomatic breakdown between the two nations.

ISSUE
How did Britain become involved in this war?

> ### The Protectorship of the Holy Places in Palestine
>
> Palestine was part of the Turkish Empire. In the early 1850s France, under its new Emperor, Napoleon III, reasserted rights, which dated back over a century, to the guardianship of the traditional Christian holy places in Jerusalem and Bethlehem. The Porte (the Turkish government) agreed to recognise these rights. However this angered the Tsar who also claimed that previous treaties had also given Russia the right to protect the members of the Russian Orthodox Church in Palestine. The Tsar now extended that claim to the right to protect all Christians living within the Ottoman Empire. Knowing that this would give Russia unlimited power to interfere in Turkish affairs, the Porte rejected Russia's claim.

This came in the 1850s for reasons which now seem very slight. One of the points often stressed by modern scholars is that while wars may have profound long-term causes, their immediate pretexts are often superficial. That was certainly the case with Britain's entry into the Crimean War in 1854. The particular dispute – the conflict between Russia and France over the guardianship of the holy places in Palestine – did not even involve Britain directly. But by the early 1850s the underlying British dislike of Russia, known to the Victorian public as 'the prison of nations', and its autocratic Tsar Nicholas I (1825–55) had become particularly intense. It had been deepened by the record of Russia's severity in helping Austria crush the Hungarian nationalists during the rising of 1848–9. When France and Russia squared up over the holy places, Britain's natural sympathies lay with the French.

Yet this was not sufficient in itself to require Britain's entry into a full-scale war. What provided a further push was the report in 1853 to Parliament by the British Ambassador in St. Petersburg of a conversation he had had with the Tsar. The key passage in the Tsar's reported statement read:

Source H The Tsars's words as reported by Sir G. Hamilton Seymour to Lord John Russell, British Foreign Secretary, January 1853.

> Now Turkey has by degrees fallen into such a state of decreptitude that, eager as we are for the continued existence of the man, he may suddenly die upon our hands; we cannot resuscitate what is dead; if the Turkish Empire falls, it falls to rise no more. It could happen that circumstances put me in a position of occupying Constantinople.

In the heightened atmosphere Parliament chose to interpret the Tsar's assertions as proof that Russia had all along been plotting the collapse of Turkey. A pro-war, anti-Russian lobby developed which claimed that Russia's designs on Turkey intensified the threat to British India. The lobby urged that Britain should join France in an anti-Russian alliance. However, while Parliament was warlike in its attitude, Lord Aberdeen and his Cabinet were less sure of themselves. Aberdeen appeared genuinely concerned to avoid war if at all possible. He was committed to the defence of Constantinople but unclear about whether Britain should take the initiative against Russia. Even when the Russians attempted to increase pressure on Turkey by occupying the Black Sea provinces of Moldavia and Wallachia in July 1853 (see the map on page 157), the British government held back.

However, its hand was forced in October when Russia retaliated to a Turkish attack on its forces in Moldavia by sinking Turkish vessels in the Black Sea. Obliged to act, Britain joined France in a joint declaration, demanding Russia's withdrawal from the Turkish provinces. When Russian declined to respond to the ultimatum, Britain and France declared war and dispatched forces to the Dardanelles. At that point Russia began a genuine, even if belated, withdrawal from Moldavia and Wallachia. Technically, therefore, Russia had met the terms of the ultimatum and there was now no longer a reason for war. But by this stage so much diplomacy and effort had been put into preparing for war that neither the French nor the British were prepared to disengage without first inflicting a military defeat on the Russians. So began a struggle that was to last a bitter three years, but which had lost its purpose before even a shot had been fired.

Palmerston had played no direct part in these events since he had been obliged to resign as Foreign Secretary in 1851. Nonetheless, he had been a leading member of the pro-war faction in Parliament. His resolute anti-Russian stance meant that when Aberdeen resigned in 1855, following his less than competent handling of the war, Palmerston was the inevitable choice as Prime Minister, unwelcome though this was to Queen Victoria. There is no doubt that Palmerston made a difference; under him there was a greater spirit and efficiency about Britain's war effort. Yet in the end, the Russian surrender in 1856 was due only in part to the British military contribution. The more important factors were the scale of the French involvement (France put four times as many troops into the field as Britain) and Austria's threat, made early in 1856, to enter the war on the Franco-British side.

Palmerston was one of the dominating influences at the Paris talks that formally ended the war. It was at his insistence that the key Article XI was included in the Treaty of Paris. This Article, which debarred warships from entering the Black Sea, appeared at first sight to be a considerable British triumph since it reimposed the

What was Palmerston's role in the Crimean War?

What was Palmerston's role in the peace making?

The Black Sea is neutralised: its waters and its ports, thrown open to the mercantile marine of every nation, are formally and in perpetuity interdicted to the flag of war, either of the powers possessing its coasts, or of any other power.

Source I Article XI of the Treaty of Paris, 30 March 1856.

Straits Convention of 1841. Yet, ironically, the very degree of success was its limitation. It was unthinkable that Tsarist Russia would accept for long the restrictions imposed on it in the Treaty of Paris. Its perception of itself as a great power required that it have free access to the Mediterranean as well as a major voice in the affairs of the Balkans and the Near East. Russia was bound, in time, to re-assert itself in the area. As we shall see in Chapter 9, the Eastern Question was far from settled.

xii) The Italian Question, 1859–60

The crushing by Austrian forces of liberal risings in the Italian states in the 1820s had left Austria in control of large parts of the peninsula. A serious challenge to that control reappeared during the 1848 revolutions. It continued in the 1850s under Count Cavour, the Piedmontese statesman, whose aim was to unite Italy under the leadership of King Victor Emmanuel of Piedmont. Cavour, judging that Austria's grip could be broken only by military means, worked to persuade Napoleon III to take up the cause of Italian nationalism. The French Emperor, eager to prove his liberalism, was keen to assist. In a series of campaigns in 1859 French troops were instrumental in driving Austrian forces out of northern Italy. Lord Derby, Palmerston's predecessor as PM, had taken a pro-Austrian line and argued for a negotiated settlement that would have left Austria still largely in control of Italy. Palmerston, however, who became PM again in the summer of 1859, had both an abiding sympathy for the cause of Italian independence and a suspicion of Napoleon III's motives. In a letter to the Queen he gave his reasons for opposing the Austrians:

Q How did Palmerston balance his support for the Italians with his distrust of the French?

Viscount Palmerston would beg to submit that there are two systems of policy which might be followed in regard to the present state of things in Italy. The one an Austrian, the other an Italian system of policy. The Austrian policy would lead to the restoration, and if possible the augmentation of Austrian supremacy in Italy. This supremacy and domination of Austria has for a long course of years been the cause of infinite misery, social, civil and political, to the nations of Italy.

The Italian system of policy, on the contrary, would tend to free the people of Italy from the thraldom of foreign control and leave them at full liberty to decide for themselves what should be their internal organisation and their condition of political existence.

Source J From a letter by Palmerston to the Queen, 6 August 1859.

Figure 42 Map of Italian states, 1815.

Palmerston's doubts concerning French aims proved well founded. Napoleon III, having gained Nice and Savoy as reward for his support of Piedmont, began to cool in his commitment to Italian nationalism. Indeed, in 1860 he tried to prevent Garibaldi, the southern Italian nationalist leader, from crossing from Sicily to the mainland in order to liberate southern Italy and link up with the

Piedmontese. This gave Palmerston the opportunity to take the initiative. He declared that the Royal Navy would guarantee Garibaldi's uninterrupted crossing. He also gave Cavour diplomatic support when the Piedmontese army moved into the Papal States, thereby removing the last barrier to the unification of Italy from north to south. So it was that without ever committing troops to the aid of the Italian nationalists, Britain under Palmerston had played a significant role in the creation of a united Italy.

xiii) The American Civil War, 1861–5

Q

Why was Britain able to preserve its neutrality throughout the war?

In 1861 civil war broke out in the USA when the slave-owning southern states, fearing domination by the industrial and anti-slavery states of the north, attempted to secede from the Union by forming their own independent Confederacy. Officially Britain remained neutral throughout the four-year struggle, but there was an interesting division of attitude among the British people. The upper classes tended to side with the aristocratic, cotton-growing, rural South while the natural sympathy of the working classes was with the industrial northern states. The problem for Britain was largely an economic one. The blockade of the Confederate ports imposed by the Union navy meant that cotton supplies to the mills of Lancashire were severely disrupted. However, the mill hands of the region won the admiration of the **abolitionists** by their willingness to suffer loss of jobs and wages rather than give support to the slave states.

THE ABOLITIONISTS
The term for those who wanted the abolition of slavery in the USA.

From the first Palmerston was an advocate of strict neutrality. He agreed with Lord John Russell, his Foreign Secretary, who urged 'for God's sake, let us keep out of it'. But this proved difficult; the Union blockade that lasted for the duration of the war interferred with British commerce and caused a number of diplomatic incidents, those over two ships, the *Trent* and the *Alabama*, proving the most dangerous. However, despite these Britain was able to retain its official detachment. By the time the American struggle ended, in 1865, Palmerston's judgment that there was no clear advantage to be gained by Britain's taking sides in the war had prevailed.

The Trent Incident

In 1861 two Confederate envoys sailed for Europe in the hope that they could persuade Britain and France to support the South. The ship they were travelling on, the *Trent*, was stopped by a Union warship and the two officials were arrested and taken into custody. Since the *Trent* was a British vessel the Union action, which took place in neutral waters, was a violation of international marine law. Palmerston angrily declared that he would not tolerate it – 'damned if I will', he told his Cabinet. The British fleet was put on alert and naval war threatened. But cooler heads prevailed. Prince Albert played his part in lessening the tension by redrafting a more conciliatory protest than the government had first drawn up. In the end, without actually apologising for the incident, William Seward, President Lincoln's Secretary of State, admitted that the arrest had been illegal. The Southern envoys were released and permitted to travel to Britain.

The Alabama *Incident*

Lincoln's government complained that British neutrality was breached by Britain's selling warships to the Southern states. One such vessel was the notorious *Alabama* which had been built on Merseyside and delivered to the Confederacy in 1862. During the next two years the *Alabama* sank or captured over sixty ships. The Union claimed compensation from Britain. Palmerston's government declined to respond and Anglo–American bitterness over the issue lasted until 1872 when Gladstone allowed the matter to go to international arbitration. Britain eventually agreed to pay the USA $15 million (equivalent to approximately £3 million) in damages.

iii) The Schleswig-Holstein Question

Bismarck, the German Chancellor, once remarked that the Schleswig-Holstein issue was so complex that only three persons ever understood it – himself, his doctor and the King of Prussia. He added that the doctor had died, the King had gone mad, and he himself had forgotten. To put it in its simplest terms, the ownership of the north German Duchies of Schleswig and Holstein was disputed between Denmark and Prussia. In 1863, the King of Denmark asserted authority over both Duchies. Despite Prussia's resisting the claim, Palmerston committed Britain to the support of the Danes. But the fact was that Prussia had gained the backing of the Austrians. This made it so strong militarily that without French help, which Palmerston had deliberately avoided gaining, there was no chance of Britain's successfully aiding Denmark. Palmerston had to climb down, leaving Prussia and Austria free to defeat the Danes and take possession of both Duchies. The result of all this was considerable embarrassment for Britain and the tarnishing of Palmerston's reputation.

Why did Palmerston's policy prove a failure over Schleswig-Holstein?

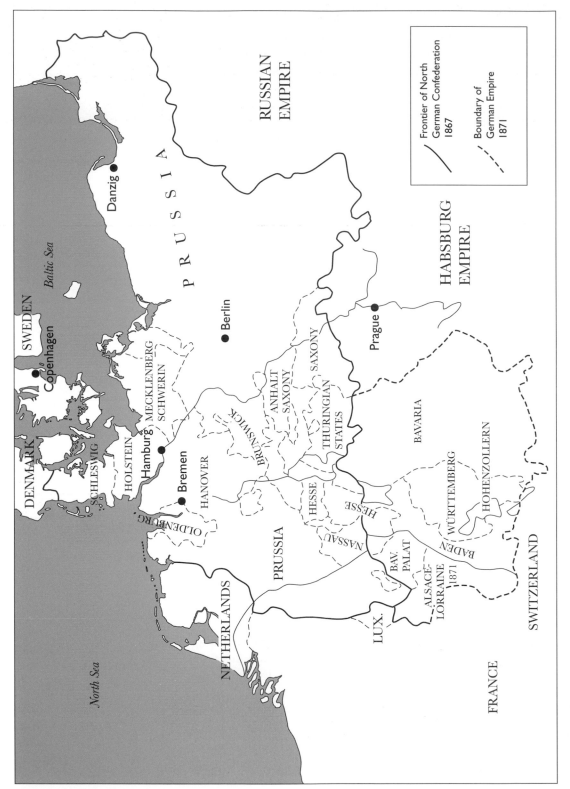

Figure 43 Map of German states 1815–71 showing the expansion of Prussian influence and indicating the position of Schleswig-Holstein.

d) Reflecting on Palmerston's Foreign Policy

ISSUE
What were the chief characteristics of his foreign policy?
How successful was he?

Palmerston's performance at the Foreign Office was nearly always spectacular. Yet except in isolated cases, as over Belgium in the 1830s, he was rarely able to dictate the course of events and he had major failures, as over Schleswig-Holstein in the 1860s. His handling of the Eastern Question had its prestigious moments and he was described by his supporters as 'the man who won the Crimean War'. But at Palmerston's death, in 1865, Russia was in a stronger position in that region than when he had first been Foreign Secretary a quarter of a century earlier. It is doubtful whether Palmerston ever fully grasped the strength of German nationalism; this may well have been because of his preoccupation with France. In line with traditional British thinking in this regard, he saw France as the main threat to the balance of power. The Anglo-French alliance during the Crimean War did not dispel this belief; Palmerston remained anxious that, in the case of Italy, the withdrawal of Austria from the peninsula should not lead to its replacement by France.

Palmerston's underlying purpose to preserve British interests above all others is most graphically shown in his response to the China question. Whatever other principles and attitudes may be ascribed to him, and however he may have been regarded by his contemporaries, radical or conservative, his overriding concern was the protection of Britain as a maritime, trading nation. In the final analysis, Palmerston's foreign policy was a matter not of pursuing general principles but of protecting British interests.

In her book *Lord Palmerston*, Muriel Chamberlain, the leading modern authority on Palmerston, describes his foreign policy as having five key features:

a) a desire for peace and stability in Europe, to be achieved by the balance of power

b) a preference for stable constitutional states because they made good trading partners for Britain

c) a wish not to engage in European affairs unless British interests were involved

d) a sympathy for liberal movements against despotic regimes, which could on occasion justify British intervention

e) a willingness to engage in dramatic gestures overseas if they involved no risk to Britain.

She stresses how large a part bluff played in Palmerston's foreign policy. But she adds that Palmerston never bluffed himself. He was a realist. 'His actions were always more cautious than his words.'

Nothing represents Palmerston's basic guiding principle in foreign policy more clearly than his words to the Queen in 1848,

ACTIVITY

Go back over the separate foreign-policy issues, i to xiii, in which Palmerston was involved and in each case consider whether they bear out Muriel Chamberlain's contention that 'his actions were always more cautious than his words'.

'England should keep herself as free as possible from unnecessary engagements and entanglements'. What impresses most in the exercise of his policy is the economy of effort on Britain's part. Involved in a multitude of issues, across a time span of thirty-five years, which touched every country in Europe and reached to the Middle East, China and the Americas, Britain nevertheless, under Palmerston's guidance, remained remarkably detached physically. Yet at the same time, he created both at home and abroad a reputation as an advocate of liberal and progressive causes in Europe, a reputation merited not by the details of his actions but by the style of his presentation.

Summary of Britain and the Wider World – Foreign Policy, 1815–65

Year	Minister and ministry	Issue or event
1812–15	Liverpool – PM Castlereagh – FS	war against USA (1812–14) war against Napoleon
1815	Liverpool – PM Castlereagh – FS	the Congress of Vienna the Congress System the Quadruple Alliance the Holy Alliance
1818	Liverpool – PM Castlereagh – FS	the Congress of Aix-la-Chapelle, 1818
1820	Liverpool – PM Castlereagh – FS	the Congress of Troppau (transferred to Laibach, 1821) Castlereagh rejected Troppau Protocol
1822	Liverpool – PM Castlereagh – FS Canning after Castlereagh's death	the Congress of Verona called to discuss risings in Spanish colonies – Castlereagh declined to attend
1823	Liverpool – PM Canning – FS	Canning supported liberals in Spain Canning accepted principle of Monroe Doctrine
1824	Liverpool – PM Canning – FS	Britain recognises independence of Spanish colonies
1825	Liverpool – PM Canning – FS	Congress of St. Petersburg Britain declined to attend
1826	Liverpool – PM Canning – FS	Britain intervened in Portugal on side of liberals
1827	Liverpool – PM Canning – FS – PM after Liverpool's retirement	Britain signed Treaty of London recognising Greek independence

Year	Minister and ministry	Issue or event
1830–9	PMs – Grey 1830–4 Melbourne 1834 Peel – 1834–5 Melbourne 1834–9 Wellington – FS 1834–5 Palmerston – FS 1830–34, 1835–9	Britain supported Belgium recognised Belgian independence in Treaty of London, 1839 Palmerston supported liberal movements in Europe
1839	Melbourne – PM Palmerston – FS	Britain goes to war with China to force Chinese to buy opium
1842	Peel – PM Aberdeen – FS	Treaty of Nanjing forced China to increase its imports of the drug and cede the port of Hong Kong to the British
1848	Russell – PM Palmerston – FS	Year of Revolution in Europe – Palmerston showed sympathy for liberal challenges to authority. He recognised the French republic that replaced Louis-Philippe
1850	Russell – PM Palmerston – FS	Palmerston used British strength to support dubious claims of Don Pacifico – he offended Austrians by supporting rough treatment of General Haynau – he further offended Austrians and the Queen by honouring the Hungarian nationalist, Kossuth
1851	Russell – PM Palmerston – FS	Palmerston outraged the Queen by recognising Napoleon III's seizure of power in France
1854	Aberdeen – PM Clarendon – FS	Britain entered the Crimean War against Russia
1855	Palmerston – PM Clarendon – FS	Palmerston prosecuted the war with great enthusiasm
1856	Palmerston – PM Clarendon – FS	Russia made peace on Franco-British terms in the Treaty of Paris which barred Russian warships from the Black Sea
1856–60	Palmerston – PM Clarendon – FS	China again humiliated at British hands in the Second China War
1859–60	Palmerston – PM Russell – FS	Palmerston supported Italian independence movement in its war against Austria
1861–4	Palmerston – PM Russell – FS	despite the *Trent* and the *Alabama* incidents, Palmerston maintained British neutrality during American Civil War
1863–5	Palmerston – PM Russell – FS	in the Schleswig-Holstein dispute between Prussia and Denmark Palmerston backed the Danes but was outmanoeuvred by Bismarck and had to climb down

▼ Working on Britain and the Wider World – Foreign Policy, 1815–65

The material in this chapter covers a wide range of incidents and topics. To avoid confusion it is important than you arrange your ideas around the major developments. To help in this, check back frequently to the summary chart. If you take the key theme linking all the policies of the period – the defence of British interests – you will have a very reliable reference point. Both Castlereagh and Canning can be best understood in relation to their attitudes towards the Congress System and towards liberal movements. You could make a set of notes comparing their policies in these areas. With Palmerston it is rather more difficult; he dominated foreign policy for so long and was concerned with so many issues. So, a suggested approach would be to build on the work you did in the last Activity (page 166). First of all list in order all the issues covered from the Belgian Question through to the Schleswig-Holstein Question. Against each of them simply record your judgment – successful or unsuccessful. Then take the five-point definition of his policies that Muriel Chamberlain provided (page 165) and select the one you think most appropriate to each particular case.

Examples might be:

issue	category	success/failure
Hungarian rising against Austria	c)	successful
Don Pacifico affair 1850	e)	successful

You could then go on to add fuller notes to explain your judgment and choice of categories. In this way you will be helping yourself both to remember the main issues and to apply your powers of analysis to them.

Answering extended writing and essay questions on Britain and the Wider World – Foreign Policy, 1815–65

You will now be very familiar with the way we break down essay questions into their types. The following list shows the style of questions you are likely to encounter on the topic of foreign policy.

Type of Issue	Examples of typical questions
1 causes/reasons/motives	Why, despite being the founder of the Quadruple Alliance, was Castlereagh unwilling to commit Britain to the Holy Alliance?
2 course of events	Examine the part played by Britain in the operation of the Congress System between 1815 and 1822.
3 consequences/results/ effects	In what ways did Palmerston's concern to safeguard the routes to India influence his conduct of foreign policy?
4 success/failure	How successfully did George Canning pursue his foreign policy objectives?
5 significance/importance	How influential was the concept of the balance of power in shaping Britain's attitude to the Eastern Question?
6 comparison	Why was Palmerston prepared to support the Italian nationalists in 1859, but not the Hungarian nationalists in 1848?
7 right/wrong (moral/ ethical judgments, assessing validity)	Consider the view that in entering the Crimean War in 1854 'Britain did the right thing for the wrong reasons'.
8 broad surveys asking for an examination of change over time	'Throughout the nineteenth century British foreign policy was based solely on the principle of protecting Britain's interests.' Examine this argument. (To be able to attempt this question you need to study Chapter 9. See the suggestions on page 254)

For our example on this occasion, let us select number 7. It is vital, as always, to look for the key terms in the question. Here we have a quotation to direct us. It contains two balanced ideas: 'right thing', 'wrong reasons'. The following suggestions should help you structure an answer around the terms:

'wrong reasons'
▼ Had the Russian withdrawal from the Danubian provinces destroyed the only justifiable reason for Britain's going to war?
▼ But was the question of the provinces merely a pretext for war?
▼ Was the conflict deliberately encouraged by the war party in the Government and in Parliament?
▼ Did Russia have a genuine right to access from the Black Sea into the Mediterranean and therefore a justifiable claim to exercise influence in the region?
▼ Was not Russia's claim to great power status as legitimate as Britain's?

'right war'
▼ Was not war with Russia unavoidable at some point in the nineteenth century, given Britain's long-term worries over the routes to India and fear that the balance of power was being disturbed by Russian expansion?

I am prepared to admit, that the independence of constitutional States whether they are powerful, like France or the United States, or of less relative political importance, such as the minor states of Germany, never can be a matter of indifference to the British Parliament, or, I should hope to the British public. Constitutional States I consider to be the natural Allies of this country; and whoever may be in office conducting the affairs of Great Britain, I am persuaded that no English Ministry will perform its duty if it be inattentive to the interests of such States.

Source K from a speech by Palmerston, in the House of Commons, August 1832.

▼ If that was the case then does that make the Russian withdrawal from the Danubian provinces immaterial?

▼ Did Britain have an equally valid claim to protect its interests as a great power which, therefore, entitled it to contemplate war when it felt these were threatened?

▼ Since war was regarded in the nineteenth century as a legitimate final step in the diplomatic process, was not Britain's involvement in the Crimean War justified?

You may well be able to think of other points that should be considered. If so, add these to the lists. Your task is then to balance the two sets of considerations to see which is the weightier.

Answering source-based questions on Britain and the Wider World – Foreign Policy, 1815–65

Read the speeches delivered by Palmerston in the Commons in August 1832 and in March 1848 (page 151). Then answer the following question:

How, according to his descriptions in sources E and K, did Palmerston interpret the role of Britain in foreign affairs? **[8 marks]**

Suggested approach

Although he came later to be celebrated as a champion of liberal movements abroad, at the early point in his career marked by the 1832 speech, Palmerston expresses an unequivocal support for constitutionalism. He does so on the grounds that Constitutional States are the most stable and, therefore, make reliable allies. Sixteen years later he modifies but does not contradict the view. Palmerston regards Britain as strong enough not to require unnecessary ties with other governments. Nonetheless, provided it is consistent with the safeguarding of her commercial and political interests, Britain's broad policy internationally will be to favour the cause of justice abroad. Such a policy pursued with moderation and judgement will, Palmerston feels, guarantee the support of powerful friends should it ever be needed. What he argues for is realism. Britain should not regard particular countries as permanent allies or enemies. The only consideration is British interests. That is the constant; other matters will be assessed in the light of circumstances. Referring to his predecessor, Canning, he asserts that for every British minister the interests of the nation should be the touchstone of his policy.

Further Reading

Books in the 'Access to History' series

Chapters 1–4 of *The Concert of Europe: International Relations 1814–70* by John Lowe provide the European dimension to the material studied in this chapter. Foreign policy under Canning and Castlereagh is described in Chapters 3 and 4 of *Tories Conservatives and Unionists 1815–1914* by Duncan Watts, and under Palmerston in the same author's *Whigs, Radicals and Liberals 1815–1914*, Chapter 4.

General

'Pax Britannica'? British Foreign Policy 1789–1914 by Muriel Chamberlain (Longman, 1988) provides an excellent coverage of all the themes in this chapter, while the best of her many studies of Palmerston's policies is *Lord Palmerston* (GPC Books, 1987). Two informed coverages of the period are *The Great Powers and the European System, 1815–1914* by F.R. Bridge and R. Bullen (Longman, 1980) and *The Foreign Policy of Victorian England, 1830–1902* by Kenneth Bourne (OUP, 1970). *Britain's Century 1815–1905* by W.D. Rubinstein (Arnold, 1998) has very informative chapters on foreign policy, as also does *The Years of Expansion Britain 1815–1914* edited by Michael Scott-Baumann (Hodder & Stoughton, 1995). Interesting biographies are *Castlereagh* by John Derry (Murray, 1976), *Canning* by W. Hinde (London, 1973), and *Palmerston* by Jane Ridley (Constable, 1970). One of the best introductory texts on the tricky subject of the Eastern Question is *Britain and the Eastern Question* by G. Clayton (University of London Press, 1971). Strongly recommended articles are: 'Europe after Napoleon – Castlereagh's Foreign Policy' by John Derry in *Modern History Review*, Feb 1993, 'Canning and the Pittite Tradition' by John Derry in *History Review*, March 1996, 'The Eastern Question' by A.L. McFie in *New Perspective*, Sept 1996, 'Pax Britannica' by Muriel Chamberlain in *Modern History Review*, Sept 1996, and '*Palmerston and Victorian Politics*' by Muriel Chamberlain in *New Perspective*, Sept 1998.

CHAPTER 7

THE RISE OF ORGANISED LABOUR

POINTS TO CONSIDER

In Chapters 1 and 4 you were introduced to the growth of industry that took place in the nineteenth century. One of the most important consequences of that growth was that it brought industrial workers together in large numbers in concentrated areas. This chapter deals with the ways in which those workers organised themselves in order to agitate for higher wages, better conditions and political rights. There are two main sections to the chapter – the Chartist Movement and the development of the trade unions. The second section is subdivided into an analysis of the 'model unions' of the middle years of the century and the 'new unions' of the later part of the period. These parts make up a continuous chronological story, so it would help your understanding if you were to work through the chapter in sequence. However, if you are interested in learning about only one of the themes, Chartism or the trade unions, you will find the appropriate sections are sufficient in themselves for your needs.

THE COMBINATION ACTS, 1799

These Acts were part of a series of repressive measures introduced by Pitt's government to prevent revolutionary movements developing in Britain as they had in France. The Acts made it illegal for two or more workers to combine in order to agitate for higher wages or better working conditions. Their effect was to make trade union activity illegal. The Acts were accompanied by a similar measure which prohibited employers from combining to keep down workers' wages. But most workers believed that this was simply an attempt on the part of the government to appear impartial. It is true that these Acts were repealed in 1824, but they were replaced by a law with similar intentions the next year, and throughout the nineteenth century the law and the courts were heavily weighted against trade unions. This was well illustrated by the notorious case of the Tolpuddle Martyrs in 1834.

Introduction

As large-scale industry and its associated transport systems developed in Britain, the workers within these sectors became very conscious of themselves as collective groups. They were in a position to discuss with each other the circumstances in their factory, workshop, mine, or shipyard and to consider ways in which they could gain better wages and conditions. The response of employers to the organisations representing workers was invariably one of suspicion. They feared that organised workers would be difficult to control and that demands for more money would threaten business profits. Since some of the most important employers were Members of Parliament, there was a strong feeling among the workers that they were at the mercy of a political system in which they were unrepresented. The idea spread among the workers that until they gained direct access to parliament they would continue to be denied the means of improving their working and living conditions since the law would always be against them. They saw the Combination Acts as a gross example of this. It was the sense of frustration and grievance with the existing political and legal system that led to the development of the first organised working-class movement in British history – Chartism.

THE TOLPUDDLE MARTYRS

In 1834 a group of agricultural labourers in Tolpuddle in Dorsetshire tried to protect themselves against severe cuts in their wages by setting up a branch of the Grand National Consolidated Trades Union (GNCTU). This was not illegal since ten years earlier the repeal of the Combination Acts had permitted trade unions to exist, although with very limited rights. But the local magistrates who were landowners were determined to make an example of the labourers. Six were tried and found guilty on the technical charge of administering illegal oaths. They were sentenced to seven years' transportation. Such was the outcry against the proceedings and the savage penalties that two years later, the Whig government, having originally backed the magistrates, reversed its attitude and pardoned the labourers. The case became part of working-class folklore and the six were seen as martyrs in the cause of trade unionism.

---

1 Chartism

a) The Origins of Chartism

The Chartist movement grew out of a deep sense of disappointment with the Great Reform Act of 1832. Many workers had hoped that parliamentary reform would enable them to have a voice in their own affairs, but it quickly became apparent that the Act had not extended voting rights to them. Hardly any workers had been added to the electoral roll and five out of six adult males still did not have the vote (see page 39). Working-class anger over this was powerfully put by Bronterre O'Brien, one of the leading Chartists.

> What a farce the present system is! The present House of Commons does not represent the people, but only those fellows who live by profits and usury [charging high interest on loans] – a rascally crew who have no interest in the real welfare of the country. Pawnbrokers are enfranchised, and two thousand brothel-owners in London all have votes, but honest folk have none.

ISSUES
Was Chartism fatally weakened by its own internal divisions?
Was Chartism a failure?
Was Chartism a class movement?

Source A From a speech by Bronterre O'Brien, April 1839.

The workers' sense of betrayal was intensified by a number of other developments in the 1830s:

▼ the introduction of the hated Poor Law Amendment Act in 1834 which as far as the workers could see was aimed deliberately at making life more miserable for them (see page 88)

KEY STAGES IN CHARTISM

1832 First reform Act;
1830s workers disillusioned with Whig reforms;
1834 failure of Grand National Consolidated Trades Union;
1836 the LWMA formed;
1838 first Charter drafted;
1839 first Charter presented and rejected;
1839 the Newport Rising;
1842 the second Charter presented and rejected; the plug plot;
1848 third Charter presented and rejected;
1858 end of Chartism as an active movement.

▼ the Tolpuddle case, 1834

▼ the failure of the factory acts to bring any real improvement in factory conditions (see page 97)

▼ the Whig reforms of the period, which included such measures as the Municipal Corporations Act and the Registration of Births, Deaths and Marriages Act, seemed an extension of government interference without any gains for the workers (see page 42)

▼ the introduction of police forces in the localities which many workers regarded as part of the government policy of repression

▼ the collapse in 1834 of Robert Owen's Grand National Consolidated Trades Union (see below)

▼ a serious economic recession that produced hardship and hunger in many parts of Britain.

Owen and Owenism

Robert Owen (1771–1858) was both an industrialist and an early socialist. A self-made man who achieved success as a textile manufacturer, he attempted to become a model employer by looking after rather than exploiting his workers. Houses and recreational facilities were provided for his employees and education for their children. He believed in the co-operative spirit; if people worked together for the common good all would benefit. He established a number of model factories in Scotland and the USA. While these were not an economic success, the co-operative principles of Owenism were an important contribution to the debate on social reform. His Grand National Consolidated Trades Union (GNCTU) was based on the idea of bringing all the existing trade and craft unions into one organisation whose size and strength would give it a formidable bargaining power. However, the GNCTU never drew more than a minority of workers into its ranks, and although it campaigned against the anti-union policies of the government, such as the Tolpuddle case, its failure when it attempted to organise a general strike in 1834 led to its collapse. Owen's ideas influenced Chartism although he never personally joined the movement since he found its methods too confrontational.

ISSUE
What were the original aims of the Charter?

b) The People's Charter

Such developments convinced many workers that unless they organised themselves effectively their grievances would continue to be ignored. They saw Parliament as the key to the problem; until the House of Commons had a large number of working-class MPs or MPs who directly represented them, the workers would never be able to improve their conditions. The great need, therefore, was for the workers to obtain the vote. In the 1830s an alliance between the London Working Men's Association (LWMA) and the Birmingham Political Union (BPU) led to the rapid growth of a nationwide movement that demanded genuine parliamentary reform. It expressed its main aims in The People's Charter, which was first drafted in 1836 and reissued in different versions over the next twelve years.

The Six Points
OF THE
PEOPLE'S
CHARTER.

1. A VOTE for every man twenty-one years of age, of sound mind, and not undergoing punishment for crime.

2. THE BALLOT.—To protect the elector in the exercise of his vote.

3. No PROPERTY QUALIFICATION for Members of Parliament —thus enabling the constituencies to return the man of their choice, be he rich or poor.

4. PAYMENT OF MEMBERS, thus enabling an honest trades-man, working man, or other person, to serve a constituency, when taken from his business to attend to the interests of the country.

5. EQUAL CONSTITUENCIES, securing the same amount of representation for the same number of electors, instead of allowing small constituencies to swamp the votes of large ones.

6. ANNUAL PARLIAMENTS, thus presenting the most effectual check to bribery and intimidation, since though a constituency might be bought once in seven years (even with the ballot), no purse could buy a constituency (under a system of universal suffrage) in each ensuing twelvemonth; and since members, when elected for a year only, would not be able to defy and betray their constituents as now.

Figure 44 *A Chartist Handbill* listing 'The Six Points of the People's Charter, 8 May 1838'. It is notable that although these demands were regarded by the authorities at the time as dangerously radical, if not revolutionary, all but point 6 had become electoral law by 1918.

ACTIVITY

To make sure that you have grasped the meaning of the Six Points, define each one briefly in your own words.

ISSUE
Why did their
presentation and
rejection cause
widespread violence?

c) The Significance of the Charters

In all, three Charters were presented to Parliament. The first was in 1839 and carried over a million signatures. The second was in 1842, signed by three and a quarter million, and the third in 1848, signed by six million, or so the Chartist leaders claimed. Neutral estimates suggest the real figure was probably only half that. But the exact number of signatories is a detail. What matters is that the three petitions indicated that Chartism was a mass movement in the major industrial areas of Britain. This was what made it different from previous working-class protests. Nor was its influence confined to the towns. Chartism also represented the grievances of agricultural workers.

In 1839, the House of Commons swiftly and contemptuously rejected the first Chartist petition by a vote of 235 to 46. Anger and violence followed. In July, riots in Birmingham, where the General Convention, the central organising body of the Chartists had moved, were crushed by the police. Many leaders were arrested including William Lovett, the founder of the LWMA. But the direct action continued. In November, the most serious disturbance so far occurred in south Wales when miners and iron workers marched on Newport in what became known as the 'Newport Rising'. It was put down but it set in motion a series of disturbances that took place sporadically throughout Britain during the following decade. The rejection of the second Chartist petition in 1842 by a Commons majority of 287 votes to 49 produced a wave of strikes known collectively as the 'plug plot'.

THE PLUG PLOT, 1842
A reference to the strikers' practice of knocking out the plugs in the boilers of factory steam engines. Since steam was the basic power source, much as electricity is today, the result was the immobilising of all the machines in the factory.

ISSUE
Why did a new form of
Chartism develop?

d) New Move Chartism

The failure of the two petitions by 1842 persuaded a number of Chartists that new ideas and new tactics were necessary. From the beginning Chartism had been divided in its strategy between physical force Chartists, those who believed in direct action, and moral force Chartists, those who believed that peaceful agitation was more effective. 'New move' Chartism, which began in 1842, was a development of the moral force argument. It stressed the need for the working classes to improve themselves by education and training. It laid stress on the Christian virtues of honesty, responsibility and sobriety and played down the idea of confrontation.

The new move was influential but it did not prevent the last major Chartist challenge to the authorities in 1848. That year saw many European countries, most notably France, affected by revolutionary ideas which often led to violent clashes between government and people. It was in this atmosphere that the third Chartist petition was prepared. The plan was for a mass demonstration to be held on Kennington Common, a large open space in south London, followed by a march to Westminster to present the Charter. Fearing serious disorder, the government forbade the march and took strong security measures, which included the enrolment of thousands of civilian volunteers as special constables. In the event, the constables were not needed since the Chartist leaders backed down and dispersed after only a short token march. This capitulation effectively marked the end of Chartism as a potentially powerful political movement even though it remained in existence for another ten years before holding its last conference in 1858.

A key factor in the history of Chartism was the attitude of the authorities. Both local and national governments showed consistent and determined resistance to the movement. The House of Commons overwhelmingly rejected the three petitions presented to it and showed no signs of accepting the Chartists' claims and arguments. The local authorities also took this strong line and always treated Chartist agitation as a threat to public order which they were not prepared to tolerate. The possibility of the movement achieving its aims was, therefore, always very remote.

How did the authorities respond to Chartism?

e) Chartist Divisions – Physical Force versus Moral Force

ISSUE
Why did splits occur within the Chartist movement?

For many Chartists the biggest obstacle they faced was not external opposition but internal division. 'We failed not because of opposition to us but because of opposition amongst us': so said a disappointed Chartist in 1860. It was certainly true that important differences between the Chartist leaders over objectives and methods had been present from the beginning. The sharpest division was between those who supported the moral force argument and those who advocated physical force. The outstanding spokesmen for the latter strategy were Feargus O'Connor and George Harney who emphasised the fundamentally violent and repressive nature of all government and argued that the tyranny of the State could be broken only by greater force being applied against it. It was such arguments that O'Connor advanced in his newspaper, *The Northern Star*, and which helped to inspire the Newport Rising of 1839 and the Plug Plot of 1842.

This appeal to violence was not supported by Chartism's first major organiser, William Lovett, who with Thomas Attwood is usually regarded as representing the moral force element. Through his London Working Men's Association, Lovett asserted that violence was self-defeating; it would excite the fears of the governing classes and would lead to greater repression. It would also deter potential supporters, especially among the propertied classes, and thus prevent the achievement of the political ends to which Chartism was dedicated. Lovett believed that what was needed was not a resort to direct action but the education of the working class into an understanding of itself as a dynamic force for the social and moral improvement of England. This was what underlay the new move Chartism of the early 1840s. O'Connor ridiculed the new move. He devoted his energies to his Chartist Land Plan.

The personal rivalry between O'Connor and Lovett, the disputes over the correct methods of achieving the Charter, and the differing aims and purposes within Chartism did much to weaken it as a movement. They show that it was never a single united force. It is also important to note there was a broad regional difference. The physical force Chartists tended to be dominant in the north of the country while the moral force moderates were influential in the south. Chartism's lack of unity and its apparent willingness to resort to violence meant it failed to gain sympathy among people of influence in the governing classes.

f) Was Chartism a Revolutionary Movement?

It is clear that historians now view Chartism as having been a critical phase in the development of working-class consciousness. They see it as a nationwide movement that expressed a wide range of ideas and grievances that had never been aired before in such an organised way. The debate is now about what the aims of the Chartists actually were. Was Chartism an economic or a political movement. Was it 'a knife and fork question', concerned with alleviating hunger and suffering, or was it a political movement that wanted to bring about a fundamental change in the structure of society? A contemporary writer, Harriet Martineau, an astute middle-class observer, had posed those same questions in 1849:

> What was the Chartist movement all about? Those who have not looked into Chartism think that it means one thing – a revolution. Some who talk as if they assumed to understand it, explain that Chartism is of two kinds – Physical Force Chartism and Moral Force Chartism – as if these were not merely two ways of pursuing an object. Those who look deeper – who go out upon the moors by torchlight, who talk with a suffering brother under the hedge, or beside the loom, who listen to the groups outside the Union workhouse, or in the public house among the Durham coal-pits, will feel long bewildered as to what Chartism is, and will conclude at last that it is another name for popular discontent – a comprehensive general term under which are included all protests against social suffering.

Source B Adapted from *History of England during the Thirty Years' Peace* by Harriet Martineau, 1849.

Martineau's view was that Chartism was not a revolution but was 'another name for popular discontent'. For her, moral force and physical force Chartism were simply two different ways of pursuing the same end – the relief of 'social suffering'. But that is not how Chartism was interpreted by an interested and highly important foreign observer – Frederick Engels. His study of the English working classes convinced him that they were essentially revolutionary, that they wished to smash the ruling class and take power for themselves. His view of the revolutionary character of Chartism is well expressed in the following passage from his published study of the working class in England, written at the height of the Chartist movement. He believed that the physical force element represented the real character of Chartism and he took very seriously the readiness of such leaders as George Harney to engage in violence. He also saw great significance in the decision of the other major protest movement of the day, the Anti-Corn Law League (see page 46), to withdraw its support from the Chartists in 1842. This for Engels was an example of the class division and therefore the underlying rivalry between the two movements. Chartism represented the **proletariat**, and the League, the **bourgeoisie**.

> Chartism was from the beginning in 1835 chiefly a movement among the working-men, though not yet sharply separated from the radical bourgeoisie. The Radicalism of the workers went hand in hand with the Radicalism of the bourgeoisie. They held their National Convention every year in common, seeming to be one party. The bourgeoisie then turned its attention to more practical projects, more profitable to itself, namely the Corn Laws. The Anti-Corn Law Association was formed in Manchester, and the consequence was a relaxation [cutting] of the tie between the Radical bourgeoisie and the proletariat. The working-men soon perceived that for them the abolition of the Corn Laws could be of little use, while very advantageous to the bourgeoisie. The fruit of the uprising (the plug plot in 1842) was the decisive separation of the proletariat from the bourgeoisie. The Chartists had not hitherto concealed their determination to carry the Charter at all costs, even that of revolution; the bourgeoisie, which now perceived, all at once, the danger with which any violent change threatened their position, refused to hear anything further of physical force, the difference between chartist democracy and all previous bourgeois democracy. Chartism is of an essentially social nature, a class movement.

THE PROLETARIAT

The Marxist term for the oppressed workers, the wage slaves produced by industrialisation, whose strength lay in their numbers and whose bitter conditions would lead them to rise up and eventually overthrow the bourgeois oppressors.

THE BOURGEOISIE

The Marxist term to describe the exploiting, capitalist class, made up of industrialists, bankers, merchants and the higher ranks of the professions. This class had taken over from the old landed [feudal] interests and was now locked in a struggle with the proletariat.

Source C The Condition of the Working Class in England by Frederick Engels, 1844.

KARL MARX AND FREDERICK ENGELS

German revolutionaries who collaborated in the writing of the *Communist Manifesto* (1848) in which they called upon the industrial workers of the world to fulfil their historical destiny by overthrowing the oppressive capitalist classes and creating a workers' state. Exiled from Prussia, the two men lived for long periods in England where they continued to develop their revolutionary theories.

ISSUES

Why did new unionism replace model unionism as the voice of organised labour? Why did the unions move towards political representation?

ACTIVITY

Re-read the quotations in this section and then answer the following:
1. What is Engel's explanation for the collapse of the alliance between working men and the bourgeoisie which had operated in the early years of the Chartist movement?
2. Which do you think is the more convincing interpretation of Chartism – Engels's or Harriet Martineau's? Explain your answer.

2 The Development of the Trade Unions

a) The Model Unions

Trade unions had been legal bodies since the Repeal of the Combination Acts in 1824, but the uncompromising attitude of the authorities during the disturbances of the Chartist years led the unions to limit their activities.

The Repeal of the Combination Acts, 1824

In the 1820s Francis Place, a prominent working-class activist, led a campaign for the removal of the Combination Acts. Success came in 1824 when a group of radical MPs, led by Joseph Hume, persuaded the Liberal Tory government to repeal the Acts. The immediate result of the new freedom was a wave of strikes. Quickly rethinking its position, the government then introduced a new Combination Act in 1825. Although this was not as restrictive as the 1799 measure, since it allowed unions to agitate for higher wages, it outlawed 'intimidation' and 'obstruction'. So, although unions were legal bodies after 1825, they were very severely restricted in what they could do.

However, the rapid decline of Chartism after 1848 meant the trade unions could resume their role as the representatives of working-class interests. 1851 saw the formation of the Amalgamated Society of Engineers (ASE), a body that set as its objectives the advancement of the interests of the skilled workers of the engineering industry. It organised itself on very efficient lines, required relatively high subscriptions from its members, and limited its membership to skilled workers. It appointed full-time, paid officials and preferred to reach agreement with employers through negotiation rather than by confrontation or strike threats. The ASE became the model for a number of other skilled-craft unions. These 'model unions', as they became known, could claim by the 1870s to have made a number of important gains for unionism. The extension of the franchise by the 1867 Reform Act to a substantial number of urban working men was seen by some of the MPs who supported it, as a reward for the responsibility shown by organised labour during the preceding twenty years. A number of Trade Union Acts in the 1870s, granted legal and financial rights to the unions. These advances together with the formation in 1868 of the Trades Union Congress (TUC) as a body representing the majority of the unions in Britain indicated that trade unionism had become a significant national movement.

But there was a problem. Most of the unions who joined the TUC were of the 'model' type, made up of skilled workers, such as engineers, masons and carpenters. Their members were proud of the skills they had acquired after long apprenticeship and training and were highly selective in admitting new members. They also protected themselves through private insurance schemes or by forming themselves into friendly societies, which were special registered bodies providing funds for the workers in the event of injury or unemployment. However, the way industry had developed, with its demand for large numbers of semi-skilled or unskilled labourers, had made these craft unions no longer representative of the emerging mass labour force. By the last quarter of the century, British industry had created a work force which was very different in attitude from the model unions.

ACTIVITY

Having read the above text, describe in your own words the essential characteristics of the model unions.

---

b) New Unionism

In the 1880s a movement developed to organise the growing ranks of unskilled workers into unions. This became known as 'new' unionism. The decade saw the formation of the National Labour Federation, the Gas Workers' Union, the Dockers' Union, and the Miners' Federation. These mass, open-entry, unskilled or semi-skilled bodies became the pattern for subsequent trade union growth. The 'new' unionism took as its immediate task the improvement of wages and conditions. A series of organised disturbances and strikes in the late-80s reached a climax with the Dockers' Strike in 1889.

KEY STAGES IN UNION DEVELOPMENT

1824 Repeal of the Combination Acts;

1834 Grand National Consolidated Trades Union;

1850s model unions grew in strength;

1867 Second Reform Acts extended the vote to most urban working men;

1868 first meeting of the Trades Union Congress;

1871 Trade Union Act gave unions legal recognition and protection of funds;

1875 Acts legalised peaceful picketing and protected unions against civil damages arising from a strike;

1880s formation of new unions;

1888 Bryant and May Match Girls' strike;

1889 the dock strike for the 'dockers' tanner';

1890s formation of employers' federations to resist unions;

1893 Independent Labour Party (ILP) formed;

1899 old unions joined new in demanding separate parliamentary representation;

1900 Labour Representation Committee (LRC) formed;

1901 the Taff Vale decision created an even greater need for the unions to be directly represented in Parliament;

1906 LRC became the Labour Party to represent union interests; large number of unions affiliated to the Labour Party;

1911 –14 marked period of industrial unrest showed the growing strength and influence of the mass unions.

The Match Girls' Strike, 1888

The female workers in the Bryant and May match factory in London struck for higher wages and in protest against their dangerous working conditions which produced such diseases as 'phossy jaw', an ulceration of the skin and softening of the bone, caused by the poison in the phosphorus with which the women were in constant contact. The strike was partially successful; the women were given a pay rise but little was done to make their conditions less hazardous.

The Dockers' Strike, 1889

In the early 1880s the gasworkers had won the 8-hour day from their employers. This encouraged the dockers to press their own claims, the principal one being the 'dockers' tanner' – sixpence ($2\frac{1}{2}$p) an hour basic pay rate. On receiving the expected rebuff from the port employers, the various dock unions, including stevedores [crane drivers], dockers [unloaders] and lightermen [those who ferry goods to and from ship to shore] declared a strike for which they had already prepared. Led by John Burns, Tom Mann and Ben Tillett, a number of appeals to the public, in the form of marches, demonstrations and press handouts, had been organised. In addition, vital relief schemes for the strikers and their families had been set up.

ISSUE
In what ways did the new unions offer an alternative form of organisation to that of the model unions?

In spite of such preparations, by the end of the fifth week, with union funds virtually exhausted, the strike seemed about to collapse. However, a welcome injection of money from sympathetic unions at home and abroad gave the dockers fresh heart. The port authorities re-opened negotiations which resulted in a measure of success for the strikers; the 'dockers' tanner' was granted as were other demands affecting working conditions. Tillett and the other strike leaders claimed this as a major victory for worker solidarity and proof of what 'new' unionism could achieve. Frederick Engels observed that it marked 'the English masses on the move'. Events in the next decade were to prove such optimism to have been premature. An economic recession caused serious unemployment among the unskilled workers and stiffened the resolve of the employers to resist union demands. Nonetheless, the excitement shown in the following extract was not entirely misplaced:

A vast congregation of upturned faces stretched from the East India Dock gates across the roadway to the payment beyond. Thousands of men were there – seedy dockers and sturdy stevedores, sailors and firemen, in the fresh enthusiasm of their new trade union, weather-stained lightermen, and coalies cleaned up for Sunday – all branches, in short, of riverside labour; and on the outskirts of the crowd stood not a few engineers and other skilled artisans ready to show their sympathy with the revolt of unskilled labour. It is a great throng that is gathering, though nothing to the huge numbers reached in later stages of the strike. Thousands of dockers are there, chiefly from the East and West India Docks, and thousands more of stevedores, whose banners add colour to the crowd. There are in all forty banners of trade and friendly societies. Many processions on other days were larger and more imposing, but it was this Monday's demonstration which first thoroughly aroused the City to the fact that something unusual was going forward in the unknown country to the east of Aldgate pump.

Source D From *The Story of the Dockers' Strike* by H. Llewellyn Smith and Vaughan Nash, 1889.

Table 14 The growth in trade union membership (calculated to the nearest thousand), 1882–1914.

Year	Number of Members
1882	404,000
1883	467,000
1884	488,000
1885	500,000
1886	515,000
1887	561,000
1888	568,000
1889	687,000
1890	1,593,000
1891	1,094,000
1892	1,155,000
1893	1,559,000
1894	1,530,000
1895	1,504,000
1896	1,608,000
1897	1,731,000
1898	1,752,000
1899	1,911,000
1907	2,513,000
1910	2,565,000
1911	3,139,000
1912	3,416,000
1913	4,135,000
1914	4,145,000

ACTIVITY

1. Having read this extract, say how far it supports Engels's view that new unionism represented 'the revolt of the unskilled workers'?
2. Study the figures in Table 14. What do they tell you about the growth of the trade unions in the period 1882–1914? What is the connection between these figures and 'new unionism'?

The industrial unrest indicated the political awareness of the new unions. They did not totally dismiss the idea of self help but their main demand was that government and Parliament take action to remedy the grievances of the workers. This immediately raised the question of party affiliation. Many of the leaders were openly socialist; they despised collaboration with the Liberal Party, which had been the policy of the 'old' unions. What they wanted was the formation of a separate party to represent the interests of the workers. The debate which this aroused proved to be a decisive phase in the growth of British trade unionism.

JOHN ELLIOT BURNS (1858–1943)

Burns was a major working-class figure in the industrial relations and politics of the late Victorian and Edwardian periods. He was also no mean cricketer. As a young man he was attracted by socialist ideas and had joined H.M. Hyndman's Social Democratic Federation. He stood unsuccessfully as a parliamentary candidate in 1885. Although he was himself a member of the ASE, he co-operated with Ben Tillett of the dockers' General Labourers' Union in the task of organising unskilled workers on a union basis. Burns became an outstanding figure in the London labour scene of the 1880s. He was an organiser of the 'Bloody Sunday' confrontation with the authorities in 1887 that led to his arrest, trial and acquittal. He modified his socialist ideas and opposed the syndicalist (violently disruptive) tactics advocated by some trade unionists. He argued that the best path was constitutional and parliamentary. He was elected to the Commons in 1892 and became the first Labour Party member to hold office when he was appointed President of the Local Government Board in the Liberal administration of 1905–14. His failure to press for the reform of the Poor Law led to his being regarded as something of a reactionary. He opposed Britain's entry into the war in 1914 and retired from politics.

The closing lines of the book which Burns had encouraged Tom Mann and Ben Tillett to write, captured the essence of his appeal that the whole trade union movement accept the new unions.

-Profile-

1858 born into a poor family in London;

1878 joined the Amalgamated Society of Engineers (ASE);

1880s associated with Hyndman's Social Democratic Federation; worked with Ben Tillet's General Labourers Union;

1887 helped to organise Bloody Sunday demonstration;

1889 established the Battersea Labour League as a base for his organisation of the London dock strike – was tried but acquitted after being charged with public order offences;

1892 became an MP;

1905 served in the Liberal
–14 government as President of the Local Government Board;

1909 became disliked because of his opposition to Poor Law reforms;

1914 his unpopularity led to his being moved to the Board of Trade;
         declined to support Britain's entry into the war; he withdrew from politics;

1943 died.

> In Conclusion, we repeat that the real difference between the 'new' and the 'old' [unions] is, that those who belong to the latter, and delight in being distinct from the policy endorsed by the 'new', do so because they do not recognise, as we do, that it is the work of <u>the trade unionist to stamp out poverty from the land</u>. Clannishness in trade matters must be superseded by a cosmopolitan spirit, brotherhood must not only be talked of but practised. What we desire to see is a unification of all, a dropping of all bickerings, and an earnest devotion to duty taking the place of the old indifference. The cause we have at heart is too sacred to admit of time being spent quarrelling amongst ourselves, and whilst we make no pretence to the possession of special virtues, we are prepared to work unceasingly for the economic emancipation of the workers.

> ***Source E*** Adapted from *The 'New' Trade Unionism*, 1890, by Tom Mann and Ben Tillett.

c) The Move towards Political Representation

In 1868 the TUC appointed a Parliamentary Committee to organise trade union representation in the House of Commons. The Committee had some success; a number of working men were elected as MPs in the period down to the end of the century. However, with the exception of Keir Hardie, all these MPs, including John Burns, gravitated towards the Liberal Party. But after the Liberals had been seriously split by the Home Rule issue in 1886, the unions began to question the value of a continued alliance with a weakened party. The matter was made urgent by ominous developments for the unions on the industrial front. During the last decade of the century, the employers, worried by the rise of 'new' unionism, mounted a counter-attack. Employers' federations imposed wage-cuts and lock-outs and took on non-union workers, all this against a background of recession and rising unemployment. Equally disturbing for labour was the obvious bias of the law against the unions. A series of court decisions in this period undermined the right to picket and threatened the legal standing of the unions. These factors added considerable weight to the case for a genuinely separate and independent set of MPs to speak for the workers. This was the objective of the Independent Labour Party which was established in 1893.

What was needed to achieve solidarity on this issue was the conversion of the traditional 'old' unionists to the necessity of separate political representation. This came in 1899 when the TUC conference voted by a large majority in favour of the union movement forming its own parliamentary party. The key resolution read:

> That this Congress, having regard to its decisions in former years, and with a view to securing a better representation of the interests of labour in the House of Commons, hereby instructs the Parliamentary Committee to invite the co-operation of all the co-operative, socialistic, trade union, and other working organisations to jointly co-operate on lines mutually agreed upon, in convening a special congress of representatives from such of the above-named organisations as may be willing to take part to devise ways and means for securing the return of an increased number of labour members to the next Parliament.

ISSUE
Why was the Liberal Party unable to satisfy union expectations?

ACTIVITY
Having read this Resolution, suggest in what sense it marked a turning point in trade union development?

Source F *Resolution of the Amalgamated Society of Railway Servants* presented at the Trades Union Congress, 1899.

The new unions voted overwhelmingly for the Resolution, but it was the support of significant numbers of 'old' unionists that was critical in carrying it. This large measure of agreement between the 'old' and the 'new' forces in trade unionism meant that from 1899 on, the movement was committed to the idea of political representation.

What gave a strong push to the campaign was a landmark legal decision against the unions, the Taff Vale ruling, in 1901.

The employees of the Taff Vale Railway Company in South Wales went on strike in June 1900. Their aim was to improve their conditions and gain recognition as a union. The Associated Society of Railway Servants (ASRS) recognised the strike as official and gave the Taff Vale workers financial assistance. The Company attempted to break the strike by bringing in non-union labour and by taking the ASRS to court for illegal picketing. Although the strike was soon called off without the strikers winning any concessions, the Company continued its legal action against the union for damages and financial loss resulting from the stoppage. The first court hearing went in favour of the Company but the Court of Appeal reversed this decision in November 1900. In turn, the House of Lords, the highest legal authority, overruled the Court of Appeal and found for the Company. The Lords' decision, delivered in July 1901, came at the end of twelve months' legal wrangling. This time span meant that the issue excited the widest interest; both the unions and the employers knew that it was a test case in industrial relations. The key part of the Lords' decision read:

Source G Lord Macnaughten, ruling on the Taff Vale case, in the House of Lords, July 1901.

> Has the legislature authorised the creation of numerous bodies of men, capable of owning great wealth and of acting by agents, with absolutely no responsibility for the wrong they may do to other persons by the use of that wealth and the employment of those agents? In my opinion Parliament has done nothing of the kind. I can find nothing in the acts of 1871 and 1875 to warrant such a notion.

What Macnaughten had ruled was that previous Trade Union Acts had not given legal protection to the unions as corporate bodies; they were responsible in law for the actions of their individual members. This interpretation was reinforced by the awarding of substantial damages and costs against the ASRS. It was now clear that the unions' right to strike and to picket had been effectively destroyed by the Macnaughten ruling. Only an Act of Parliament could reverse this in the unions' favour. But Balfour's Conservative government was resolutely set against changing the law, and the Liberals were powerless in opposition. This made the argument for a new political party to plead the unions' cause irresistible to the leaders of organised labour. The structure for such a party already existed in the form of the Labour Representation Committee (LRC), set up in February 1900, as an alliance of unions and various socialist organisations, whose declared aim was to create a separate labour group in the Commons. By 1903, 127 unions had affiliated to the LRC, a

Figure 45 'Whips for Labour's back', a Labour poster from 1906 depicting the oppression suffered by the unions at the hands of the bosses in league with the judges.

notable feature of this being that many of these, such as the Textile Workers, could be classed as moderates, thus indicating that Taff Vale had had the effect of closing the ranks of the TUC and uniting the unions formerly divided on the matter of parliamentary representation. The Taff Vale decision had stifled the doubts regarding the wisdom of unions engaging in political as opposed to industrial action and had forged the historic link between the trade union movement and the Labour Party, as the LRC became in 1906.

ACTIVITY

Examine the written and visual material on the unions in sub-section 2c.

1. How justified do you think the unions were in claiming that Parliament and the legal system had an inbuilt bias against the rights of workers?

2. Read Macnaughten's ruling and then restate the verdict in your own words.

THE TRADE DISPUTES ACT, 1906

This Act reversed the Taff Vale decision, by providing protection for union funds against claims for damages arising from strikes. It also legalised picketing and sympathetic strikes, i.e. a strike by one union in support of another.

SYNDICALISM

A revolutionary philosophy, notably influential among French and Belgian miners, which called on workers to abandon moderate methods of trying to improve their conditions and turn instead to all-out disruption, aimed at smashing the industrial-capitalist system.

d) The Crisis in Industrial Relations, 1912–14

The years preceding the First World War were a particularly troubled time for the unions, this despite the legal gains they acquired from the Trade Disputes Act of 1906. By 1912 the cost of living was 14 per cent higher than in 1906 and unemployment had risen sharply during the same period. Despite the Liberal welfare measures, the gap between rich and poor was widening (see page 197). Furthermore the presence of Labour Party MPs in the Commons did not appear to have brought the redress of worker grievances any nearer. Faced with these failures, many trade unionists began to doubt whether the existing political and parliamentary system could ever be made to respond to the needs of the workers. Their doubts were increased by the Osborne Judgement in 1910. The belief that the legal and governmental systems were fundamentally hostile to their interests encouraged a number of unions to consider direct action. The increase in trade union membership around this period may be taken as a measure of the growing frustration of the industrial workers. Few British workers were drawn to **syndicalism**, but in the charged atmosphere of pre-war Britain direct action became increasingly attractive to the more combative unions.

In 1911 the miners, who had a reputation as one of the most militant unions, went on strike to demand the right to a minimum wage. The strike was strongest in South Wales where syndicalist ideas had made their greatest impact. Asquith's Government had good reason to be disturbed by the miners' call for sympathetic action from other industrial workers; in the summer of 1911, the three major unions – the dockers, the railwaymen and the miners – came out on strike. The government regarded the situation as being so serious that they became involved in the negotiations between employers and workers. This was significant as an example of the Liberals' willingness to abandon the traditional liberal principle of non-intervention by government in industrial relations. Lloyd George helped dissuade the railway workers from continuing their strike by offering a wage increase and the recognition by the employers of their union rights. The government also offered concessions to the miners in the form of local wage boards which were empowered to fix minimum wages in each region.

The strike was called off but matters were far from settled. In 1914 another major disruption threatened when the miners linked with the transport workers and railwaymen to form a 'triple alliance'. In the event the alliance, which was never a formal agreement, did not develop into a general strike, but it had frightened the government into urging the employers to consider granting further concessions to the unions. As with the Ulster question, so it was with the industrial relations conflict, that the coming of the war in 1914 brought a temporary suspension of the troubles (see page 139).

ACTIVITY

Using the information given in this section, suggest why an increase in trade union membership occurred.

> ### THE OSBORNE JUDGMENT, 1910
> The Judgment declared it illegal for a trade union to use its funds for political purposes, i.e. to support a political party or to pay candidates or MPs. The Liberal government reversed the decision in 1913 by an Act which allowed unions to subscribe to a political party provided individual members of the union had the right to 'contract out' of paying.

Summary of The Rise of Organised Labour

Year	Key events and issues	Chartism	Trade unions
1799	Combination Laws		unions outlawed
1824	repeal of Combination Laws		unions permitted but heavily restricted
1832	Great Reform Act		
1834	Tolpuddle Martyrs case Poor Law Amended		failure of GNCTU
1830s	working class disillusioned by Whig reforms		
1836		the LWMA formed	
1838		first Charter drafted	
1839	the Newport Rising	first Charter presented and rejected	
1842	the 'plug plot'	the second Charter presented and rejected	
1848		third Charter presented and rejected	
1850s			model unions grew in strength
1858		end of Chartism as an active movement	
1867	Second Reform Act		vote extended to some of the working class
1868			first meeting of TUC
1871	Trade Union Act		unions given legal recognition
1875	1875 Acts		peaceful picketing made legal – protection of unions against civil damages
1880s			'new' mass unions formed
1888	Match Girls' strike		
1889	strike for the 'dockers' tanner'		

Year	Key events and issues	Chartism	Trade unions
1890s	formation of employers federations to resist unions		
1893			ILP formed
1899			old unions and new unions unite to demand separate parliamentary representation
1900			LRC formed
1906	Trade Disputes Act reversed the Taff Vale decision of 1901		legalised picketing and sympathetic strikes
1910	the Osborne Judgement		made it illegal for unions to use funds to support parliamentary candidates
1911–12			series of disruptive strikes
1913	Trade Union Act reversed the Osborne Judgement		
1914			the 'triple alliance' threatened a general strike

▼ Working on The Rise of Organised Labour

You would master the material in this chapter effectively if you were to take a time-line and issues approach. With both the Chartist movement and the unions you need to see their development over time. Here is where the summary chart, the chronologies on pages 174, 181, and 183 and the various issues boxes come into their own. Select what you think are the most important dates and then put beside them the relevant issues with your own accompanying questions and answers. For example:

Chartism

date	issue	question	question
1842	the new move	what was it?	why 1842?
		|	|
		answer	answer
		|	|
		the view that new ideas and tactics were necessary because confrontation had been counter productive; a development of the moral force argument.	the failure of the two petitions by 1842 and the fierce reaction of the authorities persuaded a number of Chartists that peaceful agitation might be a more productive approach.

New unionism

date	issue	question	question
1889	the Dockers' Strike	why was it called 'the revolt of the unskilled workers'? answer it marked the first major demonstration of the mass labour unions.	why 1889? answer inspired by the earlier success of the gas workers in gaining the 8-hr-day; the climax to a series of strikes in which the new unions tested the employers.

If you compile a full list in this way you will have drawn out the essential points from the chapter and tested your own understanding of them. It may be, of course, that certain issues will not easily lend themselves to a time reference except in a very broad sense. This does not matter. It is the issue that is important; the date is simply the peg. An example might be the question of whether Chartism was a failure. Clearly the time span is quite wide here, so you would be entitled to select your points as you saw fit rather than feeling obliged to obey a chronological framework.

Answering extended writing and essay questions on The Rise of Organised Labour

You will be familiar now with the way we break down essay questions into their types. The following list shows the style of questions you are likely to encounter on the topic of organised labour.

Type of Issue	Examples of typical questions
1 causes/reasons/motives	Why did the 'model' unions eventually prove incapable of representing the demands of organised labour?
2 course of events	Trace the development of the trade union movement between 1799 and 1914.
3 consequences/results/ effects	What impact did the 'new move' have on the development of Chartism?
4 success/failure	'A failure in its own time, but a success in the long term.' Consider this verdict on the Chartist movement.

Type of Issue	Examples of typical questions
5 significance/importance	What impact did the Taff Vale decision (1901) have on union attitudes towards parliamentary representation?
6 comparison	What were the essential differences between the physical-force and the moral-force forms of Chartism?
7 right/wrong (moral/ ethical judgments, assessing validity)	'The successful formation of the Labour Party in 1906 proved that the unions had been right to pursue parliamentary rather than revolutionary means to gain their objectives'. Discuss.

On this occasion, let us consider number 2, the type of question that asks you to examine a movement over a long period of time. Syllabuses and examinations have begun to lay stress on the need for students to be able to survey trends and developments that take place across a whole century. Do not be deterred by this. Clearly if you are required to consider a long period of time the amount of detail you will be expected to know and include will be less than in a question dealing with a shorter time span and asking for a more specialised analysis. If you have made adequate and accurate notes on the chapter you will be well prepared to attempt this question. Check back over the various time lines and issue boxes in this chapter which relate to the trade unions. You will also find the summary chart and the suggestions in 'Working on' the chapter very helpful. Assemble a list of the key dates and stages. Your task is to select the important developments. This is not difficult but you have to be careful not to try to include everything. The following suggestions should help you on your way.

In any question that covers a wide time range a chronological approach, putting developments in the order they occurred, is appropriate. Since you are given the date 1799 you are clearly expected to begin with the Combination Acts. State briefly what they were and how they limited the rights of the unions. This leads logically to their repeal in 1824 which legalised the unions and enabled them to make some progress in organisation. Mention of Chartism would be appropriate since its eventual failure by the late 1840s encouraged workers to turn to the unions to represent them. This point leads logically to a description of the model unions which began to develop in the 1850s. A sentence or two on the extension of the vote to the working class in 1867 and the formation of the TUC a year later would then be appropriate. The next key stage was the development of the 'new' unions which was a product of increasing industrialisation and the growth of a mass work force. The industrial troubles of the 1880s and 90s revealed both the gains made by the new unions and the considerable barriers that still stood in their way.

To surmount these problems union thoughts turned increasingly to parliamentary representation. This took trade unionism into the area of politics with the new and old unions coming together to demand the creation of a separate party to speak for the workers. The formation of the LRC in 1900, and subsequently the Labour Party, appeared to show that this objective had been achieved. This, together with their growing membership and the removal of many of the previous legal restrictions on them, made the unions more aggressive in the period of the Liberal government after 1906. One result was the fierce industrial conflicts that occurred in the years before 1914. Thus by the end of the period in question the unions had become a powerful force on the industrial front, well organised and politically represented. Yet in their own judgment they had yet to achieve full recognition of their claims and rights.

The paragraphs above suggest the lines you might follow and the key points you might select. As always, of course, you are free to make your own judgment as to what you regard as the important stages, but, whatever you select, they must conform to the requirement in the question to trace developments across time. You cannot simply set down a limited selection of events and hope they will suffice.

Answering source-based questions on The Rise of Organised Labour

Read back over the sections on Chartism, pages 173–179, and then study the passages which are on the 'New Move'. Having done that, read the sources below and answer the questions that follow them. After each question a suggested line of response is given. You would gain most if you attempted your own answers before comparing them with the given responses.

> The middle-class shop keepers promised that if we assisted them to get the Reform Bill they would get us the vote; they have broken their pledge. What is our remedy against this evil – Exclusive dealing. We have made them and we can unmake them. Our pennies make their pounds. If we cease to deal with them they will become poor, and lose their votes. They will then feel the evils they now inflict upon us and cry out for universal suffrage. Thus, while ceasing to spend our money in the shops of our enemies, we have destroyed their power.

Source H From Address on the System of Exclusive Dealing by Robert Lowery, 1839.

> The reflecting portion of our brethren are beginning to perceive the great necessity for this intellectual and moral preparation;- not as set forth by those "educationists" who seek to spread their own notions, or those who seek to train up the youthful to be submissive admirers of "things as they are"; but for establishing such a system as shall make our country intellectually great, politically free, and socially happy.
>
> There is evil to be apprehended from placing the education of our children in the hands of any government. It becomes one of the most important duties of the working and middle classes to establish a just and liberal system of education, lest the power of educating their own children be taken from them by the arbitrary act of a corrupt and exclusive government.

Source I From *Chartism* by William Lovett and John Collins, 1840.

> I am delighted with your reference to the progress of Chartist Christianity against the long-faced hypocritical pharisees whose religion consists in preaching slavery to the poor under the name of humility, and dutiful submission to the "powers that be", which are "ordained by God", although the sleek vagabonds well know that without the devil such "powers" would never have been heard of. By all means get read of these "black slugs'; by all means protect the consciences and the cabbages of the poor from the "black slugs".

Source J From a letter to the *Northern Star*, 2 January 1841.

▼ QUESTIONS ON SOURCES

1. Explain the following terms as they appear in the extracts:
   (a) 'exclusive dealing' (Source H, line 3) **[2 marks]**
   (b) 'black slugs' (Source J, line 7) **[2 marks]**
2. Using your own knowledge and drawing on the Sources describe the main features of 'New Move' Chartism. **[7 marks]**

Suggested lines of response

1. **(a)** 'exclusive dealing' is a system by which the Chartists would boycott the middle-class shopkeepers in retaliation for their failure to keep their promise to support the extension of the vote to the workers.

     (b) 'black slugs' is an unflattering reference to clergymen who are responsible for urging the poor to remain submissive.

2. All the Sources stress, either directly or by implication, the need to alter the social and political system by changing it at its roots, rather than by simply confronting it. In their various ways the sources urge a new approach to the principles that underlie the existing political and social system. Chartist self-improvement, by means of education and temperance, is seen as the key to real advancement. Draw on your own knowledge here to point out how the Chartist failures of 1839 had led to a reappraisal of the movement's strategy, which these sources illustrate. Lovett and other leaders began to campaign for the education of the workers as a path to their emancipation.

Further Reading

Books in the 'Access to History' series

Chartism by Harry Browne is an excellent study of the material in the earlier sections of this chapter. *Labour and Reform: Working-Class Movements 1815–1914* by Clive Behagg deals with Chartism (Chapter 3) and the unions and the Labour Party (Chapters 4 and 5). Chapter 4 in *The Changing Role of Women 1815–1914* by Paula Bartley has some very interesting things to say about women in the workforce and the unions.

General

The Making of the English Working Class by E.P. Thompson (Pelican, 1968) is a provocative and illuminating analysis that all students should read. *Chartists and Chartism* by Joe Finn, 1992, and *The Age of Reform* by Vyvyen Brendon, 1994 (both books in the Hodder & Stoughton 'History at Source' series), provide a very helpful introduction to Chartism. Also highly recommended on this theme are *Chartism* by Edward Royle (Longman, 1996), *Early Victorian Britain*, by J.F.C. Harrison (Fontana, 1974) and *The Chartists* by Dorothy Thompson (Temple Smith, 1984). Asa Briggs deals with Chartism in *Chartist Studies* (Macmillan, 1959). Important up-to-date studies covering the whole area are *The People and the British Economy 1830–1914* by Roderick Floud (OUP, 1998), *Britain's Century a Political and Social History 1815–1914* by W.D. Rubinstein (Arnold, 1998), and *British History 1815–1906* by Norman McCord (OUP, 1991). A very helpful short study is *The Rise of British Trade Unions 1825–1914* by Harry Browne (Longman, 1979). *The Rise of the Labour Party 1880–1945* by Paul Adelman (Longman, 1996) covers the later part of the period very effectively. *The Years of Expansion, Britain 1815–1914* edited by Michael Scott-Baumann (Hodder & Stoughton, 1995) provides coverage of both Chartism and the unions. There are helpful sections on these themes in *Britain 1815–1914* edited by Derrick Murphy (Collins, 1998). Recommended articles are: 'The Origins and Nature of Chartism' by Edward Royle in *History Review*, 1992, 'Taking Chartism Seriously' by Clive Behagg in *Modern History Review*, April 1994, and 'The Dock Strike of 1889' by Joyce Howson in *Modern History Review*, 1995.

CHAPTER 8

POLITICS AND PARTIES 3, 1886–1914

POINTS TO CONSIDER

In Chapters 2 and 3 it was suggested that political developments are best understood as reactions of the parties to the major economic and social problems of the time. This same theme is continued in the present chapter. What you will be studying are the outstanding domestic issues of the late Victorian and Edwardian periods and the way the parties attempted to grapple with them. The years covered by this chapter break down into two distinct sections: 1886–1905 which saw a period of Conservative supremacy, and 1905–14 when the Liberals held office. Although this chapter concentrates on home affairs it is necessary to remember that the Ulster question (studied in Chapter 5, pages 135–139) loomed very large on the political scene and that foreign and imperial affairs (studied in Chapter 9) were also of pressing importance.

GOVERNMENTS OF THE PERIOD

1886 Conservatives under Lord
–92 Salisbury;
1892 Liberals under Gladstone
–95 (Lord Rosebery 1894–5);
1895 Conservatives under
–1902 Salisbury;
1902 Conservatives under
–05 Arthur Balfour.

ISSUE
Why was the Liberal Party out of office for so long after 1886?

1 Conservative Ascendancy, 1886–1905

An important factor explaining why the Conservatives held power for so much of this period is that the main opposition party, the Liberals, faced profound difficulties. It is worth beginning by considering what these were.

a) The Liberals in Opposition

Some historians have described the Liberal Party after 1886 as suffering from a crisis of identity. To understand what is meant by this we have to appreciate the great social problem that overshadowed the age – poverty. As described in Chapter 1, the late nineteenth and early twentieth centuries witnessed an extraordinary increase in the size and the concentration of the British population. In the forty years after 1871, the number of people living in the major industrial areas virtually doubled. The social ills which had been present throughout the nineteenth century – overcrowding, poor sanitation, malnutrition and disease – were greatly intensified. The Poor Law and the other welfare schemes that existed were simply incapable of dealing with the widespread destitution that followed the unplanned and, therefore, uncontrolled urban growth. The squalor and deprivation that shaped the lives of the mass of people who lived in the cities were graphically revealed in a series of published reports, such as the pioneering studies produced by Charles Booth and Seebohm Rowntree.

> Widow. Four rooms. One baby. Semi-lunatic family. Receives Poor Relief. Son, who is wage earner, is weak bodily and mentally. Ditto the daughter. Nice house, but dirty. 4s. per week is received for an illegitimate child being brought up here. This house shares one closet with another house, and one water tap with three other houses.
> We are faced by the startling probability that from 25 to 30 per cent of the town population of the United Kingdom are living in poverty. In this land of abounding wealth, during a time of perhaps unexampled prosperity, probably more than one fourth of the population are living in poverty.

Source A From *Poverty: A Study of Town Life*, by Seebohm Rowntree, 1901.

The grim details of the lives of the urban poor that were now being systematically researched presented a picture of social deprivation that politicians could not ignore. It was a particular problem for the Liberals. Under Gladstone, who continued to dominate his party until his retirement in 1894, Liberalism had been preoccupied with the great moral issues of the day, such as the Irish and the Eastern Questions. Consumed by these crusades, Gladstone had neglected to give his full attention to British social problems. This had frustrated the radical Liberals who argued that the party should be dealing with the demanding domestic problems of the time. They regarded Gladstone's programme of 'peace, retrenchment and reform', as being inadequate to deal with the deprivation and poverty that blighted so much of industrial Britain. The term 'new Liberalism' began to be used to define the attitude of the radicals and progressives who wanted their party to embrace the major social questions of the time.

The New Liberals argued that the state must play the leading role in the improvement of social conditions, and that if it failed to do so the result would be the growth of socialism and class conflict. An important voice in the formulation of such thinking was J.A. Hobson. In the following passage he describes the essential change of attitude that inspired New Liberalism. He urged that the Liberal Party recognise and respond to the demands of 'the sovereignty of social welfare'.

Q What affect did the poverty issue have on politics?

Q What was New Liberalism?

Liberalism is now formally committed to a task which certainly involves a new conception of the State in its relation to the individual life and to private enterprise. From the standpoint which best presents its continuity with earlier Liberalism, it appears as a fuller appreciation and realisation of individual liberty contained in the provision of equal opportunities for self-development. But to this individual stand-point must be joined a just apprehension of the social, *viz.*, the insistence that these claims or rights of self-development must be adjusted to the sovereignty of social welfare.

Source B From *The Crisis of Liberalism* by J.A. Hobson, 1909.

SOCIALISM

Socialism has shades of meaning. It can refer to Communism, the Marxist movement that advocated revolutionary class conflict. That is the meaning it had for politicians such as Chamberlain and Lloyd George. But socialism, usually spelt with a small 's' can also refer to the radical but non-revolutionary movement which held that the power of the state should be used to correct the economic injustices and inequalities existing in society. This form of socialism was a strong influence in the early Labour Party.

Q

Why was Chamberlain important in the politics of the day?

The divisions among the Liberals were highlighted by the career of Joseph Chamberlain, the party's outstanding radical. Despairing of the apparent inability of a party led by Gladstone ever being able to adapt itself to the real needs of the nation, Chamberlain took the dramatic step in the late 1880s of abandoning the Liberals and joining the Unionists. His decision, like that of most of the Liberals who left the party after 1886, was in part a reaction against Gladstone's attempt to grant Home Rule to Ireland in 1886 (see page 134). But Chamberlain also wanted the freedom to advance his own plans for dealing with the nation's social problems. He believed that if the conditions in the urban areas were not improved there was a real danger that the masses would turn to revolutionary **socialism** and plunge Britain into class warfare. In 1885 he had challenged Gladstone's leadership by presenting his own radical 'Unauthorised Programme' of social reform.

Chamberlain's Unauthorised Programme proposed:

▼ tax on property
▼ smallholdings to be distributed to provide employment
▼ public housing to be provided
▼ free education
▼ reform of the Lords
▼ votes for all adult males
▼ payment of MPs.

Chamberlain explained the purpose behind his programme:

Politics is the art of human happiness, and the business of a statesman and of politicians is to find out how they can raise the general condition of the people. Yet surely there is some reason to doubt the perfection of our system when in this, the richest country in the world, one in thirty of the population at every moment are unable to obtain the means of subsistence without recourse to the parish [the Poor Law system of relief], and one in ten at the same time are on the verge of starvation.

Source C From a letter by Joseph Chamberlain, March 1886.

Chamberlain was well aware that his schemes would require large-scale funding but rejected the idea that this could be raised only by heavy taxation of the moneyed classes. His answer to the problem of how to relieve the poor without resorting to **redistributive taxation** was imperial federation (see page 205). Once Chamberlain had broken with the Liberals in the late 1880s and joined the Conservatives, he set himself the task of persuading his new party to adopt his scheme of tariff reform as their official economic policy.

ACTIVITY

Taxation makes an ideal topic for group discussion. Divide into two main sides, take the direct proposition that 'Redistributive taxation was an unacceptable encroachment upon the rights of the individual' and argue the case for and against. Try to view the question as it would have been seen in the late nineteenth century. This means that you should pay particular attention to the extent of poverty at that time, the powers at the command of government, and the prevailing political ideas about the role of the state. The views of Chamberlain and Hobson would be highly relevant in such a debate.

REDISTRIBUTIVE TAXATION

The notion of taking money from one group in society and transferring it to another. The obvious example is the taxing of the rich in order to provide revenue for the relief of the poor. The local poor rate (see page 84) is an illustration of this. The principle of redistributive income tax became highly controversial in the late Victorian and Edwardian periods. Its proponents said that it was an essential means of creating social justice; its opponents regarded it as a form of state robbery against which the victim had no protection.

The disputes within the Liberal Party had two important consequences. They allowed the Conservatives to dominate for twenty years after 1886 and they encouraged the development of a third force in British politics – the Labour Party.

b) The Labour Party

It had been the hope of many Liberals that the increasing number of working men who received the franchise as a result of the 1867 and 1884 parliamentary reform acts would regard the Liberal Party as able to speak for them. However, the longer the Liberals remained uncertain about whether they should become a party committed to social reform, the stronger became the argument that the working classes needed an entirely separate political party to represent their interests. The outcome was the amalgamation in 1900 of a variety of radical groups into the Labour Representation Committee, which became the Labour Party of 1906 (see page 186).

Main groups that formed the Labour Party:
▼ trade unions, who wanted a separate political party to represent them
▼ Fabians (intellectuals such as George Bernard Shaw) who wanted to spread socialism not by revolution but by propaganda and education

Q Why did a third main political party develop at the end of the century?

Q How effective was the Labour Party before 1914?

▼ the Social Democratic Federation (SDF), a Marxist group led by H.M. Hyndman, who wanted class war against the bourgeois ruling classes.

In its early days the Labour Party won too few parliamentary seats to be more than a pressure group. It saw its best means of exerting an influence to lie in co-operating with the Liberals. It was this understanding that produced the Lib–Lab pact, an agreement made in 1903 between Ramsay MacDonald and Herbert Gladstone, the respective chief whips of the Labour and Liberal parties, that their candidates would not compete against each other in parliamentary elections. Nevertheless, the implications were clear. The Liberals now had a radical rival; the presence after 1900 of a parliamentary Labour Party, although with only a small number of MPs initially, was further evidence that social issues were beginning to shape the political agenda. Some historians, notably Peter Clarke, suggest that this marks the beginning of 'class' politics in Britain; the suggestion being that the awareness of the working class of its own potential became the most significant factor in electoral politics.

ACTIVITY

Study the cartoon. How far does your reading in this section support the cartoonist's notion that Labour was a threat to the Liberals?

Figure 46 'Forced fellowship', a cartoon of 1909 showing the uneasy relations between the Liberals and Labour. The caption reads: Suspicious Looking Party: 'Any objection to my company guv'nor? I'm agoin' your way' – (aside) 'and further.'

c) The Conservatives in Office, 1886–92, and 1895–1905

ISSUES
Why were the Conservatives in office for so long?
Was it a period of legislative paralysis?

Between 1886 and 1905 the Conservatives held office for all but three years. In studying the ministries of Lord Salisbury, historians have traditionally concentrated on his role in foreign affairs. Yet though foreign and Irish questions took prominence, it would be wrong to overlook his domestic policies. Scholars now reject the notion that the Conservatives under Salisbury produced nothing significant on the social and economic front. They point to the following measures as clear evidence that the reforming policies begun under Disraeli were continued under Salisbury.

1886–92:
▼ provision made to improve working-class housing
▼ steps taken to prevent cruelty against children
▼ measures against the defrauding of customers in shops
▼ landlords rather than tenants to be responsible for paying tithes
▼ horticultural allotments made available to the public
▼ Local Government Act of 1888 established a new system of elected county councils
▼ Factory Act of 1891 improved safety condition in the mines
▼ Education Act of 1891 established free elementary education in both church and state schools
▼ Smallholdings Act of 1892 attempted to deal with the depression in farming.

1895–1902:
▼ measures to improve the conditions of shop assistants and mill workers
▼ further measures to improve housing for the poorer classes
▼ factory acts tightening safety regulations
▼ Workmen's Compensation Act of 1897 provided payments for injuries sustained at the work place
▼ a proposal to establish old age pensions was introduced but had to be abandoned because of the costs of the Anglo-Boer war.

These were obviously important measures and they make it curious that Salisbury's governments should have gained a reputation for 'legislative paralysis', as one recent study put it. The explanation is threefold: one – Salisbury's pre-eminence as an international states-man overshadowed his performance on the domestic front; two – the Irish and imperial questions dominated the parliamentary scene and distracted attention from Conservative social reforms; three – Salis-bury did not have the same 'high profile' as Disraeli and Gladstone, who had preceded him as party leaders and prime ministers.

Why have Salisbury's domestic achievements been overlooked?

ROBERT GASCOYNE-CECIL, 3rd MARQUESS OF SALISBURY, 1830–1903

-Profile-

Salisbury has been described as a natural conservative. From his youngest days he suffered from deep bouts of depression. This, plus his deep religious convictions which included the belief that human beings were flawed by original sin, tended to make him a pessimist. He considered that all change was invariably for the worse. It has been said that under him Conservatism became 'an organised rearguard action' which aimed to prevent the growing democracy of the times from becoming too disruptive. As was noted on page 59, he developed a marked distaste for Disraeli whom he regarded as an unprincipled adventurer and social upstart. Yet he came to accept the wisdom of Disraeli's belief that it was possible to win over the enfranchised working classes to the Conservative side by a policy of measured social reform. That is why Salisbury put great stress on party organisation. It was under him that the Conservative party machine with its emphasis on recruitment of supporters in the constituencies, began to take its modern shape. His success in this was shown in the Conservative victories in the general elections of 1886, 1895 and 1900. It has to be said that this period of Conservative ascendancy probably owed as much to Liberal weakness as to Conservative strength, but it would be wrong to underplay the importance of Salisbury's shrewd and responsible leadership. His particular understanding of the role of the Conservative Party was expressed in a letter he wrote to Randolph Churchill, one of his sternest critics within the Party.

> The Tory Party is composed of varying elements, and there is merely trouble and vexation of spirit in trying to make them work together. I think the 'classes and dependents of class' are the strongest ingredients in our composition, but we have so to conduct our legislation that we shall give some satisfaction to both classes and masses. This is specially difficult with the classes – because all legislation is rather unwelcome to them, as tending to disturb a state of things with which they are satisfied. Our Bills must be tentative and cautious, not sweeping and dramatic.

Source D From a letter of Salisbury's to Lord Randolph Churchill, 1886.

1830 born into one of the great aristocratic English ruling families;

1850 left Oxford with only a fourth class degree;

1850 –65 not being the family heir, he had to earn his own living as a journalist;

1865 death of an elder brother meant he inherited the family title and estates;

1866 took a minor post in the Derby–Disraeli government;

1867 resigned from the government over the Second Reform Act;

1874 joined Disraeli's government;

1878 attended the Berlin Conference as Disraeli's Foreign Secretary;

1885 became Conservative Party leader and remained so until 1902;

1885 –86 Prime Minister for the first time;

1886 –92 his second ministry;

1895 –1902 his third ministry;

1903 died.

d) Balfour's Government 1902–5

Salisbury was followed as Conservative Prime Minister by his nephew, Arthur Balfour. Historians are now beginning to suggest that both Balfour and his uncle deserve a higher reputation than they have customarily received. Jane Ridley, a modern scholar, remarked that Balfour's record of legislation during his brief three year government 'was equalled only by Gladstone's government of 1868–74; and it dealt with similar areas: education, army, licensing and Ireland.' What had diminished Balfour's reputation was that his party experienced a crushing electoral defeat at the hands of the Liberals in 1906. That the Conservatives after twenty years of political dominance should have lost so heavily eclipsed the achievements that had gone before. If we look at the reasons for the Liberal landslide we will gain further understanding of the great issues in British politics in the late Victorian and Edwardian era.

Table 15 The General Election results for 1900 and 1906 (seats won), which indicate the sharp decline in Conservative fortunes.

	1900	1906
Conservatives	402	157
Liberals	184	400
Labour (LRC in 1900)	2	30
Irish Nationalists	82	83

There is an interesting political saying: oppositions do not win elections, governments lose them. This maxim can certainly be applied to the Liberal victory of 1906, which was largely due to the mistakes of the Conservatives. Balfour inherited a number of growing problems which caused his government to become increasingly unpopular.

Q Why did the Conservatives suffer such a heavy defeat in 1906?

i) The Anglo-Boer War, 1899–1902

By the time he took over, the Conservative government's clumsy handling of the Boer War had proved a major embarrassment and caused it to be strongly criticised on financial and humanitarian grounds. See page 242 for the details of this.

ii) 'Chinese slavery'

Balfour's government was accused of having permitted large numbers of Chinese labourers, referred to as 'coolies' or slaves to be brought from Asia to work in appalling conditions for pitiful wages in the gold and diamond mines of southern Africa.

iii) Balfour's Education Act, 1902

As was pointed out on page 102, this measure was an important step forward, but since it abolished the school boards which had been establishment under the 1870 Education Act and transferred responsibility for educational provision to county and county borough councils, it created bitter resentment among the Nonconformists who complained that the rates would now be used to subsidise Anglican schools.

iv) Licensing Act, 1904

The Nonconformists also expressed moral outrage at the Government's willingness to provide substantial compensation to the brewers and the landlords who lost their licences under the new regulations governing the liquor industry.

v) Wyndham's Land Act, 1902

This made available £100 million in the form of loans to tenants in Ireland which they could use to buy out their landlords. The Act may be regarded as having ended the land problem in Ireland. However, it received only grudging thanks from the Irish nationalists who regarded it as belated recognition of their long-withheld rights, while the Irish Unionists dismissed the measure as a craven giving in to nationalist pressure (see page 136).

vi) The Taff Vale Judgment, 1901

The Conservatives did not come off well out of the controversy surrounding this legal decision against the railway union. When Balfour's government declared that it would take no steps to reverse this ruling against the trade unions it reinforced the conviction among the workers that Conservatism was fundamentally opposed to their interests (see page 186).

vii) Tariff Reform

Damaging as these problems were, it was the question of tariff reform (see pages 205 and 206) that most seriously weakened the Conservatives. In a misjudged attempt to steal a march on the Liberals on economic matters, Balfour's government adopted Joseph Chamberlain's imperial preference policies as its official programme in 1903. But few Conservatives were genuinely happy with tariff reform. They accepted it because it seemed to offer a means of raising revenue without resorting to taxation.

EDWARDIAN
Strictly speaking, the adjective Edwardian refers to the reign of Edward VII (1901–10) but it is accepted practice among historians to extend the term to include the early years of the reign of George V between his accession in 1910 and the outbreak of the First World War in 1914.

Figure 47 'History reverses itself:
Papa Joseph taking Master Arthur
a Protection walk', a *Punch* cartoon
of 1903.

ACTIVITY

As the inset shows, the cartoon is a deliberate play on the one of
sixty years earlier (see page 48). Explain the point that both
cartoonists were making. How accurate would you judge the cartoon
of 1903 to be in depiction of the conversion of the Conservatives to
tariff reform?

Tariff Reform (also known as imperial preference)

The policy, most closely associated with Joseph Chamberlain, of
protecting home produced food and manufactured goods by
imposing duties on imports from abroad with the major exception of the British dominions and colonies. Goods from these
countries would receive preferential treatment. The idea behind
this was to develop the British Empire as a worldwide protectionist trading union. The modern parallel is the European Union
which seeks to create a free-trade system between its own
members but which follows a firmly protectionist policy towards
non-member nations.

The lack of conviction with which the Conservatives presented their economic argument over tariff reform was eagerly exploited by the Liberals. They were able to project themselves as the defenders of cheap food for the people against the dear-food tariff reformers. In a clever poster campaign the Liberals contrasted the 'big loaf' of free trade, standing for plentiful and low-priced food, against the 'little loaf' of tariff reform, representing shortages and high prices. In the fierce 'free trade versus protection' debate that followed, the electorate judged that the protectionists had lost the argument. Apart from Joseph Chamberlain himself, there were few advocates of imperial preference who were able to put over a convincing case. Sceptical observers said it was clear that the Conservatives did not understand, let alone believe in, the tariff reform policy with which Chamberlain had saddled them. The result of all this was a sweeping victory for the Liberals in the 1906 election. Henry Campbell-Bannerman, who had already become Prime Minister of a minority Liberal government two months earlier, following Balfour's resignation, now headed a Liberal ministry with a majority of 243 over the Conservatives.

> ## ACTIVITY
>
> Study the posters in the light of what you have read in this section. How effectively do they present the tariff reform and free trade arguments?

DON'T WORRY YOURSELF
Over the puzzle whether
Mr. Balfour is a Chamberlainite
or
Mr. Chamberlain a Balfourite;

It's enough for you that they are
both Linked Together
AGAINST FREE TRADE.

Don't forget that whether the Tory candidate
calls himself a Balfourite or a Chamberlainite

THE ONLY WAY
to support Free Trade and no Protective Taxes
on Food is to

VOTE LIBERAL.

FREE TRADE CARTOON
Drawn for a Liberal election leaflet by F. C. Gould. 1905

Figure 48a Liberal poster attacking tariff reform.

Figure 48b A Conservative poster suggesting the harmful effects of free trade on the British working classes.

2 The Liberals, 1905–14

The years between the landslide election victory of the Liberals in 1906 and Britain's entry into the European war in 1914 ranks as one of the outstanding reforming periods in British history.

a) The Liberal Reforms

Major reforms

Social and Economic:

▼ Trade Disputes Act, 1906, reversed the Taff Vale Judgment, thus protecting union funds from claims for damages arising from strikes
▼ education measures, 1906, introduced school meals and medical examinations
▼ prison reforms of 1907 and 1912 introduced the probation service, ended imprisonment for debt, created special provisions for young offenders
▼ old age pensions, 1908
▼ national insurance, 1911

▼ Trade Boards Act, 1909, laid down minimum wages in the notorious 'sweated' industries, such as the clothing trade

▼ labour exchanges set up in 1909

▼ Development Commission set up to organise the funding of state welfare, 1909

▼ Shops Act, 1911, established the legal right of shop workers to a weekly half-day holiday

▼ Trade Union Act, 1913, legalised union funds being used for political purposes.

Constitutional:

▼ payment of MPs (£400 p.a.) introduced, 1911. This allowed people without a private income to consider standing for Parliament

▼ Parliament Act, 1911, removed the power of the House of Lords to veto Bills passed by the House of Commons

▼ Home Rule Act for Ireland, 1912

▼ The Welsh Church disestablished, 1914.

Were the reforms the implementation of New Liberalism?

New Liberalism, with its belief in the responsibility of the State to improve social conditions, seemed to have come into its own with the crushing Liberal election victory in 1906. It was Henry Campbell Bannerman, Prime Minister from 1905 to 1908, who set the Liberals on the path to reform by claiming that the 1906 election had given the party a mandate to pursue radical policies.

The pace of reform quickened still more in 1908 when Campbell Bannerman retired and was replaced by Herbert Asquith, who was to remain Prime Minister for the next eight years. What proved to be one of the new leader's most significant moves was the appointment of the radical David Lloyd George as Chancellor of the Exchequer. Lloyd George, who had already distinguished himself as President of the Board of Trade, brought a dynamic thrust to the government's programme. He and Winston Churchill, who took over at the Board of Trade, were largely responsible for the reputation that the pre-1914 Liberal government gained as a great reforming ministry. Two particular measures illustrate the character of the Liberals' approach to social welfare – old age pensions and the 'People's Budget'.

OLD AGE PENSIONS, 1908

The first pensions granted 5s (25p) a week to people over 70 years old with incomes of less than £31 10s (£31.50) a year.

The idea of pensions was not new. They had been considered by all the parties during the previous twenty years. But what made their introduction so dramatic was not the principle behind them but the method of paying for them. To meet the cost of the old age pensions Lloyd George planned to raise revenue by increasing taxation of the propertied classes. This was the purpose of his 1909 budget, which was to become known as 'the People's Budget'.

Main Terms of the 1909 Budget

▼ standard rate of income tax to be raised to 1s 3d (approx 7p) in the pound on incomes up to £3,000 p.a.

▼ a new 'super tax' of 5d (approx 2½p) in the pound on incomes over £3,000 p.a.

▼ death duties to be paid on estates valued at over £5,000

▼ a levy of 20 per cent on the unearned increase in property values when land changed hands.

It was the proposal to impose death duties and to tax increases in land values that aroused the bitter opposition of the landed interests. What gave edge to the fierce struggle that ensued between the parties was the free trade versus protection argument which was still the dominating economic issue of the day. To maintain themselves as a free-trade party it was essential for the Liberals that they paid for their welfare programme without resorting to trade tariffs. For their part, the Conservatives realised that they would lose the tariff reform argument if the Liberal government were to succeed in raising the necessary revenue through taxation. The Conservatives attacked the budget on the grounds that the unprecedentedly heavy taxation of land owners was a deliberate act of class war by Lloyd George. He retaliated by claiming that it was indeed a war budget but not of the kind described by the Conservatives:

Why did the 1909 Budget cause fierce controversy?

> This is a War Budget. It is for raising money to wage implacable warfare against poverty and squalidness. I cannot help hoping and believing that before this generation has passed away we shall have advanced a great step towards that good time when poverty and wretchedness and human degradation which always follow in its camp will be as remote to the people of this country as the wolves which once infested the forests.

Source E From a speech by Lloyd George in the House of Commons, 1909.

This was brilliant rhetoric but it hid the fact that only a portion of the proposed revenue from the budget was earmarked for pensions. The greater part of the £16 million that Lloyd George was hoping to raise was intended to pay for the government's broad reform programme and to meet the costs of the new warships that were being built for the navy.

The second great pillar of the Liberals' welfare programme was the introduction of a system of National Insurance. The measure met strong resistance. Its compulsory character was particularly disturbing to the five and half million people, many of them working class, who already paid privately into schemes run by the insurance companies and the trade unions. The workers were not easily persuaded

Figure 49 National Insurance – 'The Dawn of Hope', a Liberal Party poster, 1911. Lloyd George in his best bedside manner shows the sick patient that National Insurance will protect him.

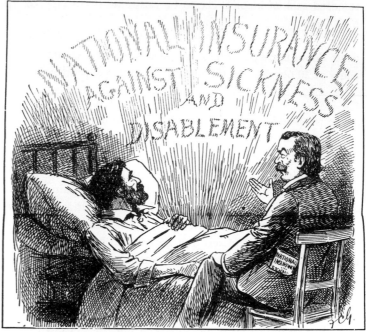

THE DAWN OF HOPE.

Mr. LLOYD GEORGE'S National Health Insurance Bill provides for the insurance of the Worker in case of Sickness.

Support the Liberal Government
in their policy of
SOCIAL REFORM.

Main Terms of the National Insurance Act, 1911

▼ cover provided against sickness and unemployment for workers aged between 16 and 70

▼ it did not apply to all industries, but was targeted at those where unemployment was consistently high

▼ the scheme to be funded by compulsory weekly contributions from the employer – 4d, the employee – 3d, and the state – 2d

▼ contributions to be deducted at source and to be paid by buying stamps which were then affixed to a card.

---

that they were going to gain more from an imposed State plan than from their own private insurance. The popular press attacked the compulsory contributions as theft from the workers' pay packets. Lloyd George responded by claiming that the workers were 'getting 9d for 4d'. As the originator of the scheme, Lloyd George showed remarkable skill in meeting the objections to it. He quietened the protests from the insurance companies, who feared competition from the State scheme, by making them an integral part of the operation of the new plans. He was also able to overcome the complaints of the Labour Party, who had wanted national insurance to be paid for by higher taxes on the wealthy. Lloyd George in effect bought off the Labour Party by promising to introduce payment for MPs, a commitment which he honoured in 1911.

The resistance of the workers and the Labour Party to measures which were supposedly in their interests is at first sight surprising. It shows that attitudes to welfare reform in the Edwardian period were often complex. It is notable that Churchill's Trade Boards Act of 1909, which aimed at providing minimum wages in the 'sweated' industries where unscrupulous employers exploited cheap labour, was also initially opposed by the unions. The reason was that they feared that the effect of a minimum wage would be job cuts by the employers. The minimum wage was also seen as interfering with the customary right of unions to negotiate differentials, that is, separate rates of pay for different levels of skill.

The fact was that many working-class people had a well-founded distrust of State intervention which they saw as patronising and disruptive. Their practical experience of officialdom in such developments as the workhouse, compulsory education, slum clearance and vaccination had seldom been a happy one. Too often they felt they were being pushed around by State-employed snoopers. Workers needed a lot of convincing that State welfare was not simply a means of keeping them in their place and making them conform. R.H. Tawney, one of the outstanding social historians of his day and a strong Labour Party supporter, explained why the intended beneficiaries of welfare reform were initially so wary:

> The middle and upper class view in social reform is that it should regulate the workers' *life* in order that he may *work* better. The working class view of economic reform is that it should regulate his *work*, in order that he may have a change of living. Hence to working people licensing reform, insurance acts, etc. seems beginning at the wrong end.

Q

Why did the working classes initially oppose the Liberal welfare reforms?

Source F R.H. Tawney writing in 1912.

ACTIVITY

From what you have read so far both in this chapter and in Chapter 4, would you judge that the working classes were right to be suspicious of state welfare?

ISSUE
Did the Liberal social reforms mark the beginning of the welfare state in Britain?

THE WELFARE STATE
The notion of the state operating a fully integrated and fully funded national scheme to provide all the essential social, health, and educational needs of all its people, regardless of their income or social status.

Q How important was the influence of the Labour Party on the Liberal reforms?

b) The Debate on the Liberal Reforms of 1906–11

The Liberal programme continues to generate historical controversy. Some writers regard the measures as marking a key stage on the path to the modern welfare state. Other commentators dispute this, preferring to see them as a set of important but piecemeal attempts to tackle particular problems. It is worth restating the main Liberal social reforms: old age pensions, labour exchanges, National Insurance, and the Development Commission. The obvious links between these measures gives them the look of a systematic programme regardless of whether or not they were originally intended to be. The system may have been rudimentary by later standards, but it did involve a considerable increase in state power and bureaucracy. It did not create a full **welfare state**; the administrative resources simply did not exist for that. But what can be said is that the Liberals had taken significant steps towards what has been termed 'the social service state', a centrally organised administration capable of improving the living and working conditions of large portions of the British population.

There was once a commonly-held view that the Liberal reforms were a response to Labour Party pressure. This view had now been largely abandoned. The Labour Party was never strong enough. The Liberals were not dependent on its support before 1910 and, even after the 1910 elections when they lost their majority, it remained inconceivable that the Labour Party would seriously consider voting against the government since that would have meant allying with the Conservatives. The Labour Party itself acknowledged that it had made little impact on Liberal Party policies before 1914.

c) The Pre-War Crises, 1911–14

The period from 1911 to 1914 was a particularly troubled time in Britain. Four major crises arose – the Lords versus Commons conflict, suffragette agitation, tensions in Ulster (examined on pages 136–39) and industrial strife (examined on pages 188–89). These problems were so disruptive that they seemed to threaten the social and political order. The seriousness of the crises has been interpreted by some observers as evidence of the failure of the Liberals to deal with the problems of their time. Before examining that view let us describe the two crises which we have not yet met in detail.

i) The Lords versus the Commons, 1909–11
A major conflict between the House of Commons and the House of Lords had become increasingly likely after the Liberals won their landslide victory in 1906. Unable to outvote the government in the

Commons, the Conservative opposition resorted to using its in-built majority in the Lords to block measures to which it objected; these included major licensing and education bills. Even some Unionists were unhappy with the recklessness with which the unelected House of Lords had begun to destroy the legislation that came from the elected Commons. Matters came to a climax in the controversy over the People's Budget of 1909.

The Unionists decided to resist the budget on the grounds that it was an unprecedented attack upon the rights of property. They argued that this entitled them to ignore the long-standing convention that the Lords did not interfere with finance bills. Lloyd George, a strong opponent of aristocratic privilege, thought the whole affair could be turned to the Liberals' advantage. They could take on the role of defenders of democracy against the forces of reaction. Lloyd George led the Liberals in denouncing the peers' attempt to maintain their privileges at the expense of the old and the poor of the nation. In a memorable turn of phrase he mocked the Lords for being not as the peers claimed, 'the watchdog of the constitution', but 'Mr. Balfour's poodle'. Lloyd George savaged the peers for opposing the will of the British people.

Why did the Unionists attack the People's Budget?

> Let them [the Lords] realise what they are doing. They are forcing a revolution and they will get it. The Lords may decree revolution, but the people will direct it. The question will be asked whether five hundred men, ordinary men chosen accidentally from among the unemployed, should override the judgement – the deliberate judgement – of millions of people who are engaged in the industry which makes the wealth of the country.

Source G From a speech by Lloyd George in the House of Commons, 1910.

ACTIVITY

Having read the details in this section, explain in your own words the point of Lloyd George's jibe that the Lords were 'Mr. Balfour's poodle'.

The Lords lost the battle that followed. In 1910, after two general elections had produced a stalemate that left the Liberals still in office though now reliant on the support of the Irish Nationalist and Labour MPs, the peers finally allowed Lloyd George's budget through. They were promptly presented with a Parliament Bill, which set out to limit their powers. For well over a year the Lords fiercely resisted the Bill. They gave in eventually only under the threat of being swamped by 500 new Liberal peers whom King

George V agreed at Asquith's request to create if the Lords' resistance could not be overcome. Even then, the narrow majority of 17 was achieved only by the decision of 37 Conservative peers to vote for the Bill rather than suffer the 'pollution' of their House.

Main terms of the Parliament Act, 1911

The Lords' absolute veto was abolished by two key clauses:
▼ the delaying power of the Lords was to be restricted to two years
▼ a Bill sent up by the Commons in three consecutive sessions to become law despite rejection by the Lords.

Q On what grounds did the Unionists resist the attempts to reduce the powers of the House of Lords between 1909 and 1911?

We noted in regard to the 1832 Reform Bill (page 41) that it is important for historical balance to appreciate the attitude of those who opposed reform. The same applies to the resistance of the Lords between 1909 and 1911. We need to understand the attitude of another of history's losing sides. The argument of the peers and their supporters was that it was not they but the Liberal government who had acted unconstitutionally by attempting to impose taxes on the landed classes in order to allow the continuation of its irresponsible free-trade policy. This, they said, was tantamount to a declaration of class war. They further stressed that Asquith's government did not have a popular mandate for the drastic measures it was proposing. It had failed to win an overall majority in the Commons in the two elections of 1910.

Table 16 Election results, 1910.

Party	Jan/Feb	December
Conservatives	273	272
Liberal	275	272
Labour	40	42
Irish Nationalists	82	84

Yet despite this, ran the Unionists' argument, the Liberals had continued to ride roughshod over the legitimate objections of the class under attack by following the 1909 Budget with a Parliament Bill which aimed to usurp the time-honoured authority of the Lords. By seeking to take away from the Upper House its traditional right to revise or reject ill-considered legislation, the Liberals were guilty of undermining the constitution. If a minority government could impose its will in such an arbitrary way on such a fundamental matter, British liberties were under threat. The peers claimed, therefore, that, far from merely defending their own privileges, they were standing for the legal and constitutional freedoms of the nation.

Added tension was created by the realisation on both sides that were the Lords' veto to be removed, there would be nothing to prevent the Liberals forcing through Irish Home Rule. Asquith's government, supported by the Irish Nationalist MPs, could carry the Bill through the Commons, with the Lords being able only to delay, not stop, its becoming law. It was the knowledge of this that gave the dispute over the Parliament Bill such a fierce edge.

ACTIVITY

The clash between the Lords and Commons is the type of topic that calls for a group discussion. You and your student colleagues could divide into two groups: one arguing the case for the government, the other for the opposition peers. An opening question might be: 'Was the resistance of the House of Lords to the People's Budget and the Parliament Bill anything more than blind reaction?' The arguments introduced in sub-section c i) will provide useful ammunition.

---

ii) The Suffragette crisis

The extension of the vote in parliamentary elections to women might be thought to have been a cause that the New Liberals would eagerly support. John Stuart Mill (1806–73), the great Liberal philosopher, had regarded it as an essential freedom in a civilised society. However, the impossibility of knowing how women would vote, made a number of the leading Liberals hesitate to commit themselves to take action. The slowness of Parliament to give its full attention to the matter led to the foundation in 1903 of the Women's Social and Political Union (WSPU). Led by the dynamic Emmeline Pankhurst, the WSPU undertook a campaign of disruption, which became progressively more violent as the Liberals persisted in their refusal to allow parliamentary time to debate the question. Between 1911 and 1914, a series of suffragette outrages, that included arson and physical assault, showed the degree of WSPU frustration. But the violence tended to alienate moderate supporters among both women and men. It also provided an excuse for the Government to impose prison sentences on the suffragettes of a severity that would have been unacceptable in less disturbed times. The issue of votes for women was no nearer to being settled when the war intervened in 1914. Mrs. Pankhurst immediately called off the suffragette campaign and committed herself and her followers totally to the war effort.

ISSUE
Why did the 'votes for women' question cause acute problems for the Liberals?

Figure 50 'The Cat and Mouse Act', a graphic poster of 1913, showing the bitterness with which the Act was regarded by the suffragettes.

THE CAT AND MOUSE ACT, 1913

This Act provided the means by which the authorities, without having to resort to the previous grim practice of force-feeding, overcame the resistance of the imprisoned suffragettes who went on hunger strike. The women were released on licence for short periods when their health deteriorated; once they had recovered they were reimprisoned.

Q Why did the suffragette crisis prove so difficult to resolve?

The struggle for female suffrage is now viewed as part of the broader campaign for female emancipation that developed in the twentieth century. Feminists interpret it as a vital stage in the gender war. However, at the time most politicians approached the matter primarily from a party political angle. Had they been confident that female suffrage would work to their advantage, they would doubtless have

found every reason for supporting it. But for them a female electorate was an unknown quantity. They feared that it would have a
harmful effect on their parliamentary strength. This worry applied to
all the parties, Conservative, Liberal and Labour. They simply did
not know how women would vote. For Labour there was the added
complication that if the franchise were to be introduced only for
selected groups of women, this would weaken the case for complete
male suffrage which was the Party's first priority. (In 1914 40 per
cent of adult males were still without the vote). It should also be
pointed out that the suffragettes were not always clear cut in their
objectives. In 1910 Mrs. Pankhurst was willing to abandon the idea of
working-class women gaining the franchise in return for Parliament
granting it to women who owned or occupied property. This was
doubtless a tactical move on her part, but it did emphasise how
ambiguous the votes for women issue could be.

Lloyd George provided a good individual example of the com-
plexities attached to the question. As an individual MP, he was in
favour of votes for women and supported the 'suffragists', the non-
violent movement for the female franchise. But as a government
minister, his approach was conditioned by political considerations.
He feared that if females were to be given the vote on the grounds of
property qualification, then only middle-class women would be eligible and that this would almost certainly benefit the Conservatives.
He concluded that if female franchise were to be granted, it had to
be to all women and not propertied groups only. His views were not
always understood by the WSPU who interpreted his reluctance to
accept half measures as a sign that he was opposed to women's suffrage on principle. In 1912, he was physically attacked by a group of
suffragettes and his house in Surrey was bombed.

The doubts that attached to Lloyd George's attitude did not apply
to the Prime Minister. Throughout the suffragette campaign,
Asquith retained a resolute stance against the granting of the female
franchise. The result was that the Liberals did not come out well in
the 'Votes for Women' issue. Their apparent reluctance to treat it as
a question of principle weakened their moral standing, and their
failure before 1914 to achieve an acceptable solution proved a political embarrassment.

d) The Debate on the Pre-War Crises of 1911–14

In the 1930s the historian, George Dangerfield, wrote a provocative
book, entitled *The Strange Death of Liberal England*, in which he argued
that the great pre-war crises indicated that by 1914 the Liberals were
incapable of dealing effectively with the social and economic pressures of the early twentieth century. He concluded that New Liberal-

ACTIVITY

Having read sub-section
c ii) dealing with the
pre-1914 crises, attempt
the following question:
Who were the more
responsible for the
political conflicts of the
period, the Conservatives
or the Liberals?

ISSUES
Did the pre-war crises
mark 'The Strange
Death of Liberal
England'?
Did they illustrate 'the
crisis of capitalism'?

ism had failed to save the Liberal Party, which by 1914 was on the point of extinction. Other historians were keen to develop his thesis. They argued that the fierce confrontations between employers and workers, the violence of the suffragettes, Ireland on the verge of civil war, and the battle between the Lords and the Commons, were all signs that Britain had entered an era of 'class politics'. It was a new form of political warfare with which the Liberal Party was not equipped to cope. References to the ideas of such Edwardian class warriors as G.D.H. Cole were made to support the argument.

A socialist view of pre-1914 Britain

Social peace! A country without strikes! Co-partnership and co-operation of worker and employer! How delightful and how soothing to the social conscience! Let it be understood once and for all that the interests of Capital and Labour are diametrically opposed, and that although it may be necessary for Labour sometimes to acquiesce in "social peace", such peace is only the lull before the storm.

Source H G.D.H. Cole, *The World of Labour*, 1913.

Many historians continue to be influenced by Dangerfield's analysis. However, there is an opposing school of thought which argues that the very fact that the Liberals were still in power in 1914 proves their strength and ability to survive. The great crises they had faced had not seriously weakened them. By 1914 they had a record of eight years of unbroken government. All challenges to their authority had been resisted, and they could boast an unprecedented range of social and economic reforms. Despite the Liberals' majority being wiped out in the 1910 elections, Asquith's government had success-fully met all the Conservatives' attacks upon it. Nor had the Labour Party been able to mount a serious political challenge to the Liber-als; it was too small and ineffectual. As things stood in 1914, there was no reason to think that the Liberal Party was in a state of irre-versible decline.

ACTIVITY

▼ Having read sub-sections c) and d), write a page or so of comments and observations to show that you understand the essential argument behind the idea that the period 1911–14 marked 'the strange death of Liberal England'.

Summary of Politics and Parties, 1886–1914

Year	Conservatives	Liberals	Labour
1886–92	under Salisbury major series of administrative and social reforms		
1892–4		under Gladstone; preoccupied with Ireland	
1893		Home Rule Bill defeated in Lords	ILP formed
1894–5		under Rosebery	
1895–1902	under Salisbury continuation of reform programme		
1899–1902	Anglo-Boer War		
1900	Khaki election victory		LRC formed
1902–5	under Balfour significant reforms: education, army, licensing and Ireland.		
1903			Lib–Lab pact
1905–8		under Campbell-Bannerman	
1906	split by tariff reform issue – lost heavily in election	won landslide victory	Labour Party formed
1908–14		under Asquith; Churchill and Lloyd George in vanguard of major reform programme – including old age pensions, national insurance	
1909	strong resistance to people's budget taxation proposals	Lloyd George's people's budget	
1911–14	Unionist resistance to Home Rule	major crises – Lords, suffragettes, industrial strife, Ulster	

▼ Working on Politics and Parties, 1886–1914

The summary chart provides the basis for structuring your study. It was suggested in the 'Points to consider' section that a logical way to examine the period is to take the central theme of how the parties reacted to the important social and economic issues of the time. Using that as your base and bearing in mind that there were two distinct periods – the Conservative ascendancy between 1886 and 1905 and the Liberals in office 1905–14 – you can construct your notes around the key questions as they appear in the chapter. The following example of how questions might be approached, with key points underlined, should help you on your way:

Main Questions
▼ Why was the Liberal Party *out of* office for so long after 1886?
▼ Why were the Conservatives *in* office for so long?

Answers
▼ Liberals, fractured over Ireland, were also <u>divided</u> in their response to social questions:
  – <u>old Gladstonian policies</u> not judged adequate by radical Liberals Hence:
  – <u>New Liberalism</u> with its emphasis on social welfare, and
  – Chamberlain's <u>Unauthorised programme</u> and <u>tariff reform</u>
▼ <u>Chamberlain's departure</u> was a sign of how serious the Liberal split had become
▼ Liberal weakness on social policy encouraged the growth <u>of a third party</u>, strongly influenced by socialist reforming ideas – <u>the Labour Party</u>
▼ The <u>Conservatives benefited from the Liberal split</u> which explains the lack of a serious electoral challenge to them before 1906
▼ Though not renowned as social reformers, the Conservatives under Salisbury and Balfour have an <u>impressive list of social reforms</u> to their credit – certainly <u>not</u> a period of legislative inactivity
▼ No issue seriously weakened the Conservatives until 1903 when their adoption of <u>tariff reform undermined</u> their <u>electoral support</u>.

A point often made in this book is that you need to be able to deal with questions across time. You may well be examined on themes that cover a century of history. One area where this is very likely is that of party politics. Three chapters in this book are devoted to this theme. Now would be a good time to refer back to 'End of Chapter Reviews' in Chapters 2 and 3 and relate the 'Working on' sections there to the notes we have just compiled above. As always with broad questions, the essential task is to look for major connecting themes rather than detail. For example, if you were responding to a question about the development of the Conservative Party between 1815 and 1914, you could not afford to indulge in too much detail. An effective linking theme would be the Party's attitude to reform.

A list of the following kind could be used to construct an outline answer covering a 100-year time span:

1815–22	Reactionary Tories opposed to reform;
1822–7	Liberal Tories pro-reform;
1827–32	Tories split over Catholic Emancipation and reform of Parliament;
1830s	Peel made the principle of limited reform the basis of Conservatism;
1841–6	Peel put his ideas into practice at the cost of splitting his party over the repeal of the Corn Laws;
1846–67	period of fragmentation and uncertainty;
1867–81	Disraeli rejuvenated the Conservative Party with a programme of measured but major social reform;
1886–1905	Salisbury and Balfour continued the Disraelian pattern of significant domestic reform though in a less spectacular manner;
1905–14	Conservative and Unionist Party becomes identified with resistance to Liberal reforms, particularly in regard to Ireland.

Answering extended writing and essay questions on Politics and Parties, 1886–1914

The following list shows the style of questions you are likely to encounter on the topic of late Victorian and Edwardian politics.

Type of Issue	Examples of typical questions
1 causes/reasons/motives	Why was the Conservative Party in office for so much of the time between 1886 and 1905?
2 course of events	Examine the development of the conflict between the House of Commons and the House of Lords in the years 1909–11
3 consequences/results/ effects	What were the political consequences for the Conservative Party of its adoption of tariff reform?
4 success/failure	How true is that 'up to 1914 the Labour Party had proved largely a failure'?
5 significance/importance	'A critical moment in late Victorian politics': Consider this comment on Joseph Chamberlain's decision to leave the Liberal Party in the late 1880s.
6 comparison	Which provides the more convincing explanation for the landslide defeat of the government in 1906 – Conservative weakness or Liberal strength?
7 right/wrong (moral/ ethical judgments)	'After the elections of 1910 had destroyed the Liberal mandate, Asquith's government was no longer justified in pursuing its radical reform programme.' Discuss this assertion.

On this occasion let us take number 6, the type of question that asks you to draw a comparison. In this instance you are being asked to decide which is the more convincing explanation of a particular historical event – the Liberal landslide victory in the election of 1906. The two factors you have to decide between are Liberal strength and Conservative weakness. Before thinking about which side you might favour it is important you are clear in your own mind about the points that make up the respective strengths and weaknesses. There is no need to look for an exact match between the lists in terms of numbers of points. Here is a case where the quality rather than the number is the important consideration. One strong factor might well outweigh a number of relatively minor points.

Conservative weaknesses:
▼ loss of reputation over the Anglo-Boer War, 1899–1902
▼ embarrassment over 'Chinese slavery'
▼ resentment aroused by Balfour's Education Act, 1902
▼ none of the Irish interests happy with Wyndham's Land Act, 1902
▼ working classes alienated by the Taff Vale Judgment, 1901
▼ tariff reform, adopted in 1903, failed to convince the electorate.

All these points, and any others you wish to include, should obviously figure in your answer since their cumulative effect was damaging to the Conservative image. But rather than just catalogue them, give some thought as to grading them in order of significance. For example, there is obviously a case for suggesting that tariff reform looms largest since it was the issue that caused the greatest controversy and excitement in the run up to the election. You might also select the Chinese slavery question and the accusations of inhumanity over the government's handling of the Boer War as being especially significant in weakening the moral standing of the Conservatives. Of course what we have listed so far have been issues. It is worth asking whether there might not be factors other than specific political issues. After all, the Conservatives by 1905, save for three years in the early 1890s, had been in office for two decades. It is observable that in all countries that operate a multi-party system, governments that stay in office for long periods tend to run low on enthusiasm and confidence. Ask yourself whether that was the case with the Conservatives by 1905.

Liberal strengths
Again you should draw up a list. A worthwhile starting point might be the suggestion that oppositions do not win elections; it is governments that lose them. Accepting that as a valid point, the most direct approach would be to set the liberal record against the list of Conservative weaknesses.

If you structure your answer on the lines suggested you will be in a position to argue for one side or the other, or indeed, to suggest that the two strengths/weaknesses arguments balance each other.

Answering source-based questions on Politics and Parties, 1886–1914

Re-read Source B on page 198 and then answer the question that follows. Our task in this instance is to judge the way in which a particular extract illustrates a general theory or principle.

Using your own knowledge and the evidence in the source, analyse this passage as a definition of 'New Liberalism'? **[8 marks]**

Suggested line of response
Hobson in this extract is arguing, in effect, that old Gladstonian Liberalism, with its limited programme of 'peace, retrenchment and reform', is no longer relevant or adequate. What the Liberal Party must now accept is that the provision of social welfare, the protection of the individual against economic misfortune, is now its primary policy. Liberty and freedom of enterprise remain valid objectives, but they must take second place to what is essentially a moral purpose. The rights of the individual must not be pursued at the expense of the general social good. Justice requires that equal opportunity must now be the goal of Liberal policies. Since equal opportunity is impossible without the reform of social conditions, the state must extend its authority to encompass social reform. Hobson specifically denies that what he is proposing is socialism; rather it is the creation of the social service state, which will prevent the development of class rivalry and bitterness. Analysts were later to define the social service state as a halfway stage between the high Liberalism of the nineteenth century and the welfare state of the later twentieth century.

Further Reading

Books in the 'Access to History' series
Whigs, Radicals and Liberals, 1815–1914 by Duncan Watts has three informative Chapters (5–7) on the Liberal problems and achievements in this period. The same author studies Conservative policies under Salisbury and Balfour in *Tories, Conservatives and Unionists 1815–1914* (Chapter 6). Chapter 7 in *Government and Reform 1815–1918* by Robert Pearce and Roger Stearn is a very helpful study of the battle over the 1911 reform of the Lords. The relationship between the Liberals and the Labour Party is covered in *Labour and*

Reform: Working-Class Movements 1815–1914 by Clive Behagg, Chapters 5 to 7. The response of the parties to social problems of late Victorian and Edwardian Britain is studied in Chapters 5 and 6 in *Poverty and Welfare* by Peter Murray. *The Industrialisation of Britain, 1780–1914* by Phil Chapple (Chapter 5) examines the economic problems of this period. The suffragette movement is the subject of *Votes for Women* by Paula Bartley who also has a helpful chapter on the same theme in her book, *The Changing Role of Women, 1815–1914*.

General

There are informative chapters giving up-to-date assessments of Chamberlain, Salisbury, Balfour, Asquith and Lloyd George in *Modern British Statesmen 1867–1945* edited by Richard Kelly and John Cantrell (Manchester UP, 1997). *The Rise of the Labour Party, 1880–1945* and *The Decline of the Liberal Party* by Paul Adelman (both published by Longman 1996 and 1995) are very helpful. A recommended long but thorough study is *The Age of Salisbury, the Conservative Party 1881–1902* by Richard Shannon (Longman, 1996). Useful short biographies on key figures are *Joseph Chamberlain, Radical and Imperialist* by Harry Browne (Longman, 1974), *Joseph Chamberlain and the Challenge of Radicalism* by Duncan Watts, and *Lloyd George and the Liberal Dilemma* by Michael Lynch, the last two books being in the 'Personalities and Powers' series (Hodder & Stoughton, 1992 and 1993). *The Evolution of the British Welfare State* by Derek Fraser (Macmillan, 1973) is very illuminating on the pre-1914 Liberal social reforms, as is *The Edwardian Age* by Vyvyen Brendon (Hodder & Stoughton, 1996). Very helpful short studies are M.E. Rose, *The Relief of Poverty, 1834–1914* (CUP, 1974) and J.R. Hay, *The Origins of the Liberal Welfare Reforms, 1906–14* (CUP, 1984). Two highly recommended analyses are *Edwardian England* by Donald Read (Harrap, 1972) and *The Edwardian Crisis, Britain 1901–1914* by David Powell (Macmillan, 1996). Two very helpful pamphlets are *Class, Party and the Political System in Britain, 1867–1914* by John Belchem (Historical Association, 1990) and *The Liberal Governments of 1905–15* by G.I.T. Machin, (University of Wales Press, 1996). The suffragette question is succinctly covered in *The British Women's Suffrage Campaign 1866–1928* by Harold L. Smith (Longman, 1998). Recommended articles are: 'Lord Salisbury and Late Victorian Conservatism' by Graham Goodlad in *History Review*, 'Joseph Chamberlain and the Liberal Unionist Party' by D.J. Dutton in *History Review*, March 1994, 'New Liberalism' by Duncan Tanner in *Modern History Review*, Nov. 1990, and 'Votes for Women' by Martin Pugh in *Modern History Review*, Sept. 1990.

FOREIGN AND IMPERIAL AFFAIRS, 1865–1914

POINTS TO CONSIDER

In this chapter foreign and imperial affairs are considered together because the overlap between them is so marked in this period. Britain's relations with the states of Europe, particularly after 1870, had as much to do with the desire to protect its Empire as it had to do with European concerns. For this reason we will examine the three key statesmen – Disraeli, Gladstone and Salisbury – whose conduct of foreign affairs gave definition to Britain's foreign and imperial policy. The first section picks up the story from where we left it in Chapter 6 by re-examining the Eastern Question in the post-Crimean War period. The second section analyses Salisbury's handling of foreign and colonial issues; the third is a study of British imperialism with emphasis on two particular features: the Scramble for Africa and the Anglo-Boer War. This is followed by a section which looks at the historical debate over the motives behind imperialism. In the final section we turn to the critical period of Britain's relations with Europe after 1900 which led to Britain's entry into the Great War in 1914. It is possible to study each of these themes separately without reference to the others. But the inter-relations between the themes are so prominent that you would gain a much sounder understanding of each theme if you were to see it in relation to the broader picture of the development of Britain's foreign and imperial policy.

1 Disraeli, Gladstone and the Eastern Question

ISSUE
To what extent was the clash between Disraeli and Gladstone over foreign policy a struggle between realism and morality?

In foreign affairs Disraeli followed very much in the footsteps of Palmerston. His overriding concern was the protection of British interests. He never shared any of Gladstone's grand ideas about countries working together in a **Concert of Europe**. This was clear from his approach to the Eastern Question. Here Disraeli's basic aim was to prevent the Russians exploiting the terminal decline of the Ottoman Empire to their own advantage. His anxiety was that, as Turkey's hold over its Balkan and Middle Eastern territories weakened, Russia would move in, thus menacing the route to India

THE CONCERT OF EUROPE

The notion that the civilised countries of Europe have much in common and that they should therefore regard themselves as friends rather than enemies. This would enable them to settle disputes between themselves without going to war and to act collectively to resolve major international issues. In Gladstone's thinking the 'concert' was not so much a formal alliance system as an attitude of mind that regarded maintaining peace as an international priority.

Source A From *The Bulgarian Horrors and the Question of the East* by W.E. Gladstone, 1876.

Q

Why did opinion in Britain become so divided over the Eastern Question?

in particular and Britain's strategic and commercial position more broadly.

Disraeli was following the established British line. Britain's entry into the Crimean War in the 1850s had been a demonstration of its anti-Russian disposition. The Treaty of Paris, which ended that war, had forbidden Russia to have warships in the Black Sea. However, in 1870 Russia had ignored that prohibition. Disraeli criticised Gladstone as Prime Minister for his failure to respond to this renewed Russian threat. In office himself after 1874, Disraeli became disturbed by news of Turkey's ill-treatment of the Christians in Bulgaria, which was part of its Empire. He feared that this might be used by Russia to justify an advance into the Balkans. So he maintained his anti-Russian position, refusing to be pushed into action by tales of Turkish barbarity. Gladstone, however, was moved not by the strategic concerns but by moral ones. When he learned of the Turkish atrocities he rose from his sick-bed, came out of retirement, and with the wrath of an Old Testament prophet, dashed off an impassioned pamphlet, denouncing the Turks for perpetrating:

> crimes and outrages so vast in scale as to exceed all modern example, and so utterly vile as well as fierce in character, that it passes the power of the heart to conceive, and of tongue and pen adequately to describe them. These are the Bulgarian horrors. An old servant of the Crown and State, I entreat my countrymen that our Government, which has been working in one direction, shall work in the other; and shall apply all its vigour to concur with the other States of Europe in obtaining the extinction of the Turkish executive power in Bulgaria.

Gladstone's thunderings gave great momentum to the anti-Turkish campaign that had started in Britain. His condemnation of Turkey for its savagery, and his contempt for Disraeli's government for allowing 'the hobgoblin of Russia' to scare it into a pro-Turkish stance, polarised opinion in Britain. The nation divided between Gladstone, the protector of oppressed peoples, and Disraeli, the guardian of the nation's interests. It became a high drama. Disraeli countered Gladstone's moral fervour with ridicule. He described Gladstone's pamphlet as 'vindictive and ill-written' and 'of all the Bulgarian horrors, perhaps the worst'. He replied to Gladstone's charge that in refusing to denounce the Turks he was sacrificing morality to expediency by asserting that in any international question Britain's interests must come first.

Although Disraeli ordered British land and sea forces to the Dardanelles in 1877, they played no part in the Russo-Turkish war that broke out in that year. Disraeli decided he would achieve more by diplomacy. When it became known that, under the Treaty of San Stefano that ended war in March 1878, the Russians had made ominous territorial gains, Disraeli was able to persuade Germany and Austria to join Britain in imposing a new settlement to cancel out Russia's advantages. The major European powers met formally at the Congress of Berlin to reconsider the Eastern Question. The gathering proved a major diplomatic success for Disraeli. Bismarck, the German Chancellor, acknowledged the British Prime Minister as the dominant influence in shaping the Treaty of Berlin, under which Russia returned the territories it had gained at San Stefano and Britain guaranteed to protect Turkey in return for the cession of Cyprus.

Figure 51a

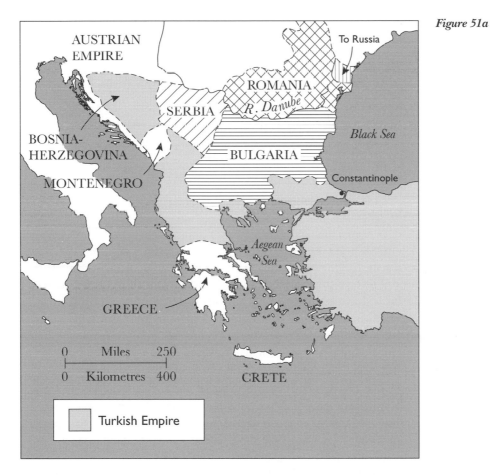

Figures 51a and 51b (overleaf) Two maps showing the territorial adjustments made by the Treaties of San Stefano and Berlin. The large bulge of the 'big Bulgaria' that Russia dominated under the terms of the San Stefano Treaty is shown in the first map. The 'little Bulgaria' of the second map shows how the Treaty of Berlin pushed back Russian influence in the region.

Figure 51b

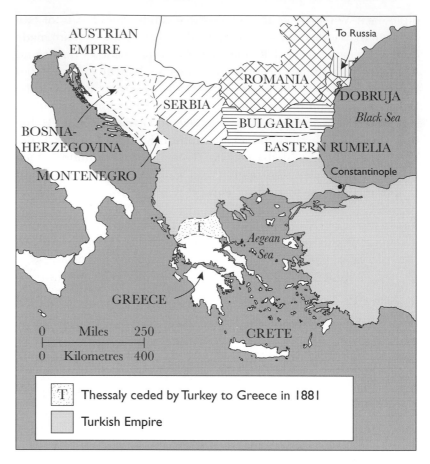

T   Thessaly ceded by Turkey to Greece in 1881

Turkish Empire

Disraeli's success in bringing back 'peace with honour' from Berlin in 1878, was greeted with huge popular acclaim. Gladstone did not join in the rejoicing; he considered Disraeli's performance at Berlin to have been based on a profound misconception of Britain's international standing. He told the Commons that Disraeli's ideas of British interests were 'perfectly fictitious and imaginary' and ignored 'the most vital realities in the world'.

> This setting up of our interests, out of place, in an exaggerated form, beyond their proper sphere, and not merely the setting up of such interests, but the mode in which they have been pursued, has greatly diminished the estimation of our moral standard of action, and consequently our moral position in the world.

Source B From a speech by Gladstone in the House of Commons, July 1878.

In view of the rapturous reception that Disraeli received in 1878, it might appear that he had got the better of Gladstone in their duel over the Eastern Question. Yet, there are grounds for suggesting that in the broader span of history Gladstone was the more progressive and enlightened. It is arguable that his anti-imperialism and his belief in the Concert of Europe showed not only higher idealism but also greater realism in acknowledging that Britain was a declining power.

But that is not the end of the story. When Gladstone came back to office in 1880, his hope was that he could rely on the Concert of Europe to maintain the European balance of power without Britain being drawn into continental engagements. What he had not fully grasped was that a major power shift had occurred as the result of the growth of Germany under Bismarck. By the early 1880s Germany had increased its influence in Europe at the expense of France, which had been humiliated by its defeat in the Franco-Prussian war of 1870–71 and left further isolated. If the Concert of Europe had ever existed in the sense that Gladstone understood it, the rise of Germany had effectively destroyed it. This suggests that there are good grounds for challenging the idea of Gladstone as a realist in international affairs.

Germany under Bismarck

A united German nation had come into being in the early 1870s. This had been largely the work of the great Prussian statesman, Otto von Bismarck, who having achieved unification then set about the task of making Germany the most powerful state in Europe. This he aimed to achieve principally by entering into a series of alliances with selected European powers that would always leave Germany in a position of strength by keeping France isolated.

BISMARCK'S ALLIANCES

1879 the Dual Alliance (Austria and Germany);
1881 the League of the Three Emperors (Russia, Austria, and Germany);
1882 the Triple Alliance (Austria, Italy and Germany).

ACTIVITY

Read the previous section and then consider the following question: Who was the more realistic in his attitude towards Britain's role in international affairs – Disraeli or Gladstone?

---

2 British Foreign Policy under Salisbury

ISSUES
What principles underlay Salisbury's foreign policy? Was he an isolationist?

Although Gladstone and Salisbury were the leaders of opposed parties, there was an interesting continuity in their approach to foreign affairs. They shared the view that Britain was a declining force in the world and that therefore it would be unwise for it to attempt to pursue an expansionist foreign policy.

Salisbury's made foreign affairs his main interest in politics. Even as Prime Minister he continued to hold the post of Foreign Secretary. As we saw on page 202, his attitude to public affairs was marked by a strong sense of fatalism. This he carried over into his conduct of foreign policy as is evident from the following passage:

> You may roughly divide the nations of the world as the living and the dying. In these dying states, disorganisation and decay are advancing almost as fast as concentration and increasing power are advancing in the living nations that stand beside them. The weak states are becoming weaker and the strong states are becoming stronger. The living nations will gradually encroach on the territory of the dying, and the seeds and causes of conflict among civilised nations will speedily appear. These things may introduce causes of fatal difference between the great nations whose mighty armies stand opposed, threatening each other.

Source C From a speech by Lord Salisbury at Crystal Palace, May 1898.

Salisbury's Main Periods of Office

Secretary of State for India – 1866–7, 1874–6
Foreign Secretary – 1878–80, 1886–92, 1895–1900
Prime Minister – 1885–6, 1886–92, 1895–1902

Salisbury had many examples to hand of the powerful nations of the world taking over the weaker. Throughout the nineteenth century Europe had been bitterly divided over the disposal of the collapsing Turkish Empire. Since 1840 China's weakness had been exploited by the Western powers. Most striking of all, Salisbury's arrival at the Foreign Office coincided with the 'scramble for Africa', the fierce competition between the European powers for African resources and territory. What is equally interesting is that Salisbury should also have regarded Britain as declining in strength relative to the other European powers. In 1900 he agreed with the following Chinese estimate of the current world situation:

Source D From a letter by Lo Fung-luh, the Chinese Minister in London, to Lord Salisbury, March 1900.

> What a calamity it is for mankind that the two greatest empires in the world, the British and the Chinese, should apparently both be entering at the same time on their decline.

What gave particular gravity and irony to Lo's observations was that 1900 was the year in which Britain joined with other European powers to crush the anti-foreigner Boxer rising in China.

Salisbury came to his main term as Foreign Secretary in the 1880s believing that Gladstone had been misguided in thinking that Britain could become a leading member of a progressive European Concert of Nations. But, since Salisbury also held that Britain had declined as a major power, he judged that it was impossible to return to the aggressive foreign policies associated with Palmerston and Disraeli. As Salisbury saw it, Britain could not direct affairs. It would have to play a waiting game, reacting to events as they occurred, and always with the safeguarding of its security as the main aim. This was evident In 1887, when he negotiated two Mediterranean agreements with the aim of limiting the influence of Russia and France in that region.

Although the two treaties were secret, they showed that at this stage Salisbury, far from isolating Britain from European engagements, was prepared to initiate them. This suggests that for Salisbury detachment was not a fixed policy. For him the question was always one of judging how British interests could best be safeguarded.

It was the same protective attitude that shaped Salisbury's attitude towards Britain's imperial role. He interpreted 'empire' not in the expansionist Disraelian sense but as a means of slowing down Britain's decline. He tended to share Joseph Chamberlain's economic understanding of imperialism (see page 199). For both men, the value of the empire was that it offered a way for Britain to avoid unnecessary commitments; it could ignore Europe on occasion by relying on its imperial resources. This did not rule out harmonious relations with the states of Europe. Indeed, Salisbury hoped that these could be maintained along with the new imperialism. An interesting example of this is to be found in his China policy.

Salisbury and China

Salisbury calculated that the fall of the Chinese Qing (Manchu) Empire would intensify the struggle between the European colonial powers, as had the weakening of the Turkish Empire. So, in 1898, in a move to protect British interests, he proposed to the Russian government that all Anglo-Russian conflicts in the Far East should be settled by an agreed policy of partition of disputed territory or interests. In the event his proposals came to nothing, largely because German expansion into China complicated the situation.

THE BOXER RISING, 1898–1901

A doomed attempt by the Chinese to end their subjection to the West. Since the 1840s China had been forced in a series of 'unequal treaties' to accept the occupation of its major cities and ports by a number of European powers, including Britain, France and Germany.

How did Salisbury approach foreign affairs?

THE MEDITERRANEAN AGREEMENTS, 1887

First agreement – February
Britain persuaded Spain and Austria to establish a system of collective consultation in the event of a Russian or French challenge to the existing international arrangements regarding the Mediterranean and Black Sea areas.

Second agreement – December
Britain, Austria and Italy drew up a contingency plan, guarding against the possible surrender to Russia by Turkey of its rights in the Balkans and Near East.

Q

How accurate is the term 'splendid isolation' to describe Salisbury's foreign policy?

THE VENEZUELA DISPUTE, 1896

Keen to win patriotic support in his 1896 election campaign, President Grover Cleveland intervened in a dispute between Britain and Venezuela over the boundary of British Guiana. Cleveland's aim was 'to twist the lion's tail' by backing the Venezuelans. He succeeded in embarrassing Britain diplomatically but when the case went eventually to arbitration all Britain's major claims were recognised. What worried Salisbury's government was the lack of international support Britain received during the dispute despite the justice of its case.

Q

Was there a revolution in British foreign policy at the beginning of the twentieth century?

The significance of Salisbury's China proposals is that they indicate his basically practical approach to foreign relations. Conscious of Britain's decline, Salisbury was attempting to be realistic. He did not abandon the idea of empire or of international co-operation but was trying to apply those concepts in such a way as to make them the practical means of defending Britain's interests.

'Splendid isolation' is one of those terms in historical writing which continues to be used long after it has outlived its appropriateness. It was never an accurate description or one that Salisbury used, except ironically, to define his foreign policy. The term was first heard in the Canadian Parliament in 1896 at the time of Britain's dispute with the USA over Venezuela. Canada, out of loyalty to Britain and a desire to impress the USA with its own independence of judgement, spoke not of Britain's but of the British Empire's being splendidly isolated. After Salisbury's retirement 'splendid isolation' was employed by commentators as a convenient, if misleading, shorthand for the foreign policy which he had followed.

Viscount Goschen, the First Lord of the Admiralty, declared in 1896: 'We have stood alone in that which is called isolation – our splendid isolation, as one of our friends was good enough to call it.' The significance of the use of the term by Goschen is that, as head of the navy in Salisbury's post-1895 government, he had good reason for emphasising the role of the Royal Navy as the traditional guardian of British independence. The freedom strategically and commercially that Britain derived from her strength at sea was a matter on which Salisbury set great store. In the later years of his premiership, he had become increasingly aware that the expansion of the German fleet, which began in earnest in 1898, was the most potent single threat to Britain's ability to exercise genuine independence in international affairs.

It used to be argued that Britain underwent a diplomatic 'revolution' in the first decade of the twentieth century, when, in a break from Salisbury's previous policy of detachment, it engaged into a series of agreements with the USA, Japan, France and Russia. However, while these agreements were certainly important responses to the changing international situation, they were not inconsistent with Salisbury's policy before 1900. The post-1900 agreements did not spring from a sudden decision on Britain's part to become more internationally minded; they were entered into in order to protect British interests. This was exactly the same motive that had lain behind Salisbury's policies. In that sense there is a clear continuity in British foreign policy before and after 1900, which makes the description of Salisbury as a 'splendid isolationist' highly misleading.

3 British Imperialism

In 1870 the interior of Africa, known to the Victorians as the 'dark continent' was still largely unexplored. By 1914 the whole vast continent had been partitioned between the major European powers. Britain was one of the leading competitors in this 'scramble for Africa'. Before looking at the reasons for this extraordinary development, we need to put the imperialism it represented in perspective.

Britain's expansion into Africa occurred at such an unprecedented pace that there is a temptation to see it as an entirely new phenomenon. That, indeed, is how many historians used to regard it. The British enthusiasm for taking over new lands in Africa and the Far East in this period was once viewed as marking a **'new imperialism'**. However, modern scholars now emphasise that though there was certainly a quickening of pace there was no sudden break in Britain's traditional colonial policy. Britain had been expanding its overseas possessions since 1815. What had encouraged historians to think in terms of a new departure was that in the preceding period, 1815–70, Britain had appeared to follow a policy of extending self-government to its colonies. This is shown in the following list:

▼ **Canada**

Based on the proposals of the Durham Report (1839), which recommended that 'responsible government' be granted, a National Federal Assembly was established with control of Canada's internal affairs. In 1867 the British North American Act gave Canada full 'Dominion' status as a self-governing colony.

▼ **Australia**

Initially regarded as a conveniently distant place to send convicts, Australia began to attract free settlers who were lured by the quality of the farmland and the discovery of gold. By 1859 South Australia, New South Wales, Victoria, Tasmania and Queensland had all adopted democratic constitutions and had been recognised as self-governing colonies by Britain. Eventually in 1901, all the states came together to form the 'Commonwealth of Australia', with the same Dominion status as Canada.

▼ **New Zealand**

Britain claimed sovereignty over the two islands in 1840. Despite conflict over land rights between British settlers and the indigenous Maori people, the six regions of the two islands that made up the country were recognised as a self-governing colony in 1856. Twenty years later a single government representing the six provinces was established at Wellington. New Zealand acquired full Dominion status in 1907.

ISSUES
What principles inspired British imperialism?
To what extent was there a 'new imperialism' at work after 1870?

NEW IMPERIALISM
An expansionist movement beginning in the 1870s that aimed to promote national prestige and stimulate commerce by a positive policy of acquiring new overseas territories or developing existing ones.

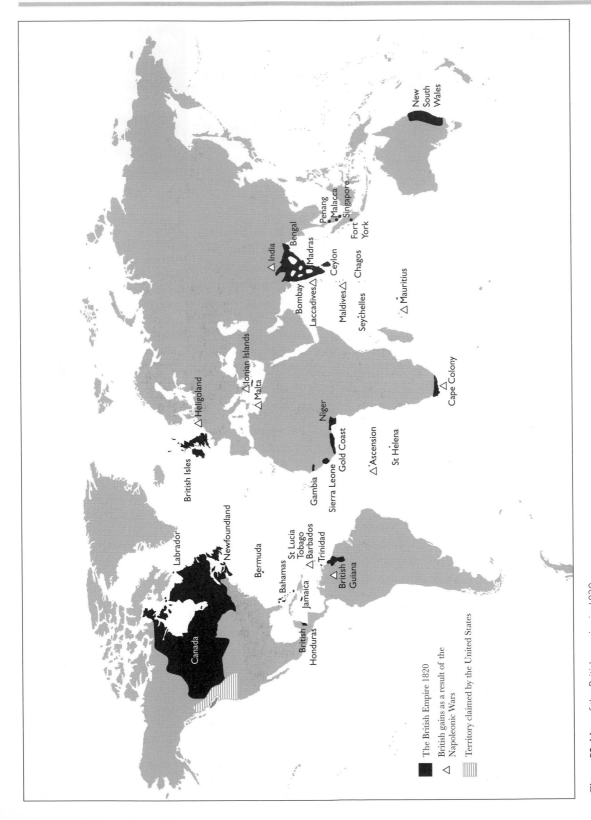

Figure 52 Map of the British empire in 1820.

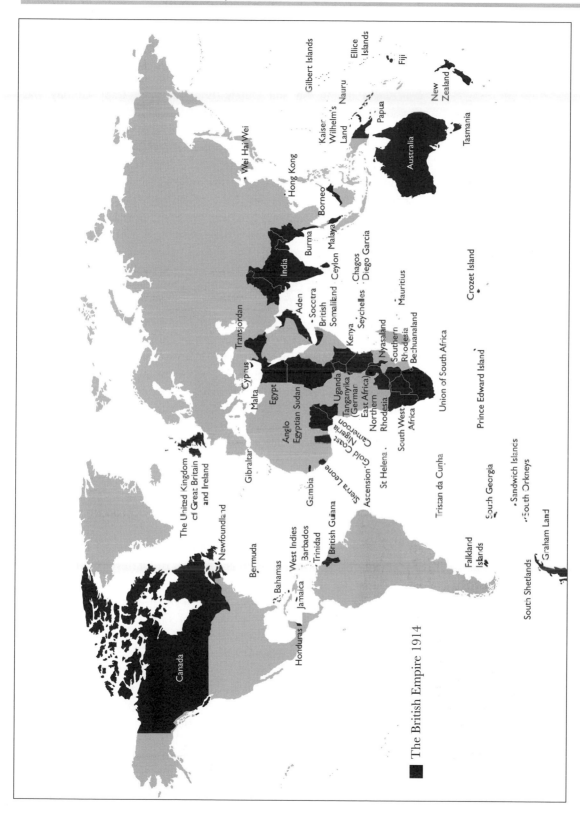

Figure 53 Map of the British empire in 1914.

▼ **Cape Colony and Natal**

Cape Colony in southern Africa had been taken from the Dutch at the end of the eighteenth century. Although this British seizure was formally sanctioned at the Congress of Vienna in 1815, friction remained between the British and Dutch (Boer) settlers. Cape Colony was granted self-government in 1872. Natal, which had been largely Zulu territory, was annexed by Britain in 1843 and was also given self-government in 1872. The Convention of Bloemfontein in 1854 recognised the Transvaal and the Orange Free State as independent Dutch republics, but it left a dangerous situation. The British and Dutch settlers regarded each other with hostility and both were resented by the native African peoples who had been forced off their land by the Europeans. Hostilities were to reach their climax in the Anglo-Boer War of 1899–1902 (see page 242). The eventual outcome was the Union of South Africa (1910), in which the two Boer republics joined the British states of Natal and Cape Colony in one self-governing Dominion.

Although this list looks impressive, it is important not to think of Britain's granting of self-determination as some great act of political generosity. The distinctive feature of British colonial policy was that it distinguished between **colonies of settlement** and **dependent colonies**. Historians often express this in terms of difference between an 'informal' and a 'formal' empire. The informal empire was those colonies over which Britain exercised only a loose control, while the formal related to the colonies over which Britain maintained direct control. But in each case Britain's attitude was governed by a concern to guard its commercial and military interests. Economic historians stress that it was no accident that Britain's quickening of interest in its empire coincided with its rise to prominence as the workshop of the world in the nineteenth century.

The centrepiece of the British Empire was undoubtedly India. British interest in, and eventual control of, India developed from the activities of the East India Company, a trading concern that first established itself on the sub-continent in the early seventeenth century. It was not until the India Act of 1784 that Britain formally asserted the authority of the British Crown over India. However, although it had been gained in this rather haphazard way, India had long been thought of by the British as 'the jewel in the Crown'. A consistent element in Britain's foreign policy was its concern to protect India and the routes to it. This is what explains the suspicion shown by all British governments towards Russia. You will remember that it was fear of Russian expansion that had motivated much of the work of Canning and Palmerston (see page 156).

It is India that provides a fascinating link between old and new imperialism. It also introduces the British statesman most closely

---

A C T I V I T Y

Having read section 3, show that you understand the difference between the notions of a formal and informal empire by listing the various colonies as shown on the maps under the appropriate heading: e.g.

Formal	Informal
Hong Kong	Canada

COLONIES OF SETTLEMENT

Areas of predominantly white British and European settlement, Canada, Australia, and New Zealand being the main examples. They were called in the foreign office language of the day 'politically advanced colonies' and regarded as capable of advancing to maturity, at which point they would be granted Dominion status as self-governing states.

Why was India so important a part of the Empire?

associated with the widening of empire after 1870 – Benjamin Disraeli. The first clear intimation of what was to become a deep commitment to expansionism was contained in a speech he made in 1857 at the time of the Indian mutiny:

> I think the great body of the population of that country [India] ought to know that there is for them a future of hope. You ought at once to tell the people of India that the relation between them and their real Ruler and Sovereign shall be drawn nearer. You ought to issue a royal proclamation to the people of India declaring that the Queen of England is not a Sovereign who will countenance the violation of treaties; that the Queen of England is not a Sovereign who will disturb the settlement of property; that the Queen of England is a Sovereign who will respect their laws, their usages, their customs and, above all, their religion. Do this, and do it not in a corner, but in a model and manner which will attract universal attention and excite the general hope of [India], and you will do as much as all your fleets and armies can achieve.

CROWN OR DEPENDENT COLONIES

Regions where no major white settlement had occurred and whose value to Britain was essentially strategic or commercial. Ports or islands such as Singapore, Hong Kong and the West Indies were examples. They were administered by British officials and were not expected to become self-governing.

Source E From a speech by Disraeli in the House of Commons, 1857.

ACTIVITY

Describe in your own words the character of the relationship that Disraeli believed existed between Britain and India.

The Indian Mutiny, 1857–58

Often referred to by such non-imperialist terms as 'the Indian national rising'; it had three main causes:

▼ the anger of the Indian peoples at the subordination of their cultures to the British
▼ the fear that traditional Indian religions, Hinduism in particular, would be undermined by the Christian missionaries working in India
▼ the growing resentment among the Indian troops (sepoys) in the British army that their traditions were being trampled on by the army command. A particular rumour that aroused Indian anger was that the sepoys were being issued with rifle cartridges that were greased with fat either from pigs (unclean animals in the Moslem religion) or from cows (sacred animals to the Hindus).

After two years' fighting the rising was eventually put down. Although British reprisals were severe, there was a growing recognition in Britain that reforms were needed. A Government of India Act in 1858 disbanded the East India Company, transferred administration to a new India Department, appointed a Viceroy and established a Legislative Council.

ISSUE
What principles underlay Disraeli's approach to the British Empire?

a) Disraeli's Imperial Policies

From the early 1870s Disraeli began to express a distinct commitment to the Empire as an essential aspect of Conservatism. He was encouraged in this by Gladstone's hostility to any form of foreign involvement. Disraeli judged that imperial expansion would prove a vote-winner with the growing electorate. He publicised his party's attitude towards the Empire in a series of powerful speeches in the early 1870s. It was part of his campaign to convince the voters that Gladstone's reforming Liberal government was engaged in destroying the nation's true character. Denouncing Liberal attempts over forty years to reduce Britain's status as an overseas and imperial power, Disraeli pledged his party to the restoration and enlargement of the Empire.

> I have referred to what I look upon as the first object of the Tory party – namely, to maintain the institutions of the country. Gentlemen, there is another and second great object of the Tory party. If you look to the history of this country since the advent of Liberalism – forty years ago – you will find that there has been no effort so continuous, so subtle, supported by so much energy, and carried on with so much ability and acumen, as the attempts of Liberalism to effect the disintegration of the Empire of England.

Source F From a speech by Disraeli at the Crystal Palace, London in June 1872.

Disraeli's translation of his imperialist ideas into practical policy is evident in four characteristic episodes which occurred during his 1874–80 administration.

i) The purchase of the Suez Canal shares, 1875

In 1875, the bankrupt Khedive of Egypt was forced to sell off his holdings in the Suez canal project, currently being constructed under French direction. Disraeli acted opportunely and swiftly. He used his influence with Rothschilds, the banking giants, to raise the necessary capital to purchase the shares for Britain. He wrote exultantly to the Queen: 'You have it, Madam; the French Government has been outgeneraled [*sic*]. The entire interest of the Khedive is now yours'.

ii) The creation of the Queen as Empress of India, 1876

The following year Disraeli introduced the Royal Titles Bill, which conferred on the Queen the title of 'Empress of India', thus making her the personification of the imperial idea and fulfilling the appeal he had made in his 1857 speech at the time of the Indian mutiny. Victoria, beguiled and delighted by Disraeli, sent him a Christmas card, signed 'Regina et Imperatrix' [Queen and Empress].

iii) The Afghan War, 1879–81

Disraeli's determination to resist any challenge to Britain's position in India, 'the Jewel in the Crown', led directly to a crisis over Afghanistan, India's north-western neighbour. Worried by Russia's expansion into southern Asia, which by the 1870s appeared to threaten India, Disraeli judged it necessary for Britain to take control of Afghanistan as a buffer state. When Sher Ali, the Afghan Amir, resisted Britain's demands that he reject Russian overtures and accept British authority, an army was dispatched from India to compel him to comply. This occasioned the Second Afghan War of 1879–81, a British success militarily but one which offended Liberal opinion and led to renewed denunciations of Disraeli's disregard of morality in state affairs. Gladstone was subsequently to reverse Britain's aggressive policy in the region.

iv) The Zulu War, 1879

In 1876, Disraeli dispatched a British army to the Transvaal in support of the Dutch Boers in their war with the native Zulus. His intention was not primarily to aid the Boers but to assert British authority in southern Africa. Things went badly at first, the Zulus inflicting a major defeat on the British forces at Isandhlwana, in 1879, before being finally overcome later that same year at Ulundi.

ACTIVITY

Examine Disraeli's imperial policies as outlined above. Then tackle the question, 'Which of these factors motivated Disraeli's actions: British commercial concerns, fear of Russia, Britain's rivalry with other powers, British prestige, the desire to expand British territory?' A paragraph on each category would be appropriate.

---

b) The Scramble for Africa, 1870–1914

ISSUE
What part did Britain play in the partition of Africa?

By intention and reputation Gladstone was a committed anti-imperialist. He condemned Disraeli for following a foreign policy that was 'deliberately designed to stifle liberty and progress'. Yet it can be argued that, ironically, it was Gladstone who set in motion the scramble for Africa by authorising the annexation of Egypt in 1882. The French who had not been consulted over this, despite having a common interest with Britain in Egypt, interpreted the seizure as an attempt to impose British authority over a key area of north Africa.

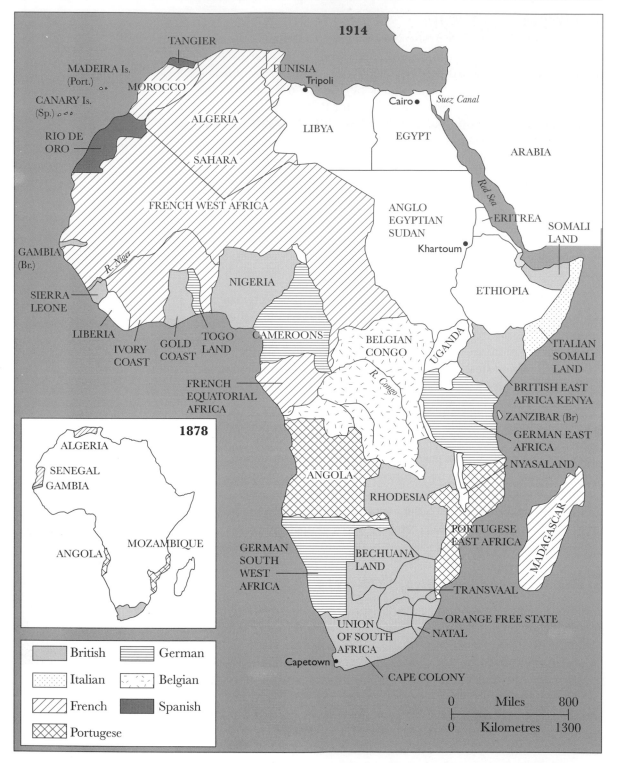

Figure 54 Maps showing the partition of Africa between the European powers, between 1878 and 1914.

ACTIVITY

Identify the following areas in Africa that Britain took over or consolidated its hold over in the period 1870–1914:

▼ west Africa – Gambia, Sierra Leone, Gold Coast, Nigeria
▼ central and southern Africa – Rhodesia, South Africa, Bechuanaland, Nyasaland
▼ east Africa – Uganda, Zanzibar, Kenya, Somaliland
▼ north Africa – Egypt, Sudan

Gladstone and Gordon, 1885

In an effort to contain the forces of the Mahdi, the troublesome Sudanese religious and nationalist leader, Gladstone's government sent a force to the region under the popular Victorian military hero, General Gordon. There was doubt and controversy over what Gordon's exact instructions were and whether he ignored them. It was believed by many in Britain that Gladstone, irritated by Gordon's refusal to follow orders, deliberately delayed sending a relief army when Gordon became besieged in Khartoum by the Mahdi's army. When Gladstone did eventually authorise the dispatch of a force it arrived too late; Gordon had already been killed. The Queen let it be known publicly that she regarded Gladstone as being largely responsible for the tragedy.

THE BRITISH TAKEOVER OF EGYPT, 1882

In 1878 a bankrupt Egypt, part of the Turkish Empire, had been rescued by a joint Anglo-French plan of financial assistance. However, the plan, which required the Egyptians to meet their debts by imposing severe economic restrictions on themselves, caused the people such suffering that it led to a national rising against Turkey and against foreign control of the economy. Rather than allow chaos, Gladstone reluctantly ordered British land and sea forces to Egypt to restore order and impose control.

Britain's military occupation of Egypt ended the uneasy Franco-British dual control that had previously operated. From 1882, the Khedive, the nominal ruler of Egypt, was under British direction. The Sudan, a key strategic area controlling the Upper Nile and bordering southern Egypt, now became a disputed region between France and Britain. British determination to maintain dominance in the face of French counter-claims is evident in the following letter from Salisbury, to Lord Cromer, the British Consul-General in Egypt.

Q What was the consequence of the British takeover of Egypt?

It is possible that a French force may be found in occupation of some portion of the Nile Valley. Should this contingency arise Her Majesty's Government entertain full confidence in Sir Herbert Kitchener's judgement and discretion. They feel assured that he will endeavour to convince the Commander of any French force with which he may come into contact that the presence of the latter in the Nile Valley is an infringement of the rights of both Great Britain and of the Khedive.

Source G Lord Salisbury to Lord Cromer, 2 August 1898.

OMDURMAN, 1898

Cromer's skilful administration of Egypt made possible the highly effective British military operations, under Sir Herbert Kitchener, C-in-C in the region, which were to culminate a month after Salisbury's letter was written in the decisive British victory at Omdurman over the Dervishes, a Sudanese resistance movement. The victory secured Anglo-Egyptian sovereignty in the Sudan.

The eventuality which Salisbury's letter anticipated duly occurred; a few days after his success at Omdurman, Kitchener came face to face with a French expeditionary force at Fashoda, a Sudanese town on the Upper Nile. This 'Fashoda Incident' was resolved precisely in accordance with Salisbury's previous instructions; the French withdrew. For a time, this blow to French imperial pride appeared to threaten war, but after a period of tension, France backed down and, in March 1899, signed an agreement recognising Anglo-Egyptian supremacy in the Sudan. When war did come for Britain in Africa it was not in the north against France but in the south against the Boers.

The Liberal Imperialists

While nearly all Conservatives supported the enlargement of the Empire, there was no single attitude among Liberals towards the issue. Many of them supported the idea of imperial expansion. Rosebery (Prime Minister 1894–5 and Liberal leader 1894–6), Herbert Asquith (Prime Minister after 1908), and Edward Grey (Foreign Secretary after 1905) were prominent among the Liberal Imperialists. Notable among those who opposed expansion were Herbert Gladstone (Liberal Chief Whip, 1899–1905), John Morley (Secretary for India 1905–10), and David Lloyd George, (Chancellor of the Exchequer, 1908–15, and Prime Minister, 1915–22). This group represented what was often referred to as the 'Little Englander' attitude, an approach associated with W.E. Gladstone and the Liberal anti-imperial tradition.

ISSUE

Was it personalities or issues that caused the war?

c) The Anglo-Boer War, 1899–1902

This struggle was in fact the second war between the British and Dutch colonists in southern Africa. An earlier conflict of 1880–1 had ended with a British defeat at Majuba Hill in 1881. This led to the London Convention in 1884 at which Gladstone's government accepted that southern Africa should be divided between the British in the Cape Province and Natal, and the Dutch Boers who would occupy the Transvaal and the Orange Free State. However, although Britain formally reognised Boer rights of self-government in the Transvaal, it continued to claim ambiguously that it exercised 'suzerainty' (authority) over the region.

This became a critical issue in 1886 when gold was discovered in the Transvaal. The Boers feared that their young and underpopulated country would be swamped by the prospectors and traders, who

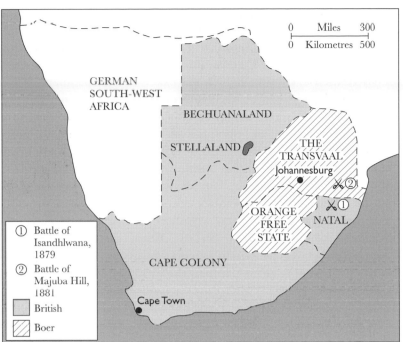

① Battle of Isandhlwana, 1879
② Battle of Majuba Hill, 1881
British
Boer

flooded in. The violent and uncivilised behaviour of the motley new-comers, who were known as **Uitlanders**, was wholly unacceptable to the sober, God-fearing Boers. Determined to protect their way of life from being destroyed, the Boers under their President, Paul Kruger, refused to extend political or electoral rights to the intruders. Relations became increasingly strained.

UITLANDER

Afrikaans (Dutch) for alien or foreigner. It was applied pejoratively by the Boers to describe the collection of prospectors and traders, mainly British and German, who, encouraged by the thought of rich pickings, swelled the population of the diamond and gold mining areas of the Transvaal, being especially numerous in Johannesburg. The issue of Uitlander civil rights became the focus of Anglo-Boer animosity.

The Jameson Raid, 1895

Cecil Rhodes, the founder of Rhodesia, was Prime Minister of the Cape Colony. As a large shareholder in gold and an imperial expansionist who wanted to see the whole of southern Africa under British control, he was determined to use the Uitlander issue to overthrow the Boers. At his instigation, Dr. Starr Jameson, the chief administrator of Rhodes' Chartered Company of South Africa, led a group of five hundred men into the Transvaal hoping to stimulate a full-scale rising against Kruger's government. The raid proved a botched affair. Jameson's force was captured and he and the ringleaders were ignominiously sent to London for trial. Rhodes resigned as Prime Minister and Anglo-Boer relations were further soured. The Boers suspected with good reason that Chamberlain had had prior knowledge of the raid and had given it his full backing.

Q

What was Joseph Chamberlain's role in the development of Anglo-Boer hostility?

It is now accepted by historians that Chamberlain, who became Colonial Secretary in 1895, was looking for an excuse to interfere. He took up the cause of the British in the Transvaal, claiming that they were entitled to full constitutional rights. This the Boers resolutely refused to consider, which was exactly what Chamberlain had hoped for. As indicated by his involvement in the Jameson Raid, he was spoiling for a fight. Chamberlain's secret correspondence with Alfred Milner, whom he appointed in 1897 as the High Commissioner in the Cape, shows beyond doubt that his deliberate aim was to manoeuvre the Boers into a position where they had no recourse but to fight. Indeed, Chamberlain had selected Milner knowing well that the Commissioner's unstable temperament and total belief in the supremacy of British claims in Southern Africa would make the breakdown of negotiations with the Boers inevitable. In 1899, Kruger, exasperated by Britain's demands, as put by Milner, abandoned any further talks. In October, the two Boer republics declared war on Britain, a war that was to last for three years.

> It seems a paradox but it is true that the only effective way of protecting our subjects is, to help them to cease to be our subjects. It is idle to talk of peace and unity. The case for intervention is overwhelming. The spectacle of thousands of British subjects kept permanently in the position of helots [slaves], constantly chafing under undoubted grievances, and calling vainly to Her Majesty's Government for redress, does steadily undermine the influence and reputation of Great Britain and the respect for the British Government with its own dominions.

Source H From a letter by Viscount Milner to Joseph Chamberlain, May 1899.

> If HM Government should decide to send an ultimatum, what should they ask for? It seems difficult to treat as *casus belli* [a justification for war] refusal by a state to which we have given complete internal independence to grant a particular form of franchise to aliens. Yet we must ask for something definite which will meet the existing situation.
>   What do you think of the following? 'the repeal of all legislation since the Convention of 1884 restrictive of the rights and privileges enjoyed by aliens when the Convention was arranged'.

Source I From a letter by Joseph Chamberlain to Viscount Milner, June 1899.

The Milner–Chamberlain letters, which clearly reveal British duplicity, justify the descriptions of the Anglo-Boer conflict as 'Milner's War' or 'Joe's War'. They show how the leading figures in the drama deliberately pushed the Boers towards a conflict. But the war did have deeper causes. The outstanding issue was who was to run South Africa. Ever since the Boers had separated from the British and set up their own republics of the Transvaal and the Orange Free State, the demanding question was who was to have the final authority. Was Southern Africa to be a British-dominated federal dominion or a Boer republic? Beneath the dispute about the rights of the Uit-landers, about whom in his quieter reflections Chamberlain expressed considerable distaste, was the matter of sovereignty. As Kruger said to Milner during the final talks at Bloemfontein before war broke out, 'it is our country you want'. For Chamberlain, British supremacy in the region was a condition of Britain's strength as an imperial power; he regarded South Africa before 1899 as the weakest link in the chain of Empire.

From the beginning there was a significant group in Britain who were deeply unhappy with the war. Referred to as 'pro-Boers', they questioned the morality of Britain's stance. Initially, however, the war was widely popular in Britain, and Prime Minister Salisbury sought to gain from this by calling an election in 1900. The Conservatives deliberately played upon the patriotism of the electorate in what became known as the 'Khaki election'. Although the Conservative majority was slightly reduced, the Government still had a comfortable majority of 218 over the Liberals. However, six years later it suffered a landslide defeat at the hands of the Liberals, who were left with a majority over the Conservatives of 243. Part of the reason for the serious falling away of support for the Conservative government was its dismal record in the Boer War. The pro-Boers drew constant attention to the failure of British forces to win the war quickly. Still more discomforting to the Government were the reports of the extreme measures which the British forces employed in trying to break Boer resistance. The most notorious of these was the internment of civilians in 'concentration' camps, where the cramped and unhygenic conditions frequently led to the spread of fatal diseases. Henry Campbell-Bannerman, who had become Liberal leader in 1899, accused Salisbury's government of employing 'the methods of barbarism'. Lloyd George declared: 'we have now taken to killing babies'. Not only did its inhumane strategy against Boer civilians prove an international scandal; the fact that it took the might of the British imperial army three long years to overcome an outnumbered and outgunned group of farmers caused embarrassment at home and aroused ridicule abroad.

THE BLOEMFONTEIN CONFERENCE, JUNE 1099

Proved to be the last major diplomatic attempt to resolve the diffences between Britain and the Boer republics. It stood little chance of success. Already strained by the scandal of the Jameson Raid into the Transvaal four years earlier, relations between the obdurate Cape Governor, Milner, and the stubborn President Kruger broke down completely over the question of Uitlander rights.

How was the Anglo-Boer War regarded in Britain?

ACTIVITY

Examine the causes of the Anglo-Boer War as described above. In your opinion, who had the stronger argument – those in Britain who supported the war or the pro-Boers who opposed it? What connection was there likely to have been between the 'little Englanders' and the pro-Boers?

ISSUE

What motivated Britain and the other European powers in their bid for empire?

Source J From *Imperialism, the Highest Stage of Capitalism* by V.I. Lenin, 1917.

SURPLUS CAPITAL

Lenin used the term to refer to the amount of capital that could not profitably be re-invested by European countries in their own markets because these had been saturated by over investment.

d) The Debate over Imperialism

Study the following passage:

> As long as capitalism remains what it is, surplus capital will be utilised not for the purpose of raising the standard of living of the masses in a given country, for this would mean a decline in profits for the capitalist, but for the purpose of increasing profits by exporting capital abroad to backward countries.

In this extract, Lenin, the Russian revolutionary, offers the classic Marxist interpretation of imperialism. For Lenin, the European scramble for Africa was the logical and inevitable outcome of the growth of capitalism. He believed that by the middle years of the nineteenth century European capitalism had reached crisis point. Over-production of capital led to fierce conflict between the advanced industrial nations for dwindling financial markets. In desperation they seized control of the world's undeveloped areas with the intention of exploiting them as regions of cheap investment. This was the driving force that explained the frantic and rapid partition of Africa after 1870. Lenin went further, claiming that the climax of such capitalist rivalry had come in 1914 with the outbreak of the final great imperialist war.

Lenin's theory of the imperialist phase of capitalism, which allows little place for motivation other than the economic in explaining the European colonisation of Africa, remains a source of considerable controversy. There are historians who continue to accept Lenin's interpretation as a convincing explanation. However, critics of this view have established that the statistics of European investment in Africa in the period covered by Lenin do not support his analysis. They point out that other factors, including, for example, militarism, religious missionary zeal, national rivalry, and the use of colonies as pawns in the game of European diplomacy, must be given as much weight as finance capitalism when interpreting a phenomenon as complex as the European scramble for Africa.

ACTIVITY

Read over the extract from Lenin and the explanation that follows. Then take each of the regions that Britain acquired for itself during the scramble for Africa and ask the question – Was the area colonised for the reasons that Lenin suggested, or were other factors involved? You will need to go outside this book to find fuller answers. The suggestions on page 257 will help you in this.

4 Britain's Entry into the First World War

Had informed Britons in 1900 been granted the foreknowledge that their country would be involved in a major European war fourteen years later, they would not have been totally shocked. But what would have surprised them would be to learn who Britain's allies and enemies would be. Most people in Britain would have anticipated that in a future war, Britain's most likely opponents would have been the major imperial powers, such as France and Russia, not Germany, which since its formation in the early 1870s had seldom represented a serious threat to Britain. The question that has to be answered, therefore, is why Britain aligned itself in 1914 with France and Russia in a war against Germany and Austria-Hungary? An easy answer that once seemed convincing was that Britain went to war as a member of an alliance that was drawn into conflict with an opposing alliance. But the notion that it was the breakdown of the alliance system that necessarily involved Britain in war overlooks the key point that Britain did not consider itself irrevocably committed to fight on any other nation's behalf. Indeed the avoidance of such a commitment had been the central purpose of Britain's foreign policy in the preceding generation. The Liberals were no keener to lock Britain into treaties than the Conservatives under Salisbury had been. While it is true that early in the twentieth century Britain entered into agreements with the USA and Japan, it did not change its stance towards Europe. Indeed, as we will see, Britain's *ententes* with France and Russia are best understood as attempts to avoid closer contacts with Europe.

The test of what the implications of the ententes actually were came with the diplomatic crisis that followed the assassination by Serbian nationalists of Franz Ferdinand, heir to the Austrian throne, in June 1914. When, a month later, a war broke out between Austria and Germany on one side and Russia and France on the other, the great question facing Britain was whether it had any legitimate reason or obligation to become involved. Remarkably, neither the Prime Minister, the Cabinet, nor even the Foreign Secretary had a precise answer to that question.

An odd feature of British foreign policy before 1914 was that it had been regarded as the individual concern of the Foreign Secretary. Cabinet scrutiny was unsystematic and, except at times of crisis, seldom demanding. Edward Grey held the position of Foreign Secretary continuously from 1905. By nature a withdrawn man, he had chosen to act alone and in secret. Reluctant to be drawn into formal

The Anglo-Japanese Alliance, 1902

Britain and Japan recognised each other's interests in China. Each agreed to remain neutral in the event of the other going to war with a third power, or to assist if the other went to war with two or more powers. The treaty was to be operative for five years with the option of renewal.

The Anglo-French Entente, 1904

Britain promised to give France a free hand in Morocco while the French returned the compliment in regard to British rights in Egypt. Although there were plentiful expressions of mutual goodwill, no formal alliance or military agreement was concluded.

Why there was such uncertainty?

The Anglo-Russian Agreement, 1907

Russia promised to refrain from interference in Afghanistan and Tibet. Both Russia and Britain promised to respect each other's 'spheres of influence' in Persia. No military matters were discussed. The agreement in effect extended the Anglo-French Entente into a triple entente.

Source K From *Twenty-Five Years, 1892–1916* by Edward Grey, 1926.

commitments, Grey tried to protect British interests by leaving the position deliberately vague. Foreign governments were known to complain that they could rarely be certain where Britain stood on international questions. The Entente with France, first entered into under Balfour's Government in 1904 and extended into the Triple Entente with the inclusion of Russia in 1907, was specifically not an alliance; at most, it was an understanding rather than a set of agreements. Since, therefore, Britain in 1914 was not formally committed to any of the European states involved in the crisis, no one could be sure what its obligations actually were.

Given the secrecy of Grey's diplomacy since 1905 and the consequent uncertainty of Britain's diplomatic position, it is little wonder that there was considerable division within the Cabinet over the question of entering the war. The Liberal Party, with its strong non-interventionist traditions in foreign policy, did not immediately incline to war. Since Britain lacked formal commitment to either France or Russia, it would require a specific issue to tilt the balance in favour of war. That issue, Grey believed, came in the form of Belgian neutrality. It was Germany's violation of that neutrality by sending its armies through Belgium in order to attack France that united the Cabinet and the nation after their initial wavering. Writing in retrospect in the 1920s Grey argued:

> The real reason for going into the war was that, if we did not stand by France and stand up for Belgium against this aggression, we should be isolated, discredited, and hated; and there would be before us nothing but a miserable and ignoble future.

Grey wrote his post-war analysis in order to establish that it had been with the highest of motives that the Liberal Government had taken Britain into what was to prove a struggle of unimagined suffering and destruction. He presented the defence of Belgium as having been the great moral purpose which animated the nation in 1914, and it is certainly true that it was the announcement of Germany's formal rejection of Britain's demand that Belgian independence be honoured that rallied the House of Commons in favour of Britain's declaration of war. Grey described the mood of the MPs:

> We felt to stand aside would mean the domination of Germany; the subordination of France and Russia; the isolation of Britain and ultimately that Germany would wield the whole power of the Continent.

Source L From *Twenty-Five Years, 1892–1916* by Edward Grey, 1926.

The opposed alliances

The Triple Alliance (the Central Powers)	*The Triple Entente* (the Allied Powers)
|	|
Germany, Austria-Hungary, Turkey	France, Russia, Britain

(Italy, an original member of the Triple Alliance, did not enter the war until 1915 and then on the side of the Allied Powers.)

This definition of what Grey called 'the true issue' is instructive. Britain, he said, could not stand aside and permit the German domination of Europe. This, it should be noted, was a consideration that applied prior to, and regardless of, the German invasion of Belgium. Effective though the image of an idealistic Britain crusading to defend gallant little Belgium was in convincing waverers that this was why Britain was going to war, the true motivation was altogether more self-interested. In keeping with tradition and, indeed, with Grey's own aims since 1905, Britain was not prepared to tolerate one nation upsetting the balance of power in Europe, thereby endangering its own security. It is difficult to see the issue of Belgian neutrality as anything other than a pretext for war. All the probabilities were that Britain would have gone to war alongside France against Germany in 1914 irrespective of the Belgian issue. As Christopher Ray, a modern historian, asked in a thought-provoking rhetorical question in 1998: 'Was it conceivable that, if the French had marched into Belgium in order to forestall an expected German attack aimed primarily at them, Britain would have joined Germany and declared war on France?'

How important was the issue of Belgian neutrality?

A further factor in the equation was the pressure applied during the decade before 1914 by the chiefs of the armed services for increased resources. The Admiralty was particularly insistent in its demand for the building of more Dreadnoughts, the great battleships that represented Britain's naval strength. The Admiralty's argument was that Germany's growing warship programme was a direct threat to British security and had to be countered by an equivalent expansion of the Royal Navy. There was a conviction among the service chiefs that Germany was bent on outstripping Britain militarily as a first step to waging an aggressive war. They believed there could be no other explanation for Germany's naval programme, which far exceeded any real defence needs it might have. Winston Churchill expressed the view of the military when he declared that, given their respective overseas commitments, Britain's navy was a necessity whereas Germany's was a luxury.

How important was the arms race?

Figure 56 'Unconquerable', a *Punch* cartoon of 1914 showing gallant little Belgium resisting German aggression.

Figure 57 A British government poster showing the signatures to the treaty of 1839 guaranteeing Belgian neutrality. Palmerston's is the first name. It was this treaty that the German Kaiser referred disparagingly to as 'the scrap of paper' when he learned that Britain was considering entering the war in accordance with its 1839 commitment.

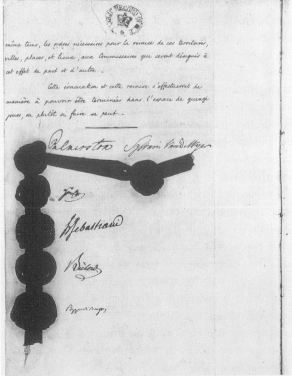

In examining the factors that disposed Britain to war in 1914, allowance has also to be made for the question of national prestige. Lloyd George, the Chancellor of the Exchequer, and one of the Liberals who had strong anti-war sentiments at the time of the Boer War, was unambiguous in declaring that there were limits to the amount of German aggression Britain would tolerate. In 1911 he warned the German government against taking a belligerent stance in foreign affairs and stated the case for possible British intervention:

> I believe it is essential in the highest interests, not merely of this country, but of the world, that Britain should at all hazards maintain her place and prestige amongst the Great Powers. If a situation were to be forced on us, in which peace could only be preserved by allowing Britain to be treated as if she were of no account in the Cabinet of nations, then I say emphatically that peace at that price would be a humiliation intolerable for a great country like ours to endure.

Source M From Lloyd George's speech at the Mansion House, London, 1911.

However, Lloyd George's precise attitude at the time of the Government's decision to declare war is not entirely clear. Official records of the Cabinet's discussions were not kept; we have to rely on the subsequent comments of those involved. At one point he appears to have been willing to resign from the Cabinet and oppose the war, should Germany draw back from violating Belgium. But there is reason to doubt his sincerity. His closest confidante at the time, Frances Stevenson, wrote in her diary account that Lloyd George's mind was already made up in favour of war and that the invasion of Belgium simply provided a 'heaven-sent excuse for supporting a declaration of war'. He himself later said that what helped persuade him to support the declaration of war was the urgent clamour for war that he witnessed among the ordinary people as he drove through the crowded streets of London. Whatever may have been the responsibility of Grey and Asquith's government for Britain's entering the war it cannot be claimed that the British people were dragged into the struggle against their will.

Q Were the British government and people eager for war in 1914?

ACTIVITY

Having read section 4 above, consider the following factors and say which one of them, or which combination of them, was the most influential in leading Britain into war in 1914:

▼ British fears of German intentions
▼ Britain's wish to preserve the balance of power
▼ the Anglo-German arms race
▼ Grey's secret diplomacy from 1905 onwards
▼ Britain's membership of the Triple Entente
▼ the popular desire in Britain for war
▼ Britain's treaty obligations to Belgium
▼ Britain's sense of honour
▼ Britain's need to protect its capitalist-imperialist interests.

Summary of Foreign and Imperial Affairs

Year	Foreign affairs	Imperial affairs
1865	death of Palmerston opened way for new approach to foreign policy	
1867		Canada received full 'Dominion' status
1868–74	Gladstone advanced the principle of the Concert of Europe	
1870	Disraeli attacked Gladstone for not reacting to Russia's breach of Black Sea clauses	
1870–1	French defeat in Franco-Prussian War left Germany dominant in Europe	
1872	Gladstone accepted international arbitration decision over the Trent affair	Disraeli began to make imperial expansion a key part of Conservatism
1875		Disraeli purchased the Suez Canal Shares
1876	Gladstone bitterly attacked Disraeli's pro-Turkish policy in the Balkans	Royal Titles Bill made the Queen the Empress of India
British army sent to Transvaal
1878	Disraeli brought back 'peace with honour' from Congress of Berlin	
1879	the Dual Alliance	the Zulu War
1879–81		the Afghan War
1881	the Three Emperors League	
1882	the Triple Alliance	British troops occupy Egypt
1884		London Convention recognised independence of Boer republic of Transvaal
1885		General Gordon killed in Khartoum
1887	Salisbury initiates the Mediterranean Agreements	

Year	Foreign affairs	Imperial affairs
1895		the Jameson Raid
1896	the Venezuela Dispute	
1898	start of German warship construction programme	British victory at Omdurman the Fashoda Incident beginning of the Boxer Rising in China
1899–1901		Anglo-Boer War
1901		Australia granted Dominion status end of the Boxer Rising
1902	the Anglo-Japanese Alliance	
1904	the Anglo-French Entente	
1906	first Dreadnought launched	
1907	the Anglo-Russian Entente	New Zealand granted Dominion status
1910		Union of South Africa formed
1914	Britain declared war on Germany	

▼ Working on Foreign and Imperial Affairs

It was suggested in the 'Points to Consider' at the start of this chapter that there is a distinct overlap between the foreign and imperial policies followed by Britain in this period. Take the main sections – 1 to 4 – and apply the same basic question to each. In what ways did imperial considerations affect the way British foreign policy was conducted? An example of the approach to the theme in section 1 might be:

The Eastern Question
British attitude towards it dictated by fear of Russian expansion at expense of Turkey
WHY? – fear for balance of power *and* routes to India [add sketch map to notes to show position]
THEREFORE – Disraeli, like Palmerston and Canning, took an anti-Russian approach
BUT – Gladstone, both an anti-imperialist and a believer in the Concert of Europe, was less concerned at the Russian threat, and was more worried about the morality of supporting a repressive Turkey
HENCE – rivalry between Gladstone and Disraeli over Russo-Turkish question.

If you compile your notes in this way linking, comparing and contrasting the points you cover by provocative leads, such as WHY, THEREFORE, HENCE, THUS, rather than just setting them down as list of points, you will clarify your thinking and sustain your interest.

Think of it as if you were having a running debate with yourself, working out the cause, course and consequences of events. If you find you cannot make the links, then it is the time to go back and check the material you have read. Never write notes that you do not really understand.

Answering extended writing and essay questions on Foreign and Imperial Affairs

The following list shows the style of questions you are likely to encounter on the topic of foreign and imperial affairs.

Type of Issue	Examples of typical questions
1 causes/reasons/motives	How true is it that Disraeli embraced imperialism not for national but for party-political reasons?
2 course of events	Trace the steps which led to the outbreak of war between Britain and the Boers in 1899.
3 consequences/results/effects	'The Anglo-Japanese Alliance of 1902 marked the beginning of 'a diplomatic revolution' for Britain.' Discuss.
4 success/failure	How accurate is the claim that Britain achieved 'peace with honour' at the Congress of Berlin in 1878?
5 significance/importance	Consider the assertion that 'the British annexation of Egypt in 1882 began the scramble for Africa'.
6 comparison	Consider the view that there were no significant differences between Gladstone and Salisbury in their approach to foreign affairs.
7 right/wrong (moral/ethical judgments)	'In the end Britain's decision to defend Belgium was taken not for strategic but for moral reasons.' How acceptable is this explanation for Britain's declaration of war on Germany in 1914?
8 covering a hundred-year time span	'Its only guiding principle was the protection in British interests.' How acceptable is this description of Britain's foreign policy between 1815 and 1914?

Let us consider number 8. This is the type of question that tests your knowledge of events and developments over time. As always when preparing an answer to a time-span question, make sure you do not get bogged down in detail. You are being asked to survey a broad pattern. In this case it is the conduct of foreign policy over a whole century. You will obviously need to check back to Chapter 6 to provide the continuity between 1815–65 and 1865–1914. The question gives you a very strong push in a particular direction. It asks you to examine the motive behind the policy that was followed in this period. You will recall that Chapters 6 and 9 took the outstanding foreign secretaries as the pegs on which to hang the foreign affairs material. In answering this question you would do well, therefore, to follow this method of analysis. Set down in chronological order the figures who dominated British policy. These should not present difficulties as Chapters 6 and 9 do this for you. Then against each figure on your the list set the question – Was his only motive the safeguarding of British interests? Let us take an example:

Castlereagh 1815–22
(Do not try to cover all the issues in which he was involved. Select just one or two to illustrate the point you are making.)
He wanted to restore the power balance in Europe after 1815
HOW? – by the congress system
WHY? – to avoid any European nation or bloc threatening the peace and thereby possibly involving Britain in further struggle
HENCE – he was not prepared to support the Holy Alliance
Canning 1822–27 – continued the policy laid down by Castlereagh
THEREFORE – he declined to co-operate with the Holy Alliance and allowed the congress system to become defunct.
Canning showed more sympathy for liberal movements in Europe and the Spanish colonies BUT never to the point of risking British interests.

The same style of analysis could be applied to Palmerston. In all the issues in which he was involved he consistently put British interests first. Even though he had a natural sympathy for liberal causes (e.g. Italian unification) his priority remained the defence of British imperial and strategic interests. You could use the relevant sections in Chapters 6 and 9 to illustrate that Disraeli, Salisbury and Grey all based their foreign policies on the same essential principle as Castlereagh, Canning and Palmerston had. Select one or two examples in each case to prove your point.

The big exception to all this was, of course, Gladstone. His belief in the Concert of Europe, his readiness to accept the principle of arbitration in international disputes and his distaste for imperial expansion, elevated his conduct of foreign policy into the realm of morality. The obvious example is his feud with Disraeli over the

Eastern Question. Does this make him fundamentally different from the other foreign ministers? Was his policy different in *practice* or only in theory? For example, did his ordering of the occupation of Egypt in 1882 mean that when it came to a crisis he was just as concerned to protect British interests as the other ministers in our list? However you answer that, your response will be highly relevant and will provide an interesting point of comparison and contrast by which to judge the trend over the whole century.

Answering source-based questions on Foreign and Imperial Affairs

Read back over sub-section 3 c) on the Anglo-Boer War, study Source H, and Source I (page 244), and then answer the questions that follow.

▼ QUESTIONS ON SOURCES

1. Explain or define the following references:
 a. 'the position of helots' (Source H) **[3 marks]**
 b. 'the Convention of 1884' (Source I) **[3 marks]**
2. Explain Milner's paradox, in Source H, 'the only effective way of protecting our subjects is, to help them to cease to be our subjects'. **[5 marks]**

Explain or define the following references:

Suggested line of response
1a. Milner's reference here is to the under-class of slaves in ancient Greece. He is dramatising what he regards as the insufferable plight of British subjects in the Transvaal, excluded from the franchise but subject to local laws and taxation.
b. Following the Boer victory over the British at Majuba Hill in 1881, Gladstone's Government had recognised Boer rights of self-government in the Transvaal but ambiguously had still claimed British 'suzerainty' in the region. To clarify the situation, the London Convention of 1884, a gathering of Boer and British representatives, granted a major concession to the Boers by restoring to the Transvaal its former title of 'South African Republic'. This left the British Cape Colonists unhappy. Source I reveals Chamberlain preparing to use the Convention settlement as a means of applying pressure on the Boers.
2. Milner's paradox is intended to point out that, in pressing Uitlander claims against the Boers in the Transvaal, Britain was asserting the rights of British subjects to full citizenship in that country. Since

the Transvaal was an independent state, and formally recognised as such by Britain on a number of occasions since the Pretoria Convention at the end of the first Boer war in 1881, Britain was, in effect, urging a new and foreign citizenship upon the Uitlanders. Thus in logic the very means by which Britain sought to protect its subjects led to their ceasing to be exclusively British subjects.

Further Reading

Books in the 'Access to History' series

All the chapters in *Britain and the European Powers 1865–1914* by Robert Pearce are relevant and to be recommended, as are those in *The British Empire 1815–1914* by Frank McDonough. Chapters 4 and 5 in *Rivalry and Accord: International Relations 1870–1914* by John Lowe relate to Britain within the broader European scene.

General

Two rewarding studies that look at British foreign and imperial policy are *Defence and Diplomacy: Britain and the Great Powers, 1815–1914* by C.J. Bartlett (Manchester University Press, 1993) and *'Pax Britannica'? British Foreign Policy 1789–1914* by Muriel Chamberlain (Longman, 1989). There are informative chapters on the foreign policies of Disraeli, Gladstone, Chamberlain, Salisbury, Balfour and Lloyd George in *Modern British Statesmen 1867–1945* edited by Richard Kelly and John Cantrell (Manchester UP, 1997). One of the most readable studies of Salisbury as a foreign statesman is *Lord Salisbury and Foreign Policy* by J.A.S. Grenville (Athlone Press, 1964). Of the many excellent studies of British imperialism the following are specially recommended: *The Scramble for Africa* by Muriel Chamberlain (Longman, 1974), *The Lion's Share: A Short History of British Imperialism, 1850–1914* (Longman, 1975), *Britain's Imperial Century 1815–1914* by Ronald Hyman (Batsford,1974), and *The Cambridge Illustrated History of the British Empire*, edited by P.J. Marshall (CUP, 1996). A difficult book but one which repays study because it has been so influential is *Africa and the Victorians: The Official Mind of Imperialism* by R.E. Robinson and J. Gallagher (Methuen, 1965). Arguably the most authoritative modern study is *British Imperialism, Innovation and Expansion 1688–1914* by Peter Kain (Longman, 1993). A detailed study of the reasons for Britain's entering the war in 1914 is *Britain and the Origins of the First World War* by Zara Steiner (Macmillan, 1977). The story of Britain's path to war in 1914 is also well, if more briefly, told in *The Edwardian Age* by Vyvyen Brendon (Hodder & Stoughton, 1996), in *Edwardian England* by Donald Read (Harrap,1972), in *Years of Expansion Britain 1815–1914*, edited by Michael Scott Baumann (Hodder & Stoughton, 1995), and in *Decisions for War, 1914* edited by Keith Wilson (UCL Press, 1995). Recommended articles are: 'The British Idea of Empire' by Kathryn Tidrick in *Modern History Review*, 'Brits, Boers and Blacks: The Boer War 1899–1902' by Keith Surridge in *Britain 1867–1918* (Heinemann), and 'Britain and the Origins of the First World War' by Christopher Ray in *History Review*, Mar 1998.

GLOSSARY

INDEX